Bubastis: city of the feline goddess

Archaeological discoveries in a metropolis of the Egyptian Nile Delta

Eva Lange-Athinodorou

Egyptian sites

This title is published by
Golden House Publications

Cover image © Bastet and Pepi I: Relief on the southern door lintel of the gateway of the *ka*-temple of Pepi I at Bubastis (JE 72133). (LANGE 2000), back cover image: Osorkon I anointing Bastet: Relief from the entrance hall of the temple of Bastet. (TELL BASTA PROJECT 2011)

A catalogue record for this book is available from the British Library

ISBN 978-1-906137-87-8

Printed in the United Kingdom
P2D Books Limited
1 Newlands Road
Westoning
Bedfordshire
MK45 5LD

London 2024

In grateful memory of MOHAMMED IBRAHIM BAKR and ERIKA ENDESFELDER

Frontispiz: Excavation of the tomb of Ankhhaf in 1984. In the foreground: MOHAMED IBRAHIM BAKR and ERIKA ENDESFELDER. (Courtesy of MOHAMMED IBRAHIM BAKR 2017)

Contents

Acknowledgements

This book could not have been written without the tireless work and friendly collaboration of the past and present team members of the TELL BASTA PROJECT, namely ALAA ABDELAZIZ, VERONIKA APPEL, DR ABDELHALEEM AWADALLAH, ALI BADAWY, SVENJA DIRKSEN, DR DINA FALTINGS, TANJA GUEHL, ALLISTER HUMPHREY, DR MANUELA LEHMANN, SAID FEKHRY MAHMOUD, MANDY MAMEDOW, DR DANIELA ROSENOW, RABEA REIMANN, AHMED EL-SAYED, DR ASHRAF ES-SENUSSI, DR JEFFREY SPENCER, JOHANNES VAETHJUNKER and many more. The same is true for the trustful and kind support of the officials and friends from the Ministry of Antiquities over many years, especially the General Secretary of the Egyptian Ministry of State for Antiquities, DR MOHAMED ISMAIL KHALED, the General Director of Foreign Missions Affairs and Permanent Committees, DR NASHWA GABR, the General Manager of the el-Sharkiya Antiquities Zone, MANAL MONEIR, the former General Manager, HISHAM MOHAMMAD ABD EL-MOAMAN EL-HEFNAWI and the Head of the Foreign Missions in the el-Sharqiya Antiquities Zone, HEND EL-ETREBY.

I am also grateful for the insight and inspiration of my colleagues and friends from the Institute of Geography and Geology at the University Wuerzburg, PROF DR ROLAND BAUMHAUER, PHILIPP GARBE, PROF DR JULIA MEISTER, DR JULIAN TRAPPE and PROF DR TOBIAS ULLMANN, as well as PROF DR AMR ABDEL-RAOUF from the Institute of Geography at the University Zagazig, and DR PENNY WILSON from the University of Durham.

At my home institution, the Institute of Egyptology of the University Wuerzburg, I owe my sincerest gratitude to PROF DR MARTIN STADLER for his determined and unwavering support of the TELL BASTA-PROJECT in all matters, and I would also like to express my thanks to PROF DR GÜNTER VITTMANN for the (ongoing) discussions on textual sources on the Nile Delta, Bubastis, Bastet and all related subjects.

Without funding, there could be no archaeological work at the site of ancient Bubastis. Therefore, I am most grateful of the support of the EGYPT EXPLORATION SOCIETY (2009-2014), the RESEARCH FUND OF THE FACULTY OF PHILOSOPHY and the UNIBUND OF THE UNIVERSITY OF WÜRZBURG (2014-2022), the GERDA HENKEL FOUNDATION (2018-2022), and the GERMAN RESEARCH FOUNDATION (DFG, since 2023).

I would also like to express my warmest thanks to DR WOLFRAM GRAJETZKI, who has graciously agreed to include this book in his famous GOLDEN HOUSE PUBLICATION series, and to PAUL WHELAN for his kind and very generous willingness to correct my English.

At last, I am deeply indebted to my parents, ROSWITHA ALBRECHT and THOMAS LANGE for their love and to my husband, ANDREAS ATHINODOROU, for his devoted and untiring support of my work, to which he has contributed so much.

List of Figures

the north. (TELL BASTA PROJECT 2014)

Fig. 20: Amenemhet III celebrating the Sed-festival. Relief on a limestone lintel from the northeastern corner of the governor's palace. (Line drawing based on VAN SICLEN 1996, fig. 11; LANGE-ATHINODOROU 2004)

Fig. 21: Ground plan of the governor's palace at Bubastis. (LANGE-ATHINODOROU 2018(a), Fig.2a)

Fig. 22: The governor's cemetery (Cemetery E) at Bubastis. View to the northwest. (TELL BASTA PROJECT 2016)

Fig. 23: Governor's cemetery (Cemetery E), tomb no 5. View to the north. (TELL BASTA PROJECT 2016)

Fig. 24: Ground plan of Cemetery E. Chronological pattern of use after VAN SICLEN's suggestion. Orange: stage 1 (earlier period), green: stage 2 (later period). (LANGE-ATHINODOROU 2015, Fig. 2)

Chapter 5:

Fig. 25: Block with an inscription of Hyksos King Apepi from the temple of Bastet. (TELL BASTA PROJECT 2011)

Chapter 6:

Fig. 26: Fragment of a papyrus column in the hypostyle hall of the temple with cartouches of Ramses II, usurped by Osorkon II. (TELL BASTA-PROJECT 2021)

Fig. 27: The block statue of Bebi from Area A east of the temple of Bastet. (TELL BASTA PROJECT 2016)

Fig. 28a: Seated statue of Ramses IV from the temple of Bastet. (TELL BASTA PROJECT 2022)

Fig. 28b: Seated statue of Ramses IV from the temple of Bastet. (TELL BASTA PROJECT 2022)

Fig. 29a: The western wall of the tomb of viceroy Hori I. (TELL BASTA PROJECT 2022)

Fig. 29b: Ground plan and section of the tomb of viceroy Hori I. (LANGE-ATHINODOROU 2024, slightly simplified version of HABACHI 1957, Fig. 27)

Fig. 30: Vessels from the Tell Basta Treasure at the Metropolitan Museum. (Metropolitan Museum, Open Access)

Chapter 7:

Fig. 31: Inscription of Osorkon I: White Light scan. (TRIGONART 2006)

Fig. 32: The temple of Bastet at Bubastis. View to the south. (TELL BASTA-PROJECT 2022)

Fig. 33: Reconstruction of the ground plan of the temple of Bastet. (LANGE-ATHINODOROU 2019(a), Abb. 2)

Fig. 34: Restored statue of Queen Karomama from the temple of Bastet. (LANGE-ATHINODOROU 2022)

Fig. 35: Throne of a seated statue of Amenemhet III, usurped by Osokon II in the temple of Bastet. (TELL BASTA-PROJECT 2014)

Fig. 36a: Relief from the entrance hall: Osorkon I offering a an Udjat-Eye to Bastet. (TELL BASTA-PROJECT 2011)

Fig. 36b: Relief from the entrance hall: Osorkon I and Hor-Hekenu. (TELL BASTA-PROJECT 2011)

Fig. 37: NAVILLE's Reconstruction of the Sed-festival gateway. (NAVILLE 1892, frontispiz)

Fig. 38: Location and orientation of the walls of the Sed-festival gateway. (LANGE-ATHINODOROU 2019(a), Abb. 3)

Fig. 39a: Relief from the Sed-festival gateway of Osorkon II, showing musicians and the royal princesses. (TELL BASTA-PROJECT 2022)

Fig. 39b: Relief from the Sed-festival gateway of Osorkon II, showing chapels of deities. (TELL BASTA PROJECT 2022) und

Fig. 39c: Head of a royal statue reused for the Sed-festival gateway of Osorkon II. Relief on the back side shows a procession of princesses. (TELL BASTA-PROJECT 2022)

Fig. 39d: Relief from the Sed-festival gateway of Osorkon II, showing a procession of princesses. (TELL BASTA PROJECT 2022)

Fig. 40: Faience Fragments Tb1b X/2 TS KF 007, 001, 004 and 003 with the cartouche of King Shoshenq Meriamun. (TELL BASTA PROJECT 2009)

Fig. 41: Suggested reconstruction of an ushabti of King Shoshenq Meriamun. (TELL BASTA PROJECT 2009)

1. The '*Eye of Ra*' in the Nile Delta: The goddess Bastet

The well-known image of the sacred cat has become an icon of ancient Egyptian religion in modern times. Its elegant and well-defined shape perfectly captures the exoticism and foreignness of this ancient civilization. However, behind the apparent clarity and coherence of the image lies a complex background of the reality of the cult of the goddess it symbolises – "*Bastet*" in ancient Egyptian. This goddess is fascinating, and the multi-layered beliefs and practices surrounding her are reflected in a multitude of sources. Despite this, our understanding of the goddess remains elusive and incomplete.

In pharaonic times, Bastet was not always worshipped as a cat, but mainly and originally as a powerful lioness. In this form, she was connected with the cult of other lioness goddesses of the Nile Delta, such as Sekhmet and Shesemtet. The origins of Bastet may actually reach back as far as the origins of ancient Egyptian civilization itself. Her earliest attestations come from the galleries under the famous step pyramid of Djoser at Saqqara near Memphis. Thousands of sherds of stone vessels from royal burials of the Second Dynasty (around 2800 BCE) were discovered there. Some have short inscriptions mentioning deities in connection with a royal name, amongst them Bastet, who is also depicted as a female with the head of a lioness. One of the inscriptions names a "*priest of Bastet*", while another mentions the provisions of a phyle of priests of Bastet. However, it remains unclear if the office of a priest of Bastet at that time was connected to a specific temple or chapel and where it was located, because, as we will see later, the earliest evidence for her cult at Bubastis dates to the end of the Old Kingdom.

It might very well be that Bastet was originally a deity of the royal residence at Memphis. The etymology of her name, a derivation of the name of the ointment jar ⌷ *bȝs.t*, suggests a connection to royal regalia. After all, the merging of the concept of a deity with a protective ointment would have perfectly aligned with the protective and mighty nature of a divine lioness as an ideological expression of ancient Egyptian royalty.[1]

The importance of Bastet in the royal ideology of the Old Kingdom is evident from her appearance in the formula "*beloved of Bastet,*" inscribed for the king on the northern door jamb of the main entrance of the Valley Temple of Chephren (Fourth Dynasty, around 2570-2530 BCE)[2]. In this inscription, Bastet is presented as a counterpart to the goddess Hathor, who appears in the same way on the southern door jamb. Interestingly, even royal princes of that period, such as Nefermaat and Hemiunu, held the title "*priest of Bastet*" associated with the priesthood for another lioness goddess, Shesemtet, and the Ram of Mendes. The connection of these titles possibly marks out a certain cult-topographic and administrative area that stretched from Memphis to Mendes, including the (later?) cult centres of Bastet and Shesemtet at Bubastis and Pi-Sopdu.[3] Already at the beginning of the Fourth Dynasty, we know of an official named Akhtyhotep who held the title "*priest of Bastet on her staircase*".[4] Although no locality is given in the title, it is interesting to note that a staircase of Bastet, denominated with the same word (*ẖnd(w)*) appears in the goddesses' epithets at Bubastis since the late New Kingdom (see Chapters 6 and 8).

A relief from the mortuary temple of King Niuserre of the Fifth Dynasty (2455-2420 BCE) shows a lioness-headed goddess with the designation: "*Bastet, lady of Ankh-Tawy, Sekhmet-Shesemtet, the One mighty of her Ba-powers, lady of Chabes*". Ankh-Tawy was either a district of Memphis or the necropolis of the city. The toponym Chabes also remains unidentified but might have been a locality in the Memphite area.[5]

Together with Sekhmet and Shesemtet, Bastet belongs to a constellation of lioness goddesses that was predominant in the Nile Delta, which may seem a surprising place for the cult of animals we would expect to find in the semi-desert regions bordering the Nile Valley. However, the earliest attestations of the cults of Sekhmet, Shesemtet, and Bastet suggest that their origins can be traced to the Southeastern Delta near the entrance to the Wadi Tumilat and in the fringes of the Western Delta close to the desert margins (see fig. 2). The Wadi Tumilat, which is a narrow valley that stretches for 52 km, may once have been a Pleistocene branch of the Nile. Sedimentological analysis of core drillings from the site of Tell el-Retaba has shown that there was a lake and other water basins fed by sparse rainfall and seasonal flooding in the centre of the Wadi. These bodies of water persisted at least until the late New Kingdom.[6] The Wadi Tumilat must therefore have had vegetated areas providing a suitable habitat for prides of lions. The same might be true for wadis at the southwestern fringes of the Delta, for example at Kom el-Hisn, where archaeological remains of a cattle raising estate have been found. The alluvial plain of the Nile Delta also offered large areas for cattle grazing, making it the preferred territory where the early centralized state of ancient Egypt established its agricultural domains for raising large herds of cattle. These, no doubt, attracted lions, especially for domains located close to their habitats at the liminal zone between cultivated land and the surrounding wilderness. These environmental characteristics, combined with economic developments, may have led to the predominance of the cults of lioness goddesses in the Nile Delta. The hunting strategies of groups of female lions would have made a strong impression on the ancient observers, creating a lasting image of ferocious lioness goddesses who played an important role in the religion of ancient Egypt. We could even speculate that long before the rise of Sekhmet, Bastet and Shesemtet, cults of lioness goddesses of names unknown to us might have already existed for as long as people have settled the Nile Delta fringes.[7]

With their predatory nature, lionesses were both feared for their wild and fiery spirit and revered for their might and protectiveness. Besides Sekhmet, Bastet, Shesemtet, and other genuinely feline goddesses, other female deities, such as Hathor, Mut, Neith, Nekhbet, and Wadjet can also appear as lionesses. With their bright amber eyes and yellowish fur, these felines were seen as forces of the sun itself, leading to their identification as '*Daughter of Ra*' or '*Eye of Ra*'. Wildlife observed at natural watering holes, where lions would often rest, led to the belief that the ambivalent and potentially dangerous goddesses required the pleasant coolness of the water. Therefore, canals or lakes were often built close to their temples, such as the sacred canals surrounding the temple of Bastet at Bubastis (see Chapter 8).[8]

Bastet was exclusively shown as a lioness from her earliest attestations until the New Kingdom. Her famed symbolisation as a cat emerged later, reflecting subtle changes in religious beliefs that occurred over many centuries of Egyptian history. In fact, a double nature of Bastet as a lioness and a cat is often expressed by her conflation with Sekhmet. This aspect of Bastet was thematised in earlier textual sources, such as the so-called '*Loyalist Teaching*' of the Twelfth Dynasty,[9] which describes the ideal character of the king thus:

> "*He is Bastet who protects the Two Lands. He who worships him will be protected by his arm. He is Sekhmet against he who transgresses his order. The one he hates will be under distress.*"

This ambivalent character of Bastet developed further in subsequent periods. The cat symbolised the gentler, more accessible, and attractive nature of the feline goddess. This re-imagining of Bastet as a gentler version of a lioness evidently led to her depiction as a cat. This shift in her depiction eliminated the potential danger that a real lioness posed to humans. Interestingly, the Middle Kingdom is also the first time in which cats, although still close to their wild form *felis silvestris,* are shown as pets in tomb paintings. From the New Kingdom onwards, the cult of Bastet and her orgiastic celebrations (see Chapter 8) enjoyed increasing popularity, especially during the later First millennium BCE when it spread outside Egypt and into the Mediterranean world.

Fig. 1: *The goddess Bastet as a lioness. Relief from the temple of Bastet. (*TELL BASTA PROJECT 2011*)*

Evidence of Bastet as the main goddess of the city of Bubastis is almost half a millennium younger than her first appearance on the stone vessels from the galleries of the step pyramid. The relief on the lintel of the *ka*-temple of King Pepi I at Bubastis from the beginning of the Sixth Dynasty (around 2270 BCE) depicts her as an anthropomorphic goddess with a lioness's head. In addition, tomb stelae and inscriptions in private tombs at Bubastis of the same period mention titles of the tomb owners that are related to the administration and cult of the local temple of Bastet. Thus, it is certain that the temple and cult of Bastet existed at Bubastis at the end of the Old Kingdom (see Chapter 2).

The goddess formed the centre of a constellation of deities at Bubastis, where other lioness goddesses of the Delta, such as Sekhmet and Shesemtet, enjoyed their own cult in the main temple. This is revealed by the titles of officials from the New Kingdom onwards, and in reliefs from the sanctuary of the temple from the time of Nectanebo II (see Chapters 6 and 8). Attested at Bubastis are also cults for the important Western Delta goddesses Wadjet, otherwise known as the main deity of Buto, who appeared in the form of a cobra and as such embodied the Red Crown of Lower Egypt, and the anthropomorphic goddess Neith, the main deity of Sais. Both belonged to the circle of the so-called '*dangerous goddesses*', a religious concept that viewed a number of female deities as ambivalent, fearsome, and protective beings, hence their association with Bastet at Bubastis.

However, there were also a number of Bubastite male deities, such as the solar god Atum in the role of Bastet's divine consort and the lion god Mahes, who was venerated in an annex temple located immediately north of the sanctuary of the main temple. Bastet, Atum, and Mahes thus formed the principal triad of Bubastis. Mahes was also closely associated with the falcon-headed Hor-Hekenu and Nefertem, who could appear either as a falcon or an anthropomorphic god with a lion head. At Bubastis, these deities also figured as manifestations of the sun god Ra and as warrior gods, and were each assumed to be the son of Bastet.[10] In addition, the cult of Bastet as the '*Eye of Ra*' and the consort of Atum furthered a close religious connection with Heliopolis and its deities, such as Horakhty, Shu and Tefnut (see Chapter 7). Inscriptions on private statues of the New Kingdom inform us that there was a cult for Osiris at Bubastis as well (see Chapter 6.1).

1.1 Bubastis: The city of Bastet over four millennia

The main cult place of the goddess Bastet was the city of Bubastis in the Southeastern Nile Delta. The archaeological site where the remains of the city are still preserved is today called '*Tell Basta*' (Arabic for "*the mound of Bastet*") and almost entirely now encroached by the modern city of Zagazig.

Bubastis was located close to the Pelusiac branch of the Nile, the most important Nile branch of the Eastern Delta. This location played a significant role in the city's prosperity. The Pelusiac branch remained active for thousands of years, ensuring Bubastis' undisturbed access to a system of connected waterways that served as ancient Egypt's most important communication routes. Previous research based on contour maps from the Survey of Egypt in the 1930s and a geoelectrical survey of the Eastern Nile Delta suggested that the Tanitic branch also passed close to Bubastis, though not as close as the Pelusiac branch.[11] However, a recent study by the geoarchaeological team of the TELL BASTA PROJECT (see below) re-examined the question of the location of the Pelusiac and Tanitic branch and integrated topographical maps with digital surface model data from the TanDEM-X Mission. The resulting digital morphometric and hydrographic modelling indicated that that the Pelusiac branch ran south of Tell Basta, but did not indicate a second major fluvial channel such as the assumed Tanitic branch to the north of Bubastis. Instead, it suggests that the Tanitic branch ran close to Kafr/Kom El-Ashraf, which is more northward than previously thought. Another possibilty would be, that there was a bifurcation of the Pelusiac branch somewhere to the southwest of Bubastis. However, it seems that two major fluvial branches marked the administrative boundaries of the Eighteenth Nome of Lower Egypt with Bubastis as the capital city since the New Kingdom.[12]

The city's proximity to the Wadi Tumilat, one of the main land routes to the Sinai, which was used for quarrying stone and minerals, as well as trade and military expeditions, was also advantageous. The city thus occupied a key position in a supra-regional communication and trade network due to its excellent geographical location.

Bubastis, like many settlements in the Eastern Nile Delta, is located on a southeast-northwest oriented sandy mound, a so-called gezira (Arabic for "*island*"). Geomorphologically, geziras

Fig. 2: *Geomorphology, hydrogeography and settlements of the Nile Delta. Dashed line: ancient coastline; yellow: coastal sand and gravels; blue: lagoons; green: marshes; pale brown: Mit Ghamr-formation. Synthesis of data from:* BIETAK 1975; COUTELLIER, STANLEY 1988; BUTZER 2002; TRISTANT, MIDANT-REYNES 2011, SPENCER 2014; PENNINGTON ET AL. 2017; ULLMANN et al. 2019 by LANGE-ATHINODOROU 2024)

are defined as peaks of the geological Mit Ghamr formation, a sediment accumulation that was deposited by the Pleistocene Pre-Nile regime (800ka-200ka BP).

The Mit Ghamr formation makes up the surface of the entire Pleistocene Delta, which is now buried beneath the Holocene sediments of the Neonile system (80ka-10ka BP). The fall of the eustatic sea level during the last glacial by up to 35 m, and the subsequent arid period, which lasted until around 12,000 BP, exposed the Pleistocene Delta surface to wind erosion while the streams of the Nile river branches carved deep rifts into the bare fluvial sediments.[13]

During the Holocene era, as the sea level rose and the Delta's river branches' gradient decreased, sediments of the so-called 'Bilqas formation' started depositing. These sediments initially accumulated in the lower-lying areas of the Northern Delta and the basin of the Central Delta and gradually covered the higher-lying areas until only the highest elevations of the Pleistocene Delta relief, the geziras, remained above the Holocene alluvial sediments. These form the sandy mounds of the Delta on which human settlements were preferentially established.[14]

The gezira of Bubastis is located on the northeastern fringes of a large Pleistocene sand accumulation in the southern Central Delta. There are indications that the gezira of Bubastis had several local elevations, called koms (Arabic for "mounds"). Recent geophysical investigations (see Chapter 8) have provided enough evidence to reconstruct some of the waterways that once flowed between these mounds.[15] These are probably the result of the above-mentioned long-term erosion of the Pleistocene Delta surface during the last global glacial maximum. While the above-described processes took place long before human occupation, they were crucial for the later development of the city of Bubastis, because they have created depressions and waterways between the elevations of the gezira, which served as natural boundaries between certain functional areas of the settlement. Natural topography thus encouraged the delineation of specific settlement zones, with local temples, cemeteries, and residential quarters built at different elevations, visibly separated by water channels and low-lying areas.

The locations of the surviving monuments and the archaeological work have enabled us to identify at least three koms at Bubastis: the Central Kom, i.e. the central plateau of the gezira, which extends to a long gradual slope to the east, the Northern Kom, and the Western Kom. The discovery of a cemetery of the Protodynastic period on the Western Kom proves that settlement activities began at Bubastis around the same time as the name of the city appears on some bone tags discovered in the tomb of a king of Dynasty 0 (around 3150 BCE) in the cemetery of Umm el-Qaab at Abydos. As the bone tags record the place of origin of contents of vessels deposited in the tomb, Bubastis seems to have been an important regional centre in the Southeastern Delta already in the Protodynastic period. The Western Kom remained the centre of the settlement also during the Old Kingdom, when a governor's palace was built there in the Fourth Dynasty (2670-2500 BCE), followed by the temples for the veneration of the royal Ka of kings Teti and Pepi I in the Sixth Dynasty (2318-2250 BCE). Thus, in the Old Kingdom, the Western Kom served as an administrative and temple zone, while a funerary zone was established on the Northern Kom, with several cemeteries dating from the Fifth Dynasty to the beginning of the First Intermediate Period (see Chapter 2).

During the Middle Kingdom, a large palace was constructed for the governors of Bubastis on the northern part of the Northern Kom. This palace was built with disregard for the former mostly funerary character of the area. However, to the immediate east of the palace, a cemetery was built for the governors residing in the palace, providing us with a very rare example of a palatial cemetery in Egypt. The palace at Bubastis may have also served as a royal mooring palace, a temporary residence for the king himself. For instance, he might have stayed there in order to take part in cultic festivities for Bastet. In fact, it is the only archaeologically preserved palace of the Middle Kingdom in all of Egypt. However, in the subsequent periods, the Northern Kom was used again for cemeteries (see Chapters 4, 5 and 6).

The temple of Bastet was erected on the Central Kom, in the middle of the highest plateau on the original surface level of the gezira. The temple had probably existed on this spot since the Old Kingdom and had remained in this position throughout the following eras. The building was never moved, it was just enlarged. The remains visible on the surface today date back to the time of the Libyan kings and the Late Dynastic period, when Bubastis had become one of the foremost cities in all of Egypt (Chapter 7-8). However, texts and depictions from the Sixth Dynasty until the end of the New Kingdom confirm its earlier existence as well (Chap. 2, 4 and 6). A characteristic feature of the temple was the above-mentioned canal system that surrounded the temple. It is along these canals that Bastet, represented by her cult-statue, would travel in her sacred barque during her famous festivals (see Chapter 8).

Traces of the domestic quarter of Bubastis can be found on the large southeastern part of the Tell, on the slope of the underlying gezira. Archaeological surveys have shown that the structures on its surface date back to the Ptolemaic and Roman period (306 BCE - Third century AD). However, the descriptions of the Greek historian Herodotus (ca. 450 BCE) inform us that the centre of Bubastis was located there from at least the Late Period. During this time, a large stone-paved processional street, the so-called Dromos, connected the temple of Bastet in the west with the so-called *Temple of Hermes* in the east. The Dromos was also the main axis of the city. Recently, the remains of the Dromos have been discovered during the excavation of Ptolemaic casemate buildings and houses adjacent to the entrance of the temple of Bastet, which was still flourishing in the time of Ptolemais Euergetes III (246-222 BCE, Chapter 8). During the Roman period, in the Third or Fourth century AD, the area in front of the temple entrance was rebuilt as an open courtyard with a single column monument (see Chapter 8). However, during the Roman dominion of Egypt, the importance of Bubastis declined and by the end of the Fourth century AD, it had become an insignificant settlement as the power shifted to the nearby city of Bilbeis.[16]

1.2 The TELL BASTA PROJECT: Continuing a long history of research
AUGUSTE MARIETTE was the first to undertake archaeological investigations at Bubastis in around 1860, but he soon turned to other projects. Unfortunately, nothing is known about the extent and results of his work, possibly due to the loss of many of his documents when his house in Cairo was flooded in 1878.[17] In 1887, ÉDOUARD NAVILLE began archaeological work at Tell Basta, which lasted for two years. He focused on the excavation and documentation of the remains of the great temple of Bastet (see Chapters 6 and 7).[18] Two deposits of Egyptian gold and silver objects from the late New Kingdom, such as bracelets, earrings, collars, and vessels, were accidently found in 1906 during track laying earthworks for a new railway line.[19] Continued work on the railway line led to the discovery in 1925 of the tomb of Hori II, the viceroy of Kush, who held office during the reign of Ramses III and his successor (see Chapter 6).[20]

In 1939, Labib Habachi conducted extensive excavations at Tell Basta, resulting in the discovery of Pepi I's *ka*-temple from the Sixth Dynasty, the temple of Mahes connected to the sanctuary of the temple of Bastet from the Twenty-second Dynasty, and the Roman open court in front of the temple of Bastet.[21] Shafik Farid from the Egyptian Antiquities Service carried out excavations on the Northern Kom from 1961-1967, and discovered the large palace of the city's governors from the Middle Kingdom and the adjoining necropolis (see Chapter 4).[22]

From 1967-1971, Ahmed El-Sawi from the Egyptian Antiquities Service conducted archaeological work on the Western Kom, in an area that is now partly covered by modern buildings. He discovered a pillar from a *ka*-temple of Teti, an administrative building of the Old Kingdom, a cat cemetery from the Late Period, and a necropolis with human burials dating from the Old to New Kingdoms. From 1978-1989, Mohamed Ibrahim Bakr from the University Zagazig in co-operation with Walter Reineke and Erika Endesfelder from the Academy of Sciences of the East German Republic, excavated the elite Old Kingdom cemeteries on the Northern Kom (see Chapter 2).[23]

In continuation of this cooperation, the University Potsdam directed by Christian Tietze carried out numerous seasons from 1990-2006, documenting the architectural remains of the temple of Bastet and starting a new archaeological survey in the temple of Pepi I (see Chapters 2, 6 and 7).[24]

As the investigation of such an important and extensive site as Tell Basta requires long-term and multi-disciplinary research, the Tell Basta Project, an international archaeological, geoarchaeological, and epigraphic project of the Institute of Egyptology at the University of Wuerzburg in cooperation with the the Egyptian Ministry of State for Antiquities, has been working towards documenting the archaeological remains of the ancient city of Bubastis since 2008. The project, directed by the author of this monograph Eva Lange-Athinodorou,[25] aims to reconstruct the history of the city and the life of its inhabitants, along with understanding its position in the network of settlements and cities of the Nile Delta throughout all historical periods.

In recent years, the Tell Basta Project has focused on the investigation of the domestic quarters of the Ptolemaic Period connecting temple and city (see Chapter 8) and the excavation of the provincial residence and *ka*-temples of the Old Kingdom on the Western Kom (see Chapter 2).

To comprehend how the city functioned and what made it thrive also requires an understanding of its natural landscape. Bubastis was a city embedded in a dynamic riverine environment with constantly changing parameters. The watery veins of Bubastis' deltaic environment, from the mighty Pelusiac branch to the small local canals, profoundly influenced the destiny of the city. Hence, geoarchaeological studies directed by Julia Meister from the Institute of Geography and Geology (Working group Geoarchaeology and Quaternary Research) at the University Wuerzburg and dedicated to reconstructing the paleo-landscape of Bubastis and its hinterland, are a vital part of the Tell Basta Project (see Chapters 2 and 8). All ongoing research is regularly published in the form of preliminary reports, research articles, and integrative studies.

Endnotes

[1] Lange 2016, 315-316.

[2] In this monograph, the reigning years of the kings are only given when they are mentioned for the first time.

[3] Lange 2016, 303-315.

[4] Meeks 2006, 240.

[5] Lange 2016, 303-304.

[6] Bietak 1975, 90, 163; Zaremba et al. 2017.

[7] Lange 2016, 317-319.

[8] Tillier, 2010, 167, 171-172; Lange-Athinodorou, 2019(b), 554-561, 580-581.

[9] Parkinson 1998, 235-245.

[10] Habachi 1957, 46-55, 117-122; Rosenow 2008, 120-121; Vicente 2016, 143-146.

[11] Bietak 1975; El-Mahmoudi, Gabr 2009.

[12] Bietak, 1975, 167 but here referring to two variants of the Pelusiac branch.

[13] Siddall et al. 2003, 856-857; Stanley, Warne 1998, 804 Fig. 8A.

[14] Wunderlich 1989, 13; Andres, Wunderlich 1991, 122, 126 Fig. 4, 12-130; Andres, Wunderlich 1992, 159 Fig. 2, 163; de Wit 1993, 310-313, 315; Pennington et al. 2016.

[15] Ullmann et al. 2019, 191-198.

[16] Habachi 1957, 3.

[17] Bierbrier et al. 1995, 275-276.

[18] Naville 1891.

[19] Edgar 1904.

[20] Gauthier 1928.

[21] Habachi 1957.

[22] Farid 1964.

[23] Bakr 1992.

[24] Tietze 2004; Lange 2006.

[25] Lange 2011; Lange-Athinodorou 2019(a); Lange-Athinodorou 2021.

2. The evolution of a Delta city: From early beginnings to residences and temples

The end of the Fourth millennium BCE saw the emergence of an Egyptian proto-state, with the development of major centres throughout Egypt. Based on archaeological discoveries, it has been a long-standing scholarly opinion that the '*Naqada civilization*' – named after the site on the west bank of the Nile in the southern Nile Valley, where FLINDERS PETRIE first excavated cemeteries and settlements with a very distinctive and uniform material culture – had established itself as the dominant force by that time. This cultural entity had assimilated earlier cultures not only in the Nile Valley but also in the Nile Delta.[1] However, recent research on the process of state formation in Egypt suggests that there was not a monolithic Naqadian culture at the outset, but rather a complex system of regional chiefdoms with diverse socio-cultural backgrounds that were each embedded within their own unique ecological environments.[2]

The transition between the indigenous Delta cultures and the Upper Egyptian Naqada culture can be reliably traced through the changing pottery repertoire of the respective sites, primarily Buto and Tell el-Farkha. At both sites, Naqada pottery appears from the Naqada IID2/ Buto IIIa phase (~3350 BCE) onwards in the settlement layers and tombs of the Delta, while the typical ware of the Delta cultures, the so-called '*Buto-Maadi*' pottery, or more recently, '*Lower Egyptian*' ware (and analogously the '*Lower Egyptian Culture*', or LEC), disappears during the same period. However, the exact details of the socio-political process that led to the transition between the Predynastic and the Early Dynastic period remain difficult to grasp based on currently available sources.[3]

Older research, which was influenced by a handful of mostly pictorial sources such as the palette of King Narmer (around 3000 BCE), had suggested that the so-called '*unification*' was a fixed and singular event that marked the beginning of Egypt's dynastic period. However, data from new excavations have rendered this view obsolete. Contrary to an explanatory model that concentrates on individual events, the newly discovered archaeological evidence indicates that the unification of Egypt was a gradual and ongoing process, undoubtedly punctuated by short-term events that influenced its course. Although these events have left hardly any material traces, they nevertheless contributed to the gradual unification of Egypt, leaving many aspects of this process open to speculation.[4]

The territorial state emerged in Egypt around 3100 BCE out of early chiefdoms that were competing for resources, territory and control in Hierakonpolis, Naqada and Abydos, the area around Memphis and the Fayum, Tell el-Farkha and Buto. The emergence of a kingship that exercised its power throughout Egypt is evident from the beginning of the Dynastic Period.[5] Textual and pictorial sources of that time show the development of royal ideology with the king as the embodiment of the divine, especially the falcon god Horus, which is reflected in the early titles of kings. The subsequent evolution of a centralized government during the first two dynasties with the further development and use of writing, enabled the king and the elite to mobilize people and use resources throughout the country for projects on a new scale, such as military and other expeditions into the Sinai and Lower Nubia, as well as monumental building projects.

The major source for the history of the First Dynasty (3150-2850 BCE)[6] comes from the royal cemetery at Umm el-Qaab at Abydos, where the tombs of several kings (Narmer, Aha, Djer, Djet, Dewen, Adjib, Semerkhet and Qa'a) were discovered. The cemetery was an extension of an older burial ground situated just to the south, the so-called 'Cemetery U', which contained tombs of rulers of the late Predynastic period. Most notable among them was a multi-chambered mud-brick tomb discovered during the excavations of the German Archaeological Institute under the direction of GÜNTER DREYER. This tomb brought to light a large number of bone labels with early hieroglyphic writings (see below).[7]

The tombs of the First Dynasty have a more advanced architecture than the earlier graves. They vary in size, but all have burial chambers made of mud-brick with floors, the lining of the walls and roofs made of wood and set into a large pit in the sand. Many of the tombs are surrounded by the subsidiary graves of relatives, court officials and servants. The tombs were covered by a low brick-lined mound of sand. Two pairs of stelae inscribed with the ruler's name marked the offering place of the royal tomb.[8] Although it is still not possible to reconstruct a detailed history of the First Dynasty, there are seal impressions and labels of goods from the royal tombs, decorated ceremonial palettes and mace heads from the temple of Horus at Hierakonpolis, rock inscriptions, and other sources that provide tantalising glimpses into the activities of these early kings. For example, they celebrated the Sed-festival, visited shrines in Sais and Buto, and conducted military campaigns as far as Southern Palestine in the northeast and Lower Nubia in the south.[9]

Information regarding the Second Dynasty (2850-2740 BCE) is quite limited, leaving doubts about the number and sequence of its rulers, as well as the length of their reign. However, research has established that Hetepsekhemwy, Raneb and Ninetjer were the first rulers, while Khasekhemwy was the last in the lineage.[10] The beginning of the Second Dynasty is marked in the archaeological record by the move of the royal burial ground to Saqqara, probably in order to connect the royal cemetery with the Memphite capital.[11] Hetepsekhemwy, Raneb and Ninetjer built a cluster of rock-cut gallery tombs in the direct vicinity of the later pyramid complex of Djoser Netjerikhet (see below). Inscriptions from the reign of Ninetjer point to internal problems in the northern part of Egypt which were answered by military action. The peculiar exchange of the falcon god Horus on top of the so-called 'serekh' (srḫ), a stylized palace façade containing the royal name, with his adversary Seth under King Peribsen in the middle of the Second Dynasty, may indicate a de facto division of the country. This is particularly evident as Peribsen chose to be buried again in the archaic cemetery at Abydos in the south. The programmatic name of the last king of the dynasty, Khasekhemwy (ḥᶜ.j sḫm.wy - "The two divine powers appear"), whose serekh also has Horus and Seth appearing together on the top, indicates a reunification of Egypt. Inscriptions on two seated statues of this ruler mention the defeat of enemies with the words: "Lower Egypt: rebels: 47.209". Additionally, several stone vessels have inscriptions stating the "Fighting and beating of Lower Egypt" accompanied with the depiction of a kneeling man with a papyrus clump on his head. These sources indicate that there was a period of civil war in Egypt, but we have no information about who Khasekhemwy's opponents were.[12]

The following period of the Third Dynasty seems to have overcome these times of unrest. Its first ruler, Netjerikhet (2720-2700 BCE), the 'Djoser' of later Egyptian sources and the son of Khasekhemwy, had the famous Step Pyramid erected at Saqqara, a visible statement marking the end of the Early Dynastic period. The building of this monument clearly shows that the centralized government now operated on a whole new level. Memphis was firmly established as the capital of the evolving state and ink inscriptions on stone vessels from the galleries under the pyramid of Djoser reveal that a network of institutions and officials operated an effective provincial administration at that time. Regular expeditions to procure raw materials, such as from the Wadi Maghara in southwestern Sinai, ensured the availability of resources for such grand building projects.[13] Prospering from the stability the rulers of the Third Dynasty had achieved, the kings of the succeeding Fourth Dynasty were able to push the monumentality of royal tombs even further. Snofru (2670-2620 BCE) constructed three pyramids at Dahshur and Meidum, while his son and successor Khufu (2620-2580 BCE) built the famous Great Pyramid on the Giza plateau on the west bank of the Nile. While Khufu's successor Djedefra (2580-2570 BCE) had his pyramid complex built at Abu Rowash, Kings Khafra (2570-2530 BCE) and Menkaura (2530-2510 BCE) returned to Giza to build the second and third pyramid there.[14]

New geoarchaeological research and the recently discovered journal of an official called Merer who was in charge of transporting limestone from Tura to the construction site of Khufu's pyramid, bear witness to the interesting fact that the desert plateau of Giza was connected to the Nile via a complex system of canals and basins. Egyptian engineers utilised these waterways, which were deep enough for cargo ships, to transport building materials and supplies. The most important of these was the so-called '*Khufu branch*', a now defunct palaeo-canal of the Nile located to the west of the modern Nile. It is possible that the gradual sedimentation of the canal led to the relocation of the royal cemetery of the Fifth Dynasty from Giza to Abusir.[15]

At Abusir, within the area of the new royal necropolis, the kings of the Fifth Dynasty, from Userkaf (2500-2490 BCE) to Menkauhor (2420-2410 BCE) introduced a new type of temple, the so-called '*sun temple*', demonstrating the ever-growing importance of the cult of the sun god and its close connection to royal ideology. Written sources indicate that every Fifth Dynasty king built such a temple, but only those of Userkaf and Niuserre (2455-2420 BCE) have been discovered so far. As papyrus archives discovered in the funerary temple of Neferirkare (2475-2465 BCE) reveal, the cult and administration of the sun temples were closely connected to that of the royal funerary temple.[16] However, Djedkare Asosi (2410-2380 BCE), reigning at the end of the Fifth Dynasty, decided to break from tradition and did not build a sun temple or his tomb at the royal necropolis at Abusir. The latter decision may have been influenced by a changing hydrogeography, similar to what happened at Giza. Geoarchaeological investigations of the Czech mission directed by MIROSLAV BARTA led to a reconstruction of the '*Lake of Abusir*', a seasonal natural water basin close to the pyramid complexes. Stratigraphic sedimentological analysis were conducted to reconstruct the depositional environment of the lake sediments. The results suggest that the lake may have dried out due to long-term changes in the palaeoclimate to drier conditions (see Chapter 3). This may finally have hindered the lake's former use as the main access route to the royal cemetery.[17]

At any rate, the pyramid of Djedkare Asosi was built at South Saqqara. The last king of the Fifth Dynasty, Unas (2380-2350 BCE), followed this example but built his tomb close to the pyramid complex of Netjerikhet Djoser. Unas' pyramid partially covers the above-mentioned tomb of Hetepsekhemwy of the Second Dynasty. The most notable feature of Unas' tomb is the innovation of inscribing the passageway, antechamber, and the burial chamber with funerary religious texts.[18]

Scholarly literature tends to outline the history of the Fourth and Fifth Dynasties along the trajectories of their impressive monumental royal tombs. The pyramid city excavated by MARK LEHNER at Giza, featuring numerous dormitories and workshops, exemplifies the scale and complexity of these construction sites.[19] It is obvious that the building of these monuments triggered an unparalleled development of the country's administration, owing to their high demand for stone, minerals and many other materials from quarries across Egypt, the adjacent deserts, the Sinai, and neighbouring countries. Consequently, textual and pictorial sources from the king's funerary temples and the officials' tombs provide information about expeditions and trade, including those as far as Punt in the reign of Sahura (2490-2475 BCE).[20] Additionally, military campaigns contributed to the growing demands of the royal court. For example, according to the annals on the so-called 'Palermo Stone', Sneferu received a large booty consisting of 7,000 captives and 200,000 head of cattle from a campaign into Lower Nubia, between the First and Second Cataract.[21]

The true backbone of the country's economy and its building projects and related activities were the provinces of Egypt where a multitude of royal and private agricultural domains were located.[22] However, high provincial officials are rarely attested in the provinces themselves. Instead, they are almost exclusively found in the Memphite necropoleis, buried close to the pyramid complex of the king they served. This custom, however, changed during the Sixth Dynasty, when royal interest in the provinces increased dramatically.[23] The available sources clearly indicate that the rise of provincial temples in terms of religious, administrative and economic importance began in the Fifth Dynasty. Although these temples did not receive significant royal patronage before, now there were royal endowments to these institutions. For example, Userkaf donated land and a temple building to the deities of Buto.[24] Thus, the introduction of exemption decrees, which freed temples from taxes and *corvée labour* since the reign of Neferirkare, is in accordance with this new course of action.[25] The rise of provincial temples was due to their evolution into efficient nexus points between residence and province, becoming part of an economic network that was formerly mainly based on provincial residences.

During the Sixth Dynasty, a new building program was implemented that involved connecting royal cult chapels (as *ka*-temples, see Chapter 2.2) to provincial temples of important towns all over Egypt, such as Dendera, Abydos, Akhmim and Bubastis. At the same time, the provincial administration was reformed and expanded, with the creation of a multitude of new offices. The high-ranking officials who were sent from the residence to govern individual nomes formed strong connections with their assigned locations, especially if they were not already from there (such as in the case of Bubastis, see Chapters 2.2.3 and 2.2.4). As a result, they were no longer buried in the Saqqara/Memphis necropoleis of the residence, but rather at their respective official residences. Elite cemeteries from the late Old Kingdom at Aswan and Elephantine, Edfu, Abydos, Deir el-Gabrawi, Akhmim, Meir in the Nile Valley and Bubastis and Mendes in the Nile Delta bear testimony to this new attitude.[26]

Teti (2318-2300 BCE) was the first ruler of the Sixth Dynasty to ascend the throne after the last king of the Fifth Dynasty. He was not the son of the previous ruler, but connected himself to the lineage of his predecessor by marrying Unas' daughter. While Teti and his successors continued building their pyramid complexes at Saqqara, they also initiated a new building program in the provinces, as mentioned above. Teti himself had a *ka*-temple at Bubastis (see Chapter 2.2.3) and Zawijet el-Meitin. After King Userkare's short reign, Pepi I (2295-2250 BCE), the son of Teti, expanded the building policy of *ka*-temples. The biographical inscription of the architect Nekhebu and other officials of provincial temples reveal that King Pepi I had no less than eight *ka*-temples at Saqqara, Assiut, Akhmim, Zawijet el-Meitin, Qus and Elkab in the Nile Valley and Akhbit, the "*City of the Lakes*" and Bubastis in the Nile Delta. Of these, the *ka*-temple at Bubastis is the only one still preserved in the archaeological record (see Chapter 2.2).[27]

The biography of Weni, from his tomb at Abydos, sheds light on internal political difficulties of the time. Weni, who was a high official and judge, mentions the interrogation of a royal wife of Pepi I who was involved in a harem conspiracy against the king. Later on, Pepi I married two daughters of a high official from Abydos, named Khui and Nebet; Weni himself was a member of this family. Both daughters were given the court name Ankhnespepi/merire. They became mothers to two later heirs to the throne, Antiemsaf Merire I and Pepi II respectively. Scholars have argued that Pepi I's marriage to these women was a reaction to the harem conspiracy led by his first queen. According to their speculations, the marriage was intended to strengthen the relationship between the royal court and the capital of one of Egypt's important provinces in the Nile Valley. This was especially true since the brother of both ladies, a provincial official named Djau, was later appointed as Vizier of Upper Egypt.[28] Without further evidence, however, this remains pure guesswork for the time being.

The biography of Weni also provides insights into various military expeditions against Asiatic Bedouins, possibly in the Sinai region. Additionally, there were quarry expeditions to Elephantine, Wadi Maghara, and another to Lower Nubia. It is known from the graffito of an official named Khnumhotep that journeys were also made to Byblos and Punt during the reign of Pepi I.[29]

After the short reign of Antiemsaf I, Pepi I's younger son and namesake, Pepi II (2245-2180 BCE) ascended the throne as a boy of no more than six years of age. He reigned for a very long time, with Manetho attributing to him the extraordinarily long reign of 94 years, while the Turin Royal Papyrus also gives him 90+x years. However, the highest securely attested date is the year following the thirty-first cattle census, which results in an equally remarkable figure of at least 63 regnal years. Pepi II apparently continued the policy of his predecessors with expeditions to Nubia and the building of *ka*-temples at the main cult centres of the country. Details of his reign come mainly from exemption decrees, such as the four decrees for the temple of Min at Coptos dealing with the allocations for the offering cult of the king's statue. Other decrees concern the pyramid city of Menkaure (whose cult was obviously still flourishing), while another concerns the funerary cult of his Queen Udjebten.[30]

The archaeological record reveals important information as well. For instance, a large governor's residence at Ain Asil in the Dakhleh oasis, excavated by the Institut français d'archéologie orientale under the direction of GEORGE SOUKIASSIAN, testifies to the country's wide-ranging network of the provincial administration and the new power of provincial governors, who had assumed the title '*head of Upper Egypt*'.[31]

Pepi II's son and successor, Antiemsaf II (2180 BCE), reigned only very briefly. After that, the royal annals have a rapid succession of a series of rulers about whom we know almost nothing. King Netjerkare Siptah, a successor of Antiemsaef II, whose name was later misread as '*Nitocris*', also belongs to this line. Mistaken for a queen, he has haunted scholarly and popular literature for a long time, especially as the Greek historian Herodotus told the legend that Nitocris was the avenging sister-wife of Antiemsaef II, who fell victim to a conspiracy.[32]

The seventeen kings in the succession of Antiemsaf II form the Eighth Dynasty (2168-2131 BCE). Though not much is known about them, it is evident that they still erected small pyramids in Saqqara, issued decrees for provincial temples, and appointed 'chiefs of Upper Egypt' from a dynasty of officials from Coptos. However, great building projects, expeditions, and military campaigns had all ceased. From an Egyptological point of view, the end of the Eighth Dynasty also marks the end of the Old Kingdom and the beginning of the First Intermediate Period.[33]

2.1 Bubastis in the Predynastic and Early Dynastic period

Upon their arrival, the earliest settlers of what would later become the city of Bubastis were struck by the sight of a large sandy hill that stretched southeast to northwest. They recognised it as a highly attractive and spacious location for a settlement foundation, as it rose several meters above the alluvial plain, and provided a safe space from the annual inundation. Close by were the mighty Pelusiac Nile branch, which could connect them with an already existing network of prosperous settlements in the Eastern Delta and their far-reaching trade connections with the Levant up to the Near East and with the Naqadian culture in the southern Nile Valley. This was a promising location for the future inhabitants of the city.[34]

Some of the oldest evidence for the existence of the settlement does not come from Bubastis but from the southern Nile Valley. As described above, the expedition of the German Archaeological Institute discovered the tomb of a Predynastic ruler in the necropolis of Umm el-Qaab at Abydos. GÜNTER DREYER identified the owner of the tomb with King Scorpion I of Dynasty 0 (around 3150 BCE). The tomb contained a large number of bone tags, inscribed with toponyms, some of which show the sign group 𓃀𓃀, an early version of the usual writing 𓎡𓃀𓋴𓏏 (b3s.t, Bubastis). The labels were once attached to grave goods, such as vessels, and indicated their place of origin, revealing that certain early central places and institutions from all over Egypt were required to provide for the funeral of the king.[35] This suggests that Bubastis was an important regional centre in the Predynastic period and participated in the trade routes between the north and south long before Egypt's unification.

Archaeological evidence of an Early Dynastic settlement at Bubastis comes from the excavations of AHMED EL-SAWI, who discovered a two-chamber shaft tomb built of mud bricks at the northern part of the Western Kom of Bubastis in 1970 (see fig. 3). Most of the funerary objects found with the burial were stone vessels of the First Dynasty.[36] In recent years, excavations of an Egyptian mission at Tell Basta under the direction of AIMAN ASHMAWY ALI have led to the discovery of a cemetery with 15 burials dating from the Protodynastic period until the Second Dynasty (ca. 3200-2686 BCE) at the western part of the Western Kom. While the earliest tombs are simple pits, dug into the sand of the underlying gezira, later burials were interred in brick lined tombs. Most of the burials were poor, but one contained a considerable amount of grave goods, consisting of stone vessels, a grinding stone used on cosmetic palettes and a bracelet of flint.[37]

Adjacent to the northeast of the First Dynasty brick tomb, EL-SAWI excavated a building in 1969 and 1970, which he dubbed the 'Great Building'. The published ground plan shows features that are typical of residential buildings, with apartments in the centre and the south, flanked by storage facilities for grain and other foodstuffs. The excavator identified the building as an administrative centre of Old Kingdom Bubastis, where staple products and grains

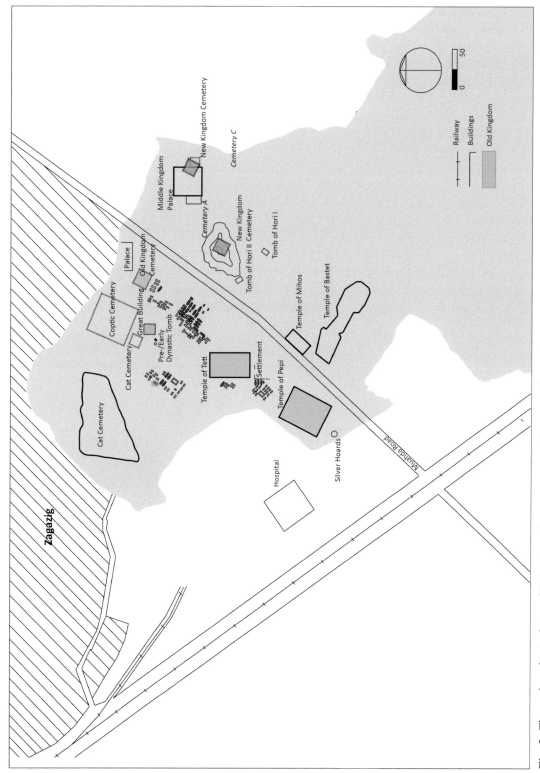

Fig. 3: *The archaeological site of Bubastis with monuments and areas of the Early Dynastic period and Old Kingdom. (TELL BASTA PROJECT 2016)*

collected from the surrounding settlements as taxes for the royal residence were stored.[38]

However, some uncertainties remain. The first concerns the exact date of the building. The pottery published by EL-SAWI ranges from a squat granite vessel with parallels from the Third Dynasty to Maidum-bowls of the Fifth and Sixth Dynasties. The lack of information on their archaeological contexts[39] makes it difficult to determine the exact period of the Old Kingdom in which the building was occupied. The other open question concerns the nature of the building. With a size of 28 by 28 m, it does not appear to have been large enough to have functioned as an administrative centre for such an important provincial centre. Bubastis would have commanded a substantial area with a correspondingly large number of satellite settlements and domains. The 'Great Building' might therefore have been the domicile of a member of the social high-ranking class of Bubastis in the Old Kingdom, possibly a provincial official with ties to the residence whose identity, however, remains unknown.

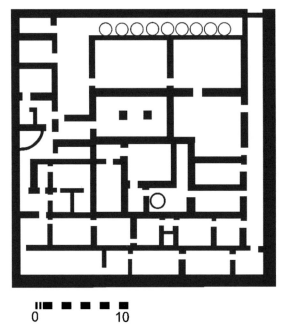

Fig. 4: *Groundplan of the 'Great Building', excavated by El-Sawi in 1970. (LANGE-ATHINODOROU 2016,based on EL-SAWI 1979, Fig. 156b)*

2.2 Bubastis in the Old Kingdom

While a great number of important settlements of the Predynastic Eastern Delta experienced decline and abandonment within the Early Dynastic period[40], Bubastis emerged as a major provincial centre of the evolving state. The location of the Old Kingdom monuments suggests that the central parts of the Old Kingdom city were located on the Western and Northern Kom, which were likely already the focal point of the Early Dynastic settlement. Later, the area underwent several functional changes. Evidence for these developments, which happened over a period of almost one millennium, has come to light during the very recent excavations of the TELL BASTA PROJECT. We now know that in the Fourth and Fifth Dynasties,

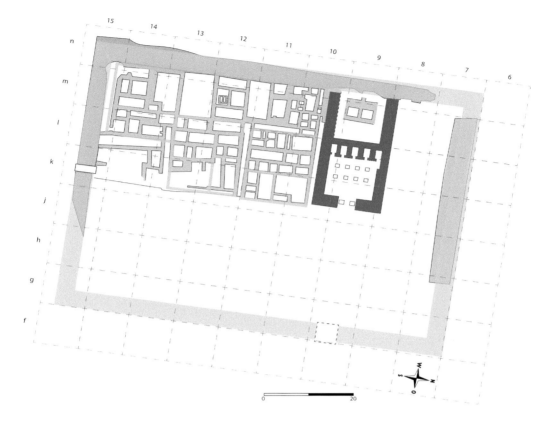

Fig. 5: *Ground plan of the ka-temple of Pepi I. Brown: HABACHI 1957; grey: JÄGER 2000; orange: reconstructed structures of the temple, i.e. enclosure wall with main entrance in the east and residential units in the southwest. (TELL BASTA PROJECT 2022)*

a provincial residence was erected there. Towards the end of the Old Kingdom, the Western Kom was the location of temples for the veneration of the royal *ka* of Kings Teti and Pepi I of the Sixth Dynasty. In a simplified way, the ancient Egyptian word *ka* (⎵ *k3*) designates a power that is inherent in humans and gods in different forms. It was believed to take the shape of a person's double and could dwell in a statue made in his image where it could receive offerings in the context of temple or funerary cults. With the establishment of royal *ka*-temples, the Western Kom was at least partly transformed from a residential zone into a temple zone.

2.2.1 Temples and residences on the Western Kom
In 1939, the renowned Egyptian archaeologist, LABIB HABACHI[41], conducted the first excavations in the area of the city of the Old Kingdom. While visiting the site of Tell Basta in March of that year, HABACHI noticed limestone blocks on the surface west of the Mo'ada road, the area now referred to as the Western Kom. The blocks were exposed during the construction of a road further southwest, and intrigued the archaeologist, leading him to do some immediate investigation:

"After a few hours of work more blocks were found close to it. When the last block to the south was cleared it proved, to my surprise, to bear a scene in relief representing Pepi I with some divinities".[42]

His interest awakened, HABACHI conducted a season in the same year and another from 1943 to 1944 where he unearthed a temple for the veneration of the *ka* of Pepi I. Apart from some elements made of limestone, the building he discovered was built of mud-bricks, oriented on a northeast to southwest axis, measuring 86.84 by 53.30 m. It was surrounded by an impressive 4.0 m thick enclosure wall. The main entrance, now lost, was in the northeast following the orientation of the sanctuary, which was turned almost 90 degrees to the main axis.

The east-west oriented sanctuary was located in the northwestern corner of the enclosure, so that the whole temple resembled the sign 𓉐 (*ḥw.t*) used in the hieroglyphic writing of the word *"temple"* and or *"ka*-temple" (𓉐𓂝 *ḥw.t-kꜣ*) (see fig 5). The sanctuary was enclosed by a wall of 16.80 by 15.25m, around 2.0 m thick, accessible by a gate on its eastern side. Two limestone bases and broken pieces of the doorjamb bearing the titles of Pepi I were all that had survived of the gate. The sanctuary's entrance was connected to the temple's main entrance near the northeastern corner of the enclosure wall, where HABACHI discovered a few undecorated limestone blocks.

The doorway of the sanctuary led to a transverse hall 8.0 m long and around 12.5 m wide. Its main feature, a double row of eight limestone pillars is still preserved. These pillars were once almost 4.0 m high and were inscribed with the titles of Pepi I. In addition, the northeasternmost pillar showed the king and the goddess Seshat engaged in the ritual action of laying out the foundations of the temple. The pillared hall was located in front of a row of sanctuary rooms consisting of either three or five chapels (see below).[43]

HABACHI also reported briefly on the excavation of further building structures in the southern part of the temple enclosure. He stated that some of these contained human burials of the Saitic Period, i.e., the Seventh to Sixth centuries BCE.[44] Unfortunately, none of these buildings were indicated on the ground plan published by HABACHI. However, new archaeological investigations of the TELL BASTA PROJECT have led to the reconstruction of some of these structures. It is now believed that they may have served as domestic units as well as storage and magazine facilities belonging to the original temple phase. These structures remained in use well into the First Intermediate Period (see below).

As mentioned above, the building's main entrance was located in the east, which is where the early temple of the Bastet was situated on the Central Kom, as will be shown below. However, HABACHI also discovered a well-preserved secondary entrance near the southeastern corner of the enclosure. The gateway, measuring 5.10 by 1.90 m, was built of limestone blocks and led through the southern enclosure wall to a corridor connected to the inner temple area. Reliefs on the doorjambs and lintels recorded by HABACHI, now in the Cairo Museum, reveal the purpose of the building and the deities connected to the veneration of the royal *ka* at Bubastis. The relief of the southern lintel depicts the central figure of the king under a winged sun disc, flanked by the goddess Bastet with the head of a lioness and wearing the White Crown to the right and the goddess Hathor with her usual headdress of a sun disc with cow horns to the left.[45] The hieroglyphic inscriptions give their names and attributes. While Hathor is identified as *"Lady of Dendera"*, Bastet has the unusual epithet *"The One, who gives all life"* without mentioning her main cult place. Nevertheless, this scene represents

Fig. 6: *Relief on the southern lintel of the lesser entrance at the ka-temple of Pepi I.* (HABACHI 1957, *Fig. 2)*

the earliest known evidence of Bastet at Bubastis. Moreover, the presence of both Hathor and Bastet in the *ka*-temple of Pepi I underlines the long-established syncretistic connections between the two goddesses. The White Crown of Bastet, which links her to Upper Egypt, may have served to emphasise her connection to Hathor, the principal deity of Dendera in the southern Nile Valley.

On the relief, Bastet is depicted approaching the king from the right, which can be interpreted in geographical terms as coming from the east, as the relief was situated on the south-

Fig. 7: *Relief on the northern lintel of the lesser entrance at the ka-temple of Pepi I.* (HABACHI 1957, *Fig. 3A)*

ern side of the entrance. Interestingly, the remains of the later temple of Bastet are located precisely in the east, indicating that a temple dedicated to this goddess had been present there since the Old Kingdom. The specifics of the spatial relationship between the two temples are, however, unknown, as any possible archaeological remains of the early temple of Bastet would be located under the later stages or may not have been preserved at all. However, let us consider some speculation on this matter: In the First millennium BCE, the main entrance to the temple of Bastet was located in the east.[46] Assuming that the Old Kingdom temple had the same orientation, the temple of Pepi I would have been situated close to the sanctuary of the goddess's temple instead of its entrance. This is reminiscent of the custom of erecting chapels at the rear wall of a temple sanctuary, the so-called '*contra temple*' we know of from later times at Karnak, Deir el-Medina, Dendera and other places. The sanctuary's rear wall was actually the closest point to the deity from the outside. Therefore, it was a place to offer petitions to the deity for those who did not have the privilege to enter the sanctuary itself.[47]

Some time ago, DAVID O'CONNOR proposed that a small-sized structure known as '*Building H*' (21.0 by 18.0 m) at Abydos could offer insides into the spatial relationship of Old Kingdom royal *ka*-temples with provincial temples. At Abydos, Building H was located in a cluster of equally modest mud-brick buildings. In front of its entrance was the base of a stela with the remains of a royal decree concerning the cult of statues of Pepi II and his family. The text on the stela describes the location of the statues as "*within the temple of Khenti-Imentiu*". BARRY KEMP thus identified Building H as the abode of the main deity of Abydos in the Old Kingdom. However, O'CONNOR believed Building H to be a *ka*-temple of Pepi II instead, comparing its size to the sanctuary of the *ka*-temple of Pepi I at Bubastis. He suggested that the actual temple of Khenti-Imentiu is located elsewhere, probably to the south of Building H.[48] Nonetheless, the lack of inscriptional references to a royal *ka*-temple at Abydos and the differences in the ground plans of the sanctuary of Pepi I's *ka*-temple at Bubastis and Building H at Abydos do not support his hypothesis.

Coming back to the central scene on the door lintel at Bubastis: Framing the king between Bastet and Hathor are two deities, Iunmutef as a divine cult servant, who is identified by his name on the right, while on the left is a fecundity figure with a clump of papyrus sprouting from his head, with the caption "*Lower Egypt, lord of provisions*". Both figures are facing a column inscribed with the royal titles. On the northern door lintel, there are three lines of an inscription that display the titles of Pepi I and the name of his temple:

> "*May live the Horus: the Beloved of the Two Lands; the Dual King, the son of Ra: Pepi, given life. May live the Two Mistresses: the Beloved of the corporate (of the gods); the Golden Horus: the most golden of falcons, whom all the gods love. May live the ka-temple of Pepi in Bubastis*".

On the eastern doorjamb of the northern side was a depiction of a fecundity figure with the caption "*Nile flood*" (*ḥp*), while on the western side was the figure of a female named "*inundation*" (*Ȝḥ.t*). Both are shown carrying a purification vessel. In their original position, they stood towards whoever entered the temple through the gateway, symbolically cleansing them.

The enclosure of Pepi I in Bubastis is the only archaeologically preserved royal *ka*-temple from the Old Kingdom. So far, no other temples of this type are known. It is therefore difficult to contextualise the architecture of the temple in any detail. Nevertheless, some interesting observations can be made when looking at Old Kingdom temples in general. Doing so, we have to keep in mind that in the Old Kingdom, only royal funerary temples were built entirely of stone. In contrast, provincial temples were modest affairs constructed mostly of mud bricks. Only certain architectural elements such as doorjambs, sills, and pillars were made of stone, consistent with the *ka*-temple of Pepi I. A good parallel is offered by an Old Kingdom building discovered under the New Kingdom temple of Osiris-Khenti-Imentiu at Abydos. It has an enclosure wall about 5 m thick with two corresponding entrances built of limestone around 1 m wide, which lead through the eastern and western walls connected by a transverse double row of three columns. During his excavations, PETRIE found a cartouche with the name *ppjj* on the inner doorframe of the western passage. PETRIE attributed the building to Pepi I, but as nothing else of the inscribed royal titles remained and both Pepi I and Pepi II had built at Abydos, it is unclear which of these kings actually erected the building.[49]

The sanctuary of the *ka*-temple of Pepi I at Bubastis is centred on a double row of pillars and adjacent chambers. According to HABACHI's plan, there are four sanctuary chambers, with the central three being of the same dimensions, while the southernmost chamber is slightly smaller. Additionally, HABACHI indicated a feature resembling a virtually destroyed narrow passageway next to the northernmost chamber. New excavations by the TELL BASTA PROJECT have led to further clarification. The central chambers (SR2-4 in fig. 9) measure 2.60 by 1.50 m, the southernmost chamber 2.34 by 0.98 m. The northernmost chamber (SR4) was not a passageway, but a room with similar dimensions to SR1, the southernmost chamber. Thus, the two smaller chambers flank the central ones. The spacing of the pillars in front of the chambers corresponds only with the entrances of SR2, SR3 and SR4, forming an architectural sub-unit that does not include chambers SR1 and SR5. This suggests that the *ka*-temple had a tripartite sanctuary with two flanking rooms rather than a sanctuary with five rooms.

Five-room sanctuaries first appeared in the temple of Khephren at Giza and afterwards became a regular feature in royal funerary temples from the time of Userkaf.[50] There are different interpretations regarding the purpose of the five chapels. LUDWIG BORCHARDT suggested that they could have housed five statues of the king, which would correspond to the five elements of the royal titulary.[51] However, this interpretation has been challenged since the final canonisation of the five elements of the royal titulary did not occur until the Middle Kingdom.[52] Nevertheless, it is certain that the chambers in the sanctuary of Pepi I's *ka*-temple were used to house statues, most likely of the king, possibly with statues of Bastet and Hathor.

Tripartite sanctuaries, on the other hand, are a well-attested feature of temples dedicated to deities. However, early examples of provincial temples comprise only one main room, such as at Tell Ibrahim Awad, Elephantine, and Abydos.[53] Interestingly, tripartite sanctuaries also appear in funerary temples built for the queens of the Sixth Dynasty. It has been suggested that the concept derived from the five-chapel rooms found in the mortuary temples of kings. In this case, the queen's tripartite sanctuary would feature three statues, each representing a different aspect of her role – such as queen, king's daughter, or king's mother.[54]

This short comparative analysis of the architecture of Pepi I's *ka*-temple shows that although it adopts individual elements from other buildings, such as the royal funerary temples, it represents a unique building type. The differences lie not so much in the selection of elements, but rather in the arrangement of the main elements, i.e., transversal hall and sanctuary rooms.

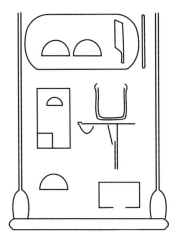

Fig. 8: *Inscription on a limestone pillar naming the building "ka-temple of Teti". (LANGE-ATHINODOROU 2022, based on EL-SAWI 1979, Fig. 165)*

While Pepi I's *ka*-temple at Bubastis is unique in terms of its archaeological preservation and architectural layout, the written record reveals that it was only one of many built throughout Egypt during the reign of this king. As mentioned above, the kings of the later Old Kingdom had a strong interest in connecting their temples to the abodes of local deities at important cult centres throughout the country. We also know of the existence of a *ka*-temple of Teti at Bubastis from an inscribed limestone pillar discovered in 1970 by EL-SAWI in an area to the adjacent north of Pepi I's temple. Due to the location of the find spot of this fragment, EL-SAWI suggested that the enclosure of Teti was situated somewhere in this area.[55] However, since there was no indication of related architecture, it is uncertain if the pillar was found in situ. Therefore, the exact location of this building, which was probably of a similar type to that of Pepi I, remains unknown (see below).

The fact that an '*inspector of the priests of the ka-temple of Teti*' existed at Zawijet el-Meitin suggests that a *ka*-temple of Teti was located there.[56] A block with annals of the kings of the Sixth Dynasty, which was reused as a sarcophagus lid for the burial of Queen Ankhnespepi, lists two *ka*-temples of Teti. Unfortunately, the part of the inscription that would have mentioned the location is mostly destroyed. However, it seems that one of the temples was located in the Heliopolitan nome. Since Bubastis was part of that nome in the Old Kingdom, there is a possibility that the inscription refers to the *ka*-temple of Teti in Bubastis.[57]

There is abundant textual evidence on the *ka*-temples of Pepi I. Most intriguingly, Cemetery C on the Northern Kom at Bubastis contains the tomb of an official named Ankhhaf who held the title "*overseer of the priests of the (ka-temple) of Pepi*" (see Chapter 2.2.3), thus offering a glimpse into the identities of the cult personnel of the *ka*-temple of Pepi I. The titles of officials and other textual evidence inform us about other *ka*-temples near Buto (*Akhbit* and the *City of the Lakes*), and at the pyramid complex of the king at Saqqara, as well as at Akhmim, El Hawawish, Elkab, Naqada/Qus, Assiut, Zawijet el-Meitin and Assiut. These *ka*-temples were linked to the temples of the respective local main deity.[58] As noted above, the number of royal *ka*-temples increased significantly in the Sixth Dynasty. This was connected to the growing importance of provincial temples, which became key elements of the provincial administration. As a result, there was new royal patronage that involved the endowment of land, dedication of statues, and establishment of royal *ka*-temples at provincial temple sites.[59]

2.2.2 New excavations: A provincial residence of the Fourth and Fifth Dynasties

As described above, HABACHI made the important discovery of the temple, but lacked sufficient time to carry out a detailed investigation of the building. A ground plan of the whole temple as well as information on its stratigraphy, including any possible earlier buildings,

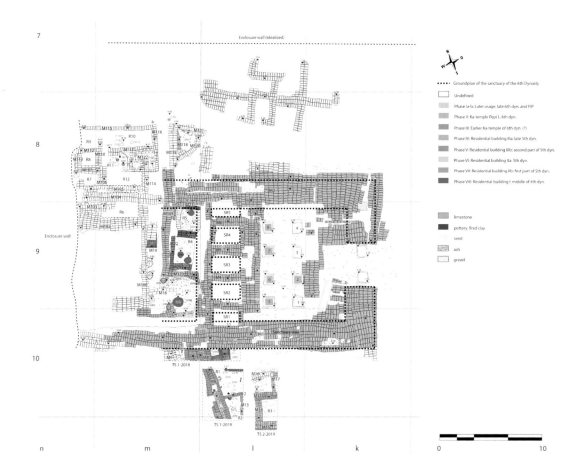

Fig. 9a: *General plan of the sanctuary of Pepi I's temple with the structures and contexts excavated from 2018-2020. (TELL BASTA PROJECT 2020)*

Fig. 9b: *Sanctuary of the ka-temple of Pepi I. View to the southwest. (TELL BASTA PROJECT 2018)*

was still missing. Another open question concerns the exact location of the *ka*-temple of Teti at Bubastis. Additionally, the area where Pepi I's temple is located is all that is left from the original much larger Western Kom, which is now mostly overbuilt. Therefore, the only place where we still have the opportunity to gather information on the early periods of Bubastis is the area where the temple of Pepi I is located. In 2018, the TELL BASTA PROJECT started new excavations there, in order to gain a fuller picture of the layout of the *ka*-temple of Pepi I and to determine if there were any earlier occupation levels beneath it.[60]

Directly to the west and southwest of the sanctuary chambers of Pepi I's temple, we were indeed able to reach earlier levels with substantial remains of a large building. Here, we detected column foundations ranging from 0.40 to 1.0 m in diameter, and north-south oriented walls. Layers of limestone chippings found close by might be the remains of column bases. The pottery associated with the earliest levels dates to the middle of the Fourth Dynasty. The dimensions of the walls and column foundations, suggest that the structure was a large provincial administrative building, which could have served as the seat of the governors of Bubastis in the Old Kingdom. Further excavations revealed that this early provincial residence building was levelled and overbuilt, undergoing numerous changes until the end of the Fifth Dynasty.

The following summary of the results from the 2018-2020 excavations, provides an overview of the main contexts and features of this building based on the reconstructed building chronology (see fig. 9a). The detailed report on the excavations and the pottery mentioned below is published elsewhere.[61]

Residential Building I: The excavation in trench TS 1-2019 revealed the presence of two column foundations, numbered 213 and 215, respectively. These foundations are made of very dark clay at 2.37-2.39 m/asl and have a diameter between 0.38 and 0.40 m. They are placed 2.82 m apart from each other on the same level. It is believed that both column foundations belong to the same building phase and were set along a north-northeast to south-southwest axis. On the same level, remains of a brick floor or wall, numbered 214, were also discovered. In addition, a large sandy column foundation, numbered 247 and measuring 0.95 m in diameter, was found further to the north in the southeastern quadrant of grid square m/9. It was

Fig. 10a: *Column foundation [247] in m/9;* **b:** *pottery associated with column foundation [247] from the southeastern and northeastern quadrant of m/9: TB 12a/1, 3-4 and TB 12a/124-126. (TELL BASTA PROJECT 2020)*

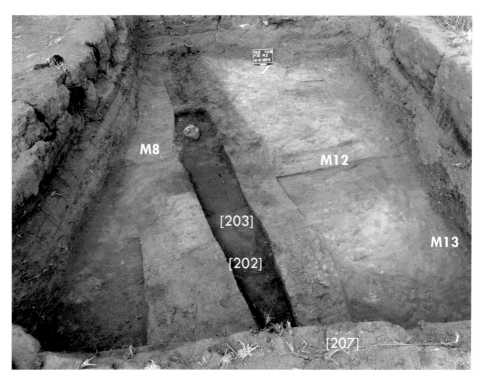

Fig. 10c: *Column foundation [203] and brick floor [204] under wall M8 from the phase of Residential building IIA, phase IV. (TELL BASTA PROJECT 2019)*

accompanied by a clay floor, numbered 248, and a layer of limestone chippings, numbered 249, in its immediate vicinity. Two more column foundations, numbered 262 and 263, were discovered as well. These column foundations have a diameter of 0.60 m and consist of dark clay. They are set at a distance of 4.40 m and have specks of a mud floor, numbered 264 and 265, at the same level. It seems that these two smaller column foundations are also part of the same building phase, but they may date to another sub-phase as they are not aligned with the large column foundation. The size of the large column foundation indicates that there was once a large open columned hall, possibly with limestone-based columns of stone or wood. Two walls in TS 1-2018, M10 and M11, are also part of this building. Only a small part of these walls could be excavated at 2.39 m/asl. The pottery associated with these contexts consists mostly of beer jars and bread moulds, dating from the middle of the Fourth to the early Fifth Dynasty.

After a period of abandonment and levelling, the courts or rooms where the columns stood were overbuilt by a new building which belongs to *Residential Building II (b-a)*. Evidence of this phase is M13 in TS 1-2019, a northeast to southwest-oriented wall, which deviates from the axis of the column foundations of the oldest phase of the building. While M13, of which only 2.0 m at 2.40 m/asl was detectable under the baulk, is probably identifiable as remains of the older sub-phase IIb, a column foundation of clayey sand of 0.38 m diameter, numbered 203, and the surrounding brick floor, numbered 202, at 2.45 m/asl, visible under a crack in the younger wall M8, represent the younger sub-phase IIa. A corresponding column foundation of dark clay, measuring 0.30 m diameter at 2.52 m/asl might have been feature 217 in TS 2-2019. According to the pottery found there, *Residential Building II* was in use from the early to mid-Fifth Dynasty. Like the older building, it encompassed columned rooms or halls.

The following stage, *Residential Building III*, also appears to have had two sub-phases. Features of this structure have so far appeared in TS 1-2018, TS 1-2019 and TS 2-2019. *Residential Building III* was a construction with a substantial wall, M8, with a width of 2.62 m at 2.47-2.70 m/asl, running 6.67 m in a north-south direction before disappearing under younger levels. M8 could have been an outer wall of the building. The east-west-oriented wall M12 at 2.55 m/asl, excavated to a length of 1.68 m, seems to have been an inner wall dividing two rooms, R1 and R2, and was filled with debris consisting of broken bricks, ashes, smashed limestone and pottery. This debris was the remnants of the backfilling of the rooms when the building of the older sub-phase (IIIb) was levelled. The remains of the following sub-phase IIIa were found in grid square m/10-9. The remains include a dark-clay column foundation, numbered 246, with dimensions of 0.50 m, which was set on a floor made of mud bricks, numbered 242, at 2.75 m/asl. An adjacent column foundation of the same size and type, numbered 245, may also belong to the same phase. The pottery found in the contexts of *Residential Building III* dates this structure and its sub-phases from the middle to the late Fifth Dynasty.

At the beginning of the Sixth Dynasty, the residential building was completely levelled and overbuilt with the *ka*-temple of Pepi I. As the ground plan in fig. 9a shows, the west-northwest to east-southeast orientation of the sanctuary clearly deviates from the general north-south orientation of the underlying residential building. As we have seen above, the orientation of the temple's sanctuary connected the royal temple to the temple of Bastet directly to the east. However, the discovery of walls west of the sanctuary and directly under the walls of Pepi I's temple with only a slight deviation to the east (M 19-23) might belong to an earlier temple building. This could either be the first stage of Pepi I's temple or maybe the *ka*-temple of his predecessor Teti.

Between the sanctuary and the western and northern enclosure walls of the temple of Pepi I, there are higher levels that have been preserved more than in other parts of the building. This area has given us the opportunity to study the remains of the late Sixth Dynasty and the First Intermediate Period re-use of the temple building. These structures consist of two small open courts (R10, R 11) measuring max. 4.28 by 1.72 m, and three small rooms (R7-9), measuring max. 1.70 by 1.66 m. The remaining walls of these structures are preserved at 4.34-4.08 m/asl and are attached to an ash-filled rectangular structure, numbered 100, measuring 2.10 by 1.72 m at 3.79 m/asl. R10 and R11 revealed several small pits with a maximum diameter of 0.30 m, which are only a few centimetres deep. These might have been used as stands for vessels with a round base.

Seeds from wild grasses (*Lolium speltum, Trifolium speltum, Chenopodium speltum, Polygonaceae*) usually found in animal dung were detected during palaeobotanical analysis of the ash that filled the rectangular brick structure (100). The ash filling (102) also contained numerous fragments of seals and dockets made of unburnt clay. In many cases, the impressions of strings or plant fibres remained on the back of the seal fragments. One of the seals bears the image of a bee incised on it. Based on parallels from the Sixth Dynasty governor's palace at Ain Asil in the Dakhleh Oasis, it was probably the stopper of a honey jar.[62] The pottery from the ash filling forms a small, yet well-secured context of large-sized body sherds from the Sixth Dynasty to the First Intermediate Period, consisting mostly of tableware and bread moulds.

To the immediate east was a silo-like structure, numbered 200, formed by a semi-circular wall M120 at 3.56-3.44 m/asl. As the pottery from the filling mostly dates to the mid-Fourth to early Fifth Dynasties, the silo probably belonged originally to the residential building, but might still have been in use later on. The silo underlines the general impression that this area was used for food storage and processing.

A building with regular rooms attached to the northern enclosure walls appeared at 3.72-3.34 m/asl. It consists of a double row of northeast-southwest-oriented rooms. The southern row had doorways at their southwestern corners. The pottery found here dates to the late Sixth Dynasty.

The newly discovered provincial residence is tangible evidence that Bubastis played a

Fig. 11: *Seal of a honey jar with incised bee (TB12a 005) from structure [100]. (TELL BASTA PROJECT 2020)*

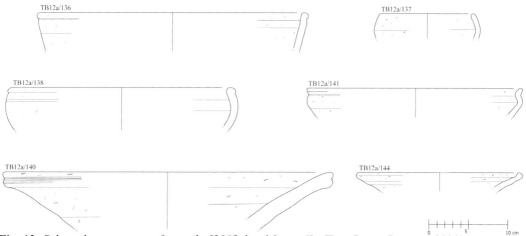

Fig. 12: *Selected pottery types from silo [200], level 2 in m/8. (TELL BASTA PROJECT 2020)*

central role in the Old Kingdom Nile Delta. Moreover, it is the first provincial residence of the Fourth and Fifth Dynasties ever discovered in Egypt. Thus, the residential building at Bubastis provides important new information about the location, architecture, use, and role of Old Kingdom provincial residences. Other archaeologically preserved provincial residences and palaces of the Third millennium BCE are either of a much earlier date, such as Buto in the North-Western Delta and at Hierakonpolis in the southern Nile Valley (both dating to the First Dynasty), or much later, such as Elephantine close to the First Cataract and at Ain Asil in the Dakhla Oasis (both dating to the Sixth Dynasty). Of these, the governor's palace at Ain Asil offers the closest architectural comparisons to the excavated parts of the residence at Bubastis, particularly in terms of the size and spacing of column foundations.[63]

In terms of its spatial situation however, the residence at Bubastis finds its best parallel in the Early Dynastic palace at Buto. At Bubastis, the residential building was located on the Western Kom and, likewise, the Early Dynastic palace at Buto was also located on the Western Kom. As archaeological investigations have shown for both sites, the Western Kom was settled on first. Consequently, in the subsequent periods, the area was considered a prime location for the erection of the prestigious buildings of the settlement, owing to its ancestral significance.

The discovery of a provincial residence of the Fourth and Fifth Dynasties at Bubastis has changed our understanding of how the city evolved, the role of residences and local temples in its development, and the processes involved in the rise of such early central places. Prior to the discovery of the residence, archaeological and epigraphic evidence suggested that the archaic city of Bubastis flourished during the late Old Kingdom, when kings of the early Sixth Dynasty built their *ka*-chapels near the temple of the local lioness goddess Bastet. This reconstruction of events linked the rise of the temple with the rise of the city, in agreement with the general scholarly model on the evolution of provincial administration, which emphasises the religious, administrative and economic influence of provincial temples on the development of central places throughout Egypt from the Fifth Dynasty onwards.[64]

However, this model heavily prioritises the importance of provincial temples while neglecting the equally significant role of provincial residences. The lack of archaeological and textual sources on the latter, particularly for the Fourth and Fifth Dynasties, may have contributed to this oversight. The existence of a provincial residence at Bubastis, which had been established in the middle of the Fourth Dynasty, indicates that the emergence of provincial temples in the latter part of the Old Kingdom was merely the concluding phase of a complex and lengthy process. From the Early Dynastic period until the latter part of the Old Kingdom, provincial residences played a crucial role in maintaining economic and administrative control on a regional level. These residences were thus the institutional forerunners to provincial temples, linking central places and settlements to the royal residence at Memphis. Over time, they evolved into administrative centres of their own and continued to be key elements of provincial administration alongside the provincial temples.

2.2.3 Elite cemeteries on the Western and Northern Kom

The Nile Delta with its rich agricultural sources, was a territory of great importance in the Old Kingdom and home to numerous settlements and cities. However, remains of that period are nowadays rarely to be found. Bubastis is arguably the Delta site where the most substantial Old Kingdom monuments are still preserved. This refers not only to the residential building and the royal *ka*-temples described above, but also to the vast cemeteries of that time. Amongst them, the elite tombs with inscribed material are of significant interest as they provide information on the status of the officials buried there within the network of Old Kingdom provincial administration and within the social matrix of the city. Furthermore, the spatial relationship between the cemeteries and other functional areas of the town, as well as the architecture of the tombs, offer rare insights into the funerary traditions of an early Delta metropolis.

We know of several Old Kingdom cemeteries located on the Western and Northern Koms. Of these, Cemeteries A, B, and C to the north of the temple of Bastet seem to have been the

Fig. 13: *Structures from the later Sixth Dynasty and First Intermediate Period northwest of the sanctuary. View to the east. (TELL BASTA PROJECT 2020)*

most extensive. On the Western Kom, to the north of the *ka*-temple of Pepi I, was a large burial ground with tombs from the Early Dynastic to the Ptolemaic Period. While excavating this area, EL-SAWI discovered four tombs of the Old Kingdom with burial chambers made of limestone and one mud-brick tomb with a vaulted roof. However, only the latter can be securely dated due to the discovery of inscribed surgical instruments of copper with the name and title of their owner, the sole friend *mr(.jj)-(mrjj-rᶜw)*|.[65] Since the name of the deceased contains the throne name of Pepi I, his tomb can be dated to somewhere in the later reign of Pepi I or the early years of Pepi II's reign.

The Northern Kom was the main funerary zone of the city for most of its lifetime, i.e., from at least the Old Kingdom until the Ptolemaic Period. From 1978-1988, MOHAMED IBRAHIM BAKR excavated two cemeteries of the Old Kingdom, now labelled Cemetery A and C, while in the early 1990s, excavations conducted by MAHMUD OMAR brought to light another cluster of Old Kingdom tombs, possibly an extension of Cemetery A to the north (Cemetery B, see fig. 14).[66]

Cemetery A consists of 22 north-northeast to south-southwest oriented tombs of mudbrick around 350 m northwest of the temple of Bastet. It was partly overbuilt by a necropolis of the Nineteenth Dynasty. The excavation of a 30 by 40m area revealed just a part of Cemetery A. Further tombs still extend under the later levels to the north, south and west.

All the tombs consist of a vaulted rectangular mud-brick enclosure, ranging in size from a maximal 7.15 by 5.80 m to 1.60 by 1.20 m, with the exception of a large mastaba, the so-called '*family tomb*', which measures 15.50 by 12 m. The inner structure of the tombs consists of either a single or multiple (two to four) burial chambers, with shafts on the northern side providing access. After the interment, the shafts were filled with debris. The vaulted chambers of the large mastaba contained several burials. BAKR recorded two vaults on its northern side and one vault on its southern side. During the new documentation of the tomb in 2015 by the TELL BASTA PROJECT it became clear that there were two additional vaults in the southwestern corner of the mastaba tomb. However, after the intended tomb owners were laid to rest, the massive eastern and southern walls of the mastaba were reused for 30 secondary burials, some lying on top of each other. The outer brickwork of the tomb was covered in white plaster, imitating the appearance of the stone mastabas of high officials in the Memphite region, which were dressed with limestone blocks.[67]

Three tombs on the northwestern side of the cemetery had recesses in their eastern walls with limestone stelae set in, completed by rectangular basins made of mud bricks to serve as a place for offerings for the deceased. From the stelae inscriptions we know of the names and titles of the tomb owners. At tomb no. 1, this was the "*overseer of the (singers of) praise* [68], *inspector of the priests of Bastet, Nebsen*". Another "*overseer of the priests of Bastet*", named Tjemem (?) was buried in tomb no. 4. Owner of tomb no. 17 was "*inspector of the priests, inspector of the sealers of the treasury and privy to the secrets of the god's treasure, Meshetj*".[69]

As no detailed information on the excavated grave goods and pottery is available, dating the tombs in Cemetery A is difficult. Fortunately, the palaeography of the inscriptions provides some clues. For example, the writing of certain significant groups, such as the opening of the offering formula invoking Anubis with 🔺 and his epithet ✝🔺 (*jm.j-wt*) indicates that the tombs with the stelae in question were built at the end of the Fifth or the early Sixth Dynasty.[70] In addition, as part of the TELL BASTA PROJECT's re-documentation of Cemetery A in 2015, ASHRAF ES-SENUSSI conducted an analysis of a number of diagnostic sherds from the bricks of tombs no. 3, 5, 10-12, 15, 17-18 and the '*family tomb*'. The majority of sherds date in the late Fifth to Sixth Dynasty, which is in agreement with the results of the palaeographic analysis. However, there were exceptions; the bricks of tombs no. 3, 15, and 18 contained sherds of pottery types dating to the late Sixth Dynasty until the First Intermediate Period. This suggests that these tombs were later additions to the original cemetery, which is not surprising since cemeteries were usually in use over certain periods of time.

Around 30 m to the north of Cemetery A is an area of approximately 22 by 18 m with twelve northeast-southwest oriented tombs of the same kind of architecture found in Cemetery A. While it is possible that this is a continuation of Cemetery A, the slightly different orientation of the tombs suggests that they were constructed during a different time period. The cemetery (B) was excavated in the early 1990's by MAHMUD OMAR, but the results remain unpublished, making it challenging to determine the precise date of the tombs. However, a date to end of the Old Kingdom or the beginning of the First Intermediate Period is likely. The excavation trench profile indicates that the cemetery extends into the unexcavated area to the south.[71]

At a distance of 140 m to the east of Cemetery B, and directly to the east of the palace of the Middle Kingdom (see Chapter 4.1), BAKR discovered another Old Kingdom cemetery (Cemetery C) in 1985. The excavated area of 35 by 37 m contained a multitude of northeast

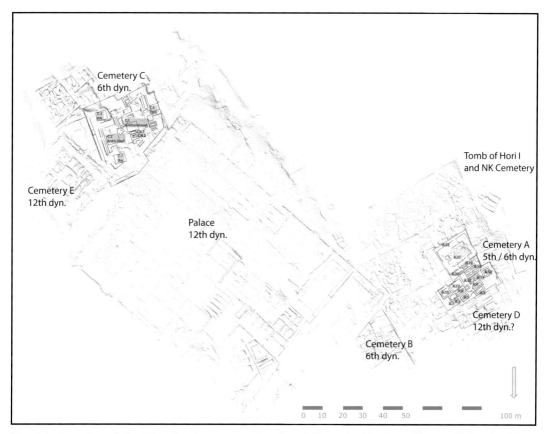

Fig. 14: *Location of the Old Kingdom cemeteries A and C on the Northern Kom at Bubastis. (Tell Basta Project 2014)*

Fig. 15: *Vaulted tombs in Cemetery A on the Northern Kom. View to the south. (Tell Basta Project 2022)*

to southwest oriented mudbrick tombs. They were clustered around five main tombs with decorated burial chambers built of limestone blocks. All tombs appear to have had vaulted roofs, but due to unpublished excavation records and the disturbed state of many tombs, nothing can be said for sure. [72]

The TELL BASTA-PROJECT conducted a preliminary survey of the cemetery and epigraphic work from 2013-2015. It found that the main tombs were accessible by means of a sloping passage from the north, with the chambers being closed off by an undecorated slab of limestone. The tombs consisted of a two-storeyed burial chamber with an average size of 3.46 by 1.60 by 1.19 m. The upper chamber was decorated with reliefs or paintings, while the lower chamber, where the actual burial was located, was undecorated. Smaller subsidiary tombs were attached to the main tombs, some of which contained undecorated limestone burial chambers. The inscriptions in the main tombs allowed for the identification of their owners as follows: Ihy, the "*governor, sealer of the king of Lower Egypt, the sole companion and overseer of the priests*" (Tomb TB C.1); Ankhhaf, the "*governor, sealer of the king of Lower Egypt, overseer of the place of production, the sole companion and overseer of the priests of (the ka-temple of) Pepi*" (Tomb TB C.2); Ankhembaset, the "*sealer of the king of Lower Egypt, overseer of the priests, personal scribe of royal records, overseer of scribes of the registry, sole companion, overseer of provisions*" (Tomb TB C.4) and Khenti/Tjeti, the "*priestess of Bastet, mistress of Bubastis, ornament of the king*" (Tomb TB C.5).[73] The title 'governor' is actually a functional interpretation of the well-known title: $ḥȝtj-ᶜ$ (lit: "*he, who is foremost of arm*").[74] It was also the highest title of the governors of Bubastis during the Middle Kingdom (see Chapter 4.3). Given that Ankhhaf was the overseer of the priests of the *ka*-temple of Pepi I, Cemetery C dates to the Sixth Dynasty. Furthermore, the arrangements of the panels of decoration in these tombs suggest that the cemetery was in use until the end of the Sixth Dynasty.[75]

The above-listed titles are highly interesting in terms of the position of the tomb owners within the network of the provincial administration of that time. However, we are faced with the unfortunate fact that we have limited information on the structure of provincial administration of the late Old Kingdom Nile Delta. This is especially true when compared to the Nile Valley. While we can identify a rather clear hierarchy of offices, such as nomarchs (*ḥqȝ spȝ.t*), who were led by an '*overseer of Upper Egypt*' (*jm.j-rȝ šmᶜ*),[76] things were different in the Delta. It is evident that at the time of the early Old Kingdom, the title *ᶜḏ-mr* (only provisionally translatable as "*district administrator*"), was linked solely to the administration of the Delta.[77] However, the office encompassed diverse areas of duty that were very different from the office of the Upper Egyptian '*leader of the land*' (*sšm-tȝ*) during the same period.[78] Therefore, it is far from certain that an *ᶜḏ-mr* should be understood as a nomarch of the Delta.

During the Fifth Dynasty, the title of an '*overseer of the nomes of the Lower Egypt*' (*jm.j-rȝ spȝ.wt tȝ mḥw*) appears, which was linked to the office of an '*overseer of the production place*' (*jm.j-rȝ gs-pr*).[79] However, those who held these titles preferred to be buried in the residential cemeteries at Memphis instead of the provinces.[80] Provincial cemeteries usually housed officials of the next lower level of provincial administration. This changed during the Sixth Dynasty, and it is possible that officials such as Ankhembaset, who held the title of a *jm.j-rȝ gs-pr*, may have been directly associated with the office of the *jm.j-rȝ spȝ.wt tȝ mḥw*.

Fig. 16: *Upper chamber of the tomb of Ankhembaset. View to the north. (TELL BASTA PROJECT 2013)*

Fig. 17: *Detail of the western wall of the tomb of Ankhembaset. (TELL BASTA PROJECT 2013)*

2.2.4 Provincial and court elites in an Old Kingdom Delta city

Cemeteries A and C provide valuable insights into the social hierarchy of Bubastis and the rise of provincial elites in the later Old Kingdom. As per the Egyptian funerary tradition, the tomb owners of these cemeteries defined themselves by listing their titles of rank and office in their tomb chambers. In Cemetery A, the tomb owners only mention their positions at the temple of Bastet to illustrate their own status in the social matrix of the local community. However, none of them held any titles related to the royal court. The stelae inscriptions in Cemetery A reveal another interesting detail: In several cases, the name of the goddess Bastet was determined with the representation of an enthroned lioness goddess. This image could possibly be based on a real cult image of the goddess that was present in the temple at that time. Those buried in Cemetery A would have been familiar with the appearance of the cult image through their official duties in the temple.

The officials of the later Sixth Dynasty buried in Cemetery C, on the other hand, no longer considered the local temple as the primary ranking reference for their social status. Instead, titles connected to local priestly duties were subordinate to impressive titles of rank at the royal court. Ihy and Ankhhaf, for example, combine the titles 'sealer of the king of Lower Egypt, sole friend'. These titles were typically given to high court officials at the royal residence. Moreover, Ankhembaset had a direct connection to the king as he was a 'personal scribe of royal records'. This indicates that the governors of Old Kingdom Bubastis had close ties to the royal residence at Memphis. As a result, they also held the highest positions in the local hierarchy. It is interesting to note, that they had access to richer resources than the officials of Cemetery A. This is evidenced by the fact that limestone tomb stelae were replaced by decorated stone chambers, which provided more space for self-expression. Ihy, Ankhhaf, Ankhmebaset, and Tjeti were representatives of a new social class at Bubastis, which was not limited to the provincial town but was closely connected with the royal residence where they started their careers. They continued to hold offices there while simultaneously acting as governors of a provincial centre in the Nile Delta.

The location of Cemetery C provides further evidence for this change. It is situated directly east of the governor's palace of the Twelfth Dynasty (see Chapter 4.1). This palace may have been built over a large structure of the Sixth Dynasty, which could have served as the official residence of a local dynasty of governors during that time. This would have replaced the governor's palace on the Western Kom, which was already abandoned by the end of the Fifth Dynasty (see above). Thus, Cemetery C was the burial place of the governors of the late Old Kingdom, and it is no coincidence that the cemetery of the governors of Bubastis of the Twelfth Dynasty lies directly to its north (Cemetery E, fig. 14, see Chapter 4.2).

In conclusion, during the reign of Pepi I, there was probably an administrative reorganisation in Bubastis. The older elites without high court rank titles and no direct connection to the residence were replaced by a new social class of high court officials. These officials were transferred to Bubastis to run the provincial administration. This changed allowed high court officials to replace the older local elites without direct ties to the residence, and gave the king better access to the growing economic potential of the provincial temples. This course of action is in line with the above-described rising royal interest in the provinces of Egypt during the early Sixth Dynasty. Such officials, albeit appointed by the residence, would be linked in a special way to their place of service, even if they did not hail from these cities. An example of the latter could be the governor

Ankhembaset with his programmatic name: *"He who lives in Bubastis"*.

As high officials of the king, the governors acted as a link between the royal residence in Memphis and the local city of Bubastis. They brought with them aspects of the elite culture of the residence and merged it with local traditions. While it is broadly accepted that the gradual empowerment of provincial elites led to their final *de facto* independence from the royal residence and the king during the late Old Kingdom (see Chapter 3), this was not the case at Bubastis. Instead, under the direction of the royal residence, officials who had held offices at the royal court were sent as governors to Bubastis under the authority of Memphis, and they rapidly displaced the older local elite. It remains unclear to what extent the latter participated in these changes (for example, through family connections).[81]

Endnotes

[1] Petrie, Quibell 1896; Kaiser 1956; Kaiser 1990; Spencer 1993, 27-33.

[2] Köhler 2017, 335-356.

[3] Faltings 1998, 373; Köhler 1998, 61; Hendrickx 2006; Mączyńska 2011; Mączyńska 2013, 19 Table 3; Jucha 2014, 22-25.

[4] Koehler 2020.

[5] Koehler 2017, 347.

[6] Kahl 2006, 95-101 (also for Dynasty "0").

[7] Dreyer 1998.

[8] Petrie 1900-1901; Spencer 1993, 71-91; For the ongoing research on the royal tombs at Abydos see the excavation reports of Kaiser and Dreyer et al. in *Mitteilungen des Deutschen Archäologischen Instituts Kairo* (since 1979).

[9] Wilkinson 1999, 66-81.

[10] Wilkinson 1999, 82-94; Kahl 2006, 102-108.

[11] On the capital zone see Moeller 2016, 158-161.

[12] Quibell 1900, Pl. XXXVIII-XLI; Spencer 1993, 67-71; Wilkinson 1999, 91-94; Endesfelder 2011, 91.

[13] Spencer 1993, 98-109; Wilkinson 1999, 95-98; Moreno Garcia 2013, 87-94.

[14] Wilkinson 1999, 94-105; Baud 2010, 73-74; Lehner, Hawass 2017.

[15] Tallet 2017; Lehner 2020; Sheisha et al. 2022.

[16] Posener-Krieger 1976; Verner 2020, 381-389; Baud 2010, 74-76; Nuzzolo 2018; Barta 2019, 102-113.

[17] Cílek et al. 2012; Bárta 2013.

[18] Verner 2020, 263-280.

[19] Tavares 2011; Lehner 2016.

[20] Awady 2009; Khaled 2020.

[21] Urk. I, 236.10 (= Palermo stone r.VI.2): Wilkinson 2000, 141; Baud 2010, 73-76.

[22] Papazian 2013.

[23] Moreno Garcia 2013, 94-121.

[24] Urk. I, 241.13-15 (= Palermo stone v.II.2): Wilkinson 2000, 153; Moreno Garcia 2013, 107-111.

[25] Goedicke 1967, 22-26; Bussmann 2010, 468, 583.

[26] Baud 2010, 77; Alexanian 2016.

[27] Lange 2006, 128-133.

[28] Urk I, 100.13-101.7: Strudwick 2005, 357-358; Kanawati 2003.

[29] Urk I, 101.9-103.5, 104.10-105.4, 106.14-109.11: Strudwick 2005, 340; Schneider 2015, 436. Cf. Richards 2002.

[30] Goedicke 1967, 81-157.

[31] Moeller 2016, 241-244; Jeuthe 2018, 125-127; Martinet 2019, 136-189, 537-538; Soukiassian 2022.

[32] Hd. II, 100,1: Wilson, 2015, 181-182; Nesselrath, 2017, 162; Ryholt 2000.

[33] The Seventh Dynasty, which the Egyptian priest and historian Manetho summarizes as: "*70 kings in 70 days*", is nowadays omitted: Baud 2006; Papazian 2015.

[34] Lange et al. 2016, 385.

[35] Dreyer 1998.

[36] El-Sawi 1979, 63, Fig. 102, 104-109; Kroeper 1988, 18-19, Fig. 210-213; Lange et al. 2016, 378.

[37] Ashmawy 2021.

[38] El-Sawi 1979, 74-75.

[39] El-Sawi 1979, 74-75, Fig. 156-163. I would like to thank ASHRAF ES-SENUSSI for the new dating of the pottery published by El-Sawi.

[40] For instance: Tell el-Farkha (Chłodnicki 2014; Ciałowicz 2017) and Minshat Abu Omar (Krzyżaniak 1993; Kroeper, Wildung 1994; Tristant 2020, 119-120). For a detailed overview on the development of settlement processes in the Nile Delta from the Neolithic Period until the end of the Old Kingdom see Lange-Athinodorou, forthcoming.

[41] Kamil 2007.

[42] Habachi 1957, 11.

[43] Habachi 1957, 13-32.

[44] Habachi 1957, 33-36.

[45] Cairo JE 72133, JE 72132 B and JE 72132 C: Habachi 1957, 13-18, Fig. 2, 3.

[46] Lange-Athinodorou 2019(a), 8-10.

[47] Arnold 1994, 91.

[48] Kemp 1968, 149-150; O'Connor 1992, 89-96; Lange 2006, 134-137.

[49] Petrie 1903, 11, pl. XLVII.4; Kemp 1968, 149.

[50] Stadelmann 1997, 8; Jánosi 1996, 145 n. 915.

[51] Borchardt 1909, 8; Cf. Junker, Giza 1943, 9.

[52] Ricke 1950, 36.

[53] Elephantine: Dreyer 1986, Taf. 2a. Tell Ibrahim Awad: Eigner 2000, 18-22. Abydos, Building F: Petrie 1903, 8.

[54] Jánosi 1996, 148.

[55] El-Sawi, 1979, 75-76.

[56] Jones 2000, 941.

[57] Baud, Dobrev 1995, 30-31, Fig. 4.

[58] Lange 2006, 129-132.

[59] Seidlmayer 1996, 213-214; Bussmann 2010, 3-12; 509-512; Papazian 2012, 18-25, 37-54; Moreno Garcia 2013, 116-117.

[60] Lange-Athinodorou, Es-Senussi 2018.

[61] Lange-Athinodorou, Es-Senussi 2022.

[62] Pantalacci 2022, 26.

[63] For a detailed comparative analysis cf. Lange-Athinodorou 2023; Buto: Hartung 2018, 104-108, 109-110; Ain Asil: Jeuthe 2018, 127-134, 131 Fig. 4.

[64] Bussmann 2010, 3-12; 509-512; Papazian 2012, 18-25, 37-54. Cf. Moreno Garcia 2013, 116-117.

[65] El-Sawi 1979, 19, 64, 72-74.

[66] Bakr 1982, 154-163; Bakr 1992, 19-21; Bakr, Brandl 2010, 15-26; Bakr, Lange 2017.

[67] Bakr 1989, 35-49; Bakr 1992.

[68] This interpretation of *m3t* seems more likely than the "*overseer of the granite*" Bakr 1992, 92-94 suggested. I would like to thank STEPHAN SEIDLMAYER for bringing this to my attention.

[69] Bakr 1989, 35-49; Bakr 1992; Bakr, Lange 2017. Cf. also Alexanians typology: 2016, 246-247.

[70] Bakr, Lange 2017, 39-41.

[71] Bakr, Lange 2017, 32-33.

[72] Bakr 1989, 31-35; Bakr, Lange 2017, 41-43.

[73] Bakr, Lange 2017, 33, 35-36, 41-42.

[74] Grajetzki 2000, 221, 223.

[75] Bakr, Lange 2017, 42.

[76] Since the Fifth Dynasty: Moreno Garcia 2013, 88; Martinet 2019, 45-56, 432.

[77] Pardey 1976, 43-54; Jones 2000, 354.1316.

[78] Moreno Garcia 2013, 106-107.

[79] Moreno Garcia 2013, 117; Martinet 2019, 45-46.
[80] Moreno Garcia 2013, 125; Martinet 2019, 46-47.
[81] Bakr, Lange 2017, 42-46.

3. The Dark Ages in the Nile Delta? Bubastis in the First Intermediate Period

At the end of the Old Kingdom late in the Third millennium BCE, Egypt was heading towards a time of territorial and political fragmentation. Scholars have attempted to explain the reasons behind this development, suggesting that the unusually long reign of Pepi II of at least sixty-four years weakened the power of the royal family. This was due to subsequent struggles for succession by the many potential heirs fathered by Pepi II. Additionally, the governmental reforms of the late Fifth and early Sixth Dynasties saw the provinces gain more importance than ever before. This shift in power created a new and powerful elite group of officials, especially in Upper Egypt who, from the Fifth Dynasty, headed provincial nomes as nomarchs (*ḥqꜣ-spꜣ.t,* "*chief of the nome*").[1] They are believed to have gradually gained independence, causing a severe erosion of the monarch's authority and a decline of the political organisation of Egypt towards the end of the Sixth Dynasty.[2] This time of disintegration of royal power occurring between two periods of a strongly centralised government, the Old and the Middle Kingdom, is called the First Intermediate Period.

Egyptologists have long been intrigued by the disappearance of the great monumental buildings after the end of the reign of Pepi II, as well as by some literary sources from the Middle Kingdom. These sources, especially the so-called '*Admonitions of Ipuwer*'[3] and the '*Words of Neferti*'[4], portray the preceding period as a time of famine, anarchy and civil war. Biographical inscriptions of the First Intermediate Period, the most famous coming from the tomb of Ankhtifi, the nomarch of the three southernmost nomes of Egypt, mentioning famines and military campaigns of local warlords, add further colour to the picture.[5] Such texts were the major contributing factor for the long-standing negative connotation in Egyptology of that period, which was considered to be a time of general disintegration and weakening of the culture of ancient Egypt in all matters and forms; a period for which the term '*dark age*' was coined.[6] The possible causes for this period became the topic of many scholarly discussions. For instance, FLINDERS PETRIE was convinced that the end of the Old Kingdom was triggered by the invasion of the Delta by West Semitic peoples.[7]

Besides external causes, internal social and political developments were also discussed. Already in 1885, ADOLF ERMAN referred to textual evidence of a "*certain decentralisation of the country*" under Pepi II. This explanation was widely accepted and still forms the general theoretical framework in which other approaches are embedded. However, the situation is more complex. While there is evidence to suggest that the provinces became increasingly independent from the royal residence, maybe limiting the latter's access to provincial resources,[8] archaeological research has revealed that the decline of the royal dynasty and residence did not necessarily lead to a deterioration in the quality of life in the provinces. In fact, STEPHAN SEIDLMAYER's work on cemeteries of the First Intermediate Period has shown quite the opposite. It seems that as the kingship weakened and the drain of provincial resources for large royal building projects lessened as a result, the provincial population gained wealth in inverse proportion. Therefore, we should expect to see a change in social norms and the emergence of new social classes. An example of this is observable at the end of the Old Kingdom when provincial cemeteries grew in size, and tombs were equipped with numerous objects of funerary material culture for the deceased of different social strata. These burials were far richer than those of the provincial cemeteries of the Fourth and Fifth Dynasties, indicating an increase in prosperity among the people living in the provinces.[9]

In addition, elite tomb architecture of the late Old Kingdom follows regional traditions, differing from the uniform layout of the earlier dynasties. Also very interesting is the fact that during this period, tomb structures reveal the existence of a social hierarchy that extends beyond immediate family. Tombs now contain multiple burial chambers, arranged according to a system that reflects a social hierarchy in life, with a so-called '*patron*' at the top and members of his family, but also including people without blood-ties, i.e., his '*clients*', forming a social unit.[10] The information from the provincial cemeteries provides insight into social relations and networks far from the court, which are unknown for the preceding dynasties.

However, there were also indications of other external factors adding to the process of state dissolution. In 1971, the astronomer BARBARA BELL published proxy data that indicated a severe and abrupt climate change as the main cause of the end of the Old Kingdom. BELL based her study on KARL BUTZER's earlier reconstruction of the climatic chronology of the North African region from the Late Pleistocene to the Holocene.[11] This model postulated an end of the rainfall of the Neolithic pluvial around 5000 BCE followed by a long period of aridisation. BELL also made extensive use of ancient Egyptian literary texts, first and foremost the above-mentioned '*Admonitions*', but also the biographical tomb inscription of Ankhtifi in Mo'alla and other biographical texts of this period.

Although BELL's data sets were still limited – derived from geological outcrops of Nile terraces, Lake Fayum levels and historical Nile levels – geoarchaeological research saw a significant boost from the 1980s onwards. For example, the drilling campaigns of the Mediterranean Basin Program (MEDIBA) of the Smithsonian Institute under the direction of JEAN-DANIEL STANLEY, with eighty-seven boreholes in the North Delta, both onshore and offshore, generated large amounts of new data on late Pleistocene and Holocene lithostratigraphies and numerous C14 dates.[12] The stratigraphic and sedimentological analysis of these data led to the reconstruction of the palaeogeography of the Mediterranean coast of the Nile Delta and its river system.[13] Petrological and isotopic analysis of these cores also showed a decreasing ratio of isotopes of certain elements (for instance 86Sr/87Sr) for the time around 2200 BCE, which indicates a reduction of the sediments deposited in the Delta from the White Nile catchment area, revealing that there was a progressive reduction of the water supply from this Nile tributary. These findings were recently corroborated for other isotope ratios in sediments from the Nile upper continental slope and the Lake Burullus, here indicating an extreme decrease in Blue Nile sediment deposition and flood discharge.[14] A distinct iron and manganese hydroxide layer in cores from the Central Delta also provides evidence for the long-term exposure and desiccation of riverbed sediments around 2300-2100 BCE.[15]

Similar geoarchaeological investigations worldwide have found traces of this climatic phenomenon in Holocene geoarchives from the Levant, North Africa, North and South America to the Middle East, China and Antarctica dating to a time span of about 4.2 to 3.9 ka BP, i.e., from about 2250 to 1950 BCE.[16] At that time, a particularly dry climate prevailed, which is regarded as the extreme culmination of the previously mentioned progressive aridisation process since the end of the Neolithic pluvial. The main cause of climate change was the southward shift of the inner-tropical convergence zone (ITCZ) that began in the mid-

Holocene. This precipitation zone near the equator shifts seasonally, but also over larger time periods. The shift resulted in a decrease in the amount of monsoon rainfall in the Ethiopian highlands. This, in turn, resulted in lower annual water levels in the catchment areas of the White and Blue Nile, as well as the Atbara River. In a kind of chain reaction, the Nile floods in Egypt were either lower than usual or did not occur at all.[17]

The geoarchaeological proxy data also suggest that the period around 2200 BCE was characterised by strong aeolian activity, i.e., sandstorms and the general desertification of former vegetated surfaces in combination with short-term heavy rainfall. Telling examples are for instance a terrace at a cemetery of the late Old Kingdom at Sakkara-West, where thick slope deposits accumulated in the period of 4.6-4.1 ka BP, resulting from torrent rainfall.[18] Dune formation observed in geoarchaeological records in Memphis and Dahshur from the end of the Old Kingdom points in the same direction.[19] In geoarchaeology, these climatic events are nowadays subsumed under the term '*the 4.2 ka event*' and are regarded as the stratigraphic epoch boundary between the Middle and Late Holocene.[20]

While the reality of palaeo-climate change is evident from the multitude of, still growing, hydro-climatic proxy data, disagreement has arisen over the question of whether the climate change was really one of the main reasons for the end of the Old Kingdom as Bell originally stated and as other Egyptologists subsequently argued.[21] It has been argued that climate change could not have been the sole cause of societal collapse in the ancient Near East and Egypt. Critics, such as Nadine Moeller, question deterministic models that attribute collapse solely to climate change. She suggests that while climate change did occur, it may have had a slower transformative effect on society rather than an immediate collapse.[22] The discussion however is impeded by the fact, that it is currently difficult to establish an absolute chronology for the climatic events around the 4.2ka time window in Egypt due to the lack of C14 data and also the general problem of identifying short-time extreme climatic events in archaeological records.[23] As a result, it is still unclear how much climate change contributed to the end of the Old Kingdom.

Around 2160 BCE, the central power continued to dissolve with a series of ephemeral kings of the Eighth Dynasty, whose realm was gradually limited to the northern part of Egypt. At that time, for unresolved reasons, the rulers abandoned Memphis and moved to Herakleopolis at the south of the entrance to the Faiyum. Thus, their territory is referred to as the Herakleopolitan kingdom (Ninth and Tenth Dynasties, 2131-1990 BCE).

Local powerful families emerged at the same time in the provinces of the Central and Southern Nile Valley. Some were allied to the former royal dynasty at Memphis, later Herakleopolis. This was the case with the above-mentioned nomarch Ankhtifi, whose biographical tomb inscription is one of the main sources for reconstructing the historical events of that period. Other nomarchs formed new centres of power, like those in Thebes. The First Intermediate Period lasted for about 200 years, although its precise length is difficult to determine.[24]

At around the time of the later Herakleopolitan Dynasty, the ambitious nomarchs of the province of Thebes in the south (Eleventh Dynasty from 2081 BCE) started a long-term military conquest. They subdued the provinces loyal to the Herakleopolitans and expanded their territory to the north, eventually defeating the Herakleopolitan Kings. Mentuhotep II (2008-1957 BCE), a descendant of this line of Theban rulers, reunited Egypt again. The following period of the Middle Kingdom saw a return to a centralised government, much like the Old Kingdom (see Chapter 4).

Unfortunately, there is not much information available on the social and political history of the First Intermediate Period in general, and even less so for the Nile Delta. In fact, the absence of information has caused the recent revival of the above-mentioned theory put forward by PETRIE in 1894. This theory suggests that foreign invaders from the Eastern Levant overpowering the Egyptian dominion of the Delta were the primary cause of the downfall of the Old Kingdom and the abandonment of Memphis.[25] It is true that there are literary texts dating to the Middle Kingdom that speak of the troublesome arrival and presence of '*Asiatics*' (*ꜥꜣm.w*) in the Nile Delta, such as the so-called '*Words of Neferti*'. Although the composition of the text most probably dates to the early Middle Kingdom, the passages referring to the Asiatics might not. They could stem from older oral or literary traditions reflecting conditions of the First Intermediate Period. A particularly telling paragraph reads:

> '*A foreign bird will breed in the marshes of the Delta after he has built nests in the vicinity of the citizens, after they have led him come close out of necessity. All those good things are truly destroyed: these winding lakes, which were full of slaughter and overflowed with fish and fowl. All good things have vanished as the land is thrown down in misfortune because of those sustenances for the Asiatics roaming the land. Rebels have arisen in the East, Asiatics have descended to Egypt.*'[26]

However, what little archaeological evidence there is does not support the idea of more or less permanent presence of communities of Syrian-Palestine origin in the Delta. First Intermediate Period domestic and funerary contexts such as at Mendes, Bubastis (see below), Tell Ibrahim Awad[27], and Kom el-Hisn[28] have not produced any non-Egyptian pottery or other material culture that one would expect to find had that been the case. On the other hand, the archaeological record is very sketchy and large areas of the Delta are still terra incognita in terms of basic archaeological investigations, including almost the entire Central Delta. Therefore, at present, we have simply no way of knowing how many settlements of the First Intermediate Period existed and what material culture they might have contained. The high degree to which we depend on chance finds is well illustrated by a little-known group of false doors and offering tables accidentally discovered in 1928 at Kom el-Akhdar, probably the necropolis of ancient Busiris. The group included a limestone architrave of a provincial high official of the late Sixth Dynasty or even the early First Intermediate Period. The ethnical names of his sons, *ꜥꜣm* ('*Asiatic*') and *sḏ-rtnnw* ('*The crusher of Retjenu*'), have an especially interesting ring given the above-mentioned references to people from the region of Syria-Palestine settling in the Nile Delta in the '*Words of Neferti*'. Could they indicate an already ongoing acknowledgement of the provincial elite's situation from the late Old Kingdom onwards?[29]

The depiction of the attack on a fortress clearly defended by Asiatics in the Theban tomb of Intef (TT 386), a military commander of Mentuhotep II, could be proof that there were, indeed, Asiatic strongholds in the Delta at least at the end of the First Intermediate Period. Compelling arguments for the location of this fortress being in the Delta and not in the Levant have been proposed principally because there is no evidence of a military campaign of this king in the region of Syria-Palestine, nor is there evidence of fortresses in the Levant at that time.[30] Consequently, if Mentuhotep II had to overcome Asiatic-dominated cities in the Delta, these must have existed in the First Intermediate Period. In any case, this would raise the question as to whether they were allies, client kings or outright enemies of the neighbouring Herakleopolitan Kings. Strong indications that Asians were in fact on unfriendly terms with the Herakleopolitans, who were in a constant struggle to maintain control over the Delta, can be found in the so-called 'Teachings for Merikare'. Within the text, a king named Khety, one of the later rulers of the Herakleopolitan Dynasty, refers to his actions against foreigners pouring into the Delta:

> "I rose as lord of the city whose heart was destroyed because of the Delta: (i.e.,) ḥw.t-šnw belongs to it up to bqȝ. Its southern border is at the canal of the two mullets. I pacified the whole Western Delta up to the coastal lakes. (...) Behold, the mooring post is set up in the territory that I made (accessible) in the East(ern Delta). From Hebenu, to the way of Horus, founded with cities, filled with people of the choicest of the whole land to ward off the (hostile) arms of them."[31]

A stela of the Twelfth Dynasty discovered at Tell el-Dab'a, the site of the ancient city of Avaris in the Northeastern Delta, provides further information on the activities of the Herakleopolitan King Khety in this area. According to the stela's text, the name of the settlement of the early Twelfth Dynasty south of Ezbet Rushdi was "the house of rȝ-wȝ.ty (of) Khety". This indicates that Avaris could have originally been a Herakleopolitan settlement, founded by a ruler named Khety. The state-planned settlement had a regular layout with uniform dwellings, most likely built to accommodate individuals cultivating and colonising the land and guarding the borders of the Eastern Delta, exactly as it is stated in the 'Teachings for Merikare'.[32] There may have been similar state-planned settlements of the Herakleopolitan Dynasty in the Delta which have not yet been found.

As it is true for the whole Delta, few archaeological remains dating to the First Intermediate Period have so far come to light at Bubastis. It is therefore impossible to gain a coherent picture of how the city and its occupants were affected by the changes at that time. As was discussed in the previous chapter, the city thrived especially at the end of the Old Kingdom, with a new local elite who maintained strong ties with the residence and the king. Due to its established role as a major provincial centre of the Southeastern Delta, it is possible that it was able to keep its high rank in the network of settlements of that area well into the First Intermediate Period. In theory, the Herakleopolitans, who governed the Nile Delta, would have had a vested interest in Bubastis as a strategic stronghold. However, we lack any information to confirm this assumption.

At present, the only evidence for Bubastis in the First Intermediate Period comes from the *ka*-temple of Pepi I, which remained in use long after the reign of this king. Close to the northern enclosure wall, the excavations of the last few years revealed a building of regular layout, which probably had an administrative function, possibly combined with the storage of products. While it seems that the building originally belonged to the temple of Pepi I, large numbers of sherds and whole vessels dating to the first half of the First Intermediate Period discovered on its latest level show that it continued in use after the cult for Pepi I had come to an end (see Chapter 2 and fig. 13).

To gain a better understanding of the happenings in the Eastern Delta at that time, it is beneficial to examine the archaeological evidence at Mendes. This city, located in the Northeastern Delta on the Mendesian Nile branch, was equally as important as Bubastis. Mendes had been inhabited since the very end of the Neolithic era (end of the Fifth millennium) and subsequently developed into a major economic and religious centre of the Old Kingdom. So far, excavations have focused on the area around the temple of the local ram god Banebdjedet, revealing Early Dynastic levels of domestic occupation and temple bakeries of the Fourth and Fifth Dynasties. Located close to the temple are the cemeteries which boast mud-brick mastaba tombs with decorated limestone chambers for the local elite of the late Fifth and Sixth Dynasties, comparable to the elite tombs of the late Sixth Dynasty at Bubastis.[33]

The temple's forecourt has yielded a fascinating discovery: thirty-five skeletons have been unearthed. Anthropological examinations revealed that they were young and old men and women who had been killed on the spot and lain unburied, partly even covered by fallen walls. Based on seals and pottery finds, the time of this event can be narrowed down to the end of the Sixth Dynasty (from the end of the reign of Pepi II) to the Eighth Dynasty. In view of the destruction of the nearby mastabas, which dates in the same time span, DONALD REDFORD, the excavator of the city, interprets this finding as evidence of a violent confrontation followed by the destruction of the centre of Mendes.[34]

Even with a cautious assessment of the archaeological findings from Mendes, one cannot help but notice that here, after a period of great prosperity of the city in the Old Kingdom, gruesome events followed, matching the descriptions of destruction and plunder we find in the literary works cited above. However, the settlement continued throughout the Herakleopolitan Period. On top of the destruction level to the east of the temple, two buildings were erected, showing at least three occupation phases. The publication, however, describes only one of them in detail. The uncovered part of the building measured 30 x 40 m. Its ground plan shows that it had a bi-part transverse central room with two column bases surrounded by several smaller rooms. It could have been an administrative building or the residence of a member of the local elite, perhaps both combined. MATTHEW ADAMS has pointed out that there are similarities between the Mendes building and the ground plan of the so-called 'Great Bbuilding' at Bubastis (see Chapter 2). According to ADAMS, the pottery from the building at Mendes dates to the late First Intermediate Period, i.e., the first half of the Eleventh Dynasty, which probably corresponds to the latest phase of the building.[35] Around the same time, the cemeteries around the temple were re-established, containing simple burials as well mastaba tombs and tombs with vaulted roofs.[36]

The existence of administrative buildings and elite burials at Mendes in the First Intermediate Period shows that the city saw a revival in the (later) First Intermediate Period rather than a decline. As mentioned above, the 'Teachings for Merikare' highlights the keen interest of the Herakleopolitans in securing the Eastern Delta under their rule. It is possible that this interest prompted the rebuilding of important centres in this region, with Mendes being a prime location due to its proximity to the Eastern Delta border. The archaeological record of that time, although limited, corroborates this notion. Similarly, the geographical position of Bubastis and its importance during the Old Kingdom made it a prime candidate to attract the interest of the ruling Herakleopolitan dynasty. However, it remains unclear whether the city was a target of any such royal activities. Only future discoveries can shed more light on this question.

Endnotes

[1] Moreno Garcia 2013, 88; Martinet 2019, 45-56, 432.

[2] Martin-Pardey 1976, 50; Baud 2010, 77-80; Seidlmayer 2000. For a critical overview and literature see Jansen-Winkeln 2010, 276-282.

[3] Parkinson 2002, 308-309; Hassan 2007.

[4] Parkinson 2002, 303-304.

[5] Vandier 1950; Schenkel 1965; Morenz 2010, 544-547; Willems 2010, 82-83.

[6] Bell 1971.

[7] Petrie 1939, 121.

[8] Müller-Wollermann 1986. For a critical discussion, see Jansen-Winkeln 2010.

[9] Seidlmayer 1990, 2000. On the development of provincial tombs since the Fourth Dynasty see Alexanian 2016, 479-486.

[10] Seidlmayer 1990, 399-405; Willems 2010, 83.

[11] Butzer 1958; Butzer 1959(a-b); Butzer 1961; Bell 1971.

[12] Stanley et al. 1996.

[13] Coutellier, Stanley 1987; Arbouille, Stanley 1991; Stanley, Jorstadt 2006.

[14] Revel et al. 2015; Marks et al. 2022.

[15] Stanley 2019.

[16] Walker et al. 2012, 649-659.

[17] Welc, Marks, 2014, 124-126; Dee 2017; Stanley, Wedl 2021.

[18] Welc, Marks 2014, 126-130.

[19] Lourenço Gonçalves 2019, 56, 219-224, 223 Fig. 43; Alexanian et al. 2012, 28-29; Bunbury 2019, 64.

[20] Walker et al. 2012; Walker et al. 2019.

[21] Hassan 2007; Welc, Marks 2014; Hamdan et al. 2016; Morris 2023.

[22] Moeller 2005.

[23] Dee 2013; Dee 2017; Cordova 2018, 224-226.

[24] Seidlmayer 2006; Strudwick 2020.

[25] Jansen-Winkeln 2010.

[26] Papyrus Petersburg 1116B verso, 29-32: Parkinson 1997, 131-143; Parkinson 2002, 303-304. On general problems of dating literary texts see: Quack 2013, 405-469.

[27] Eigner 2000.

[28] Wenke et al. 2016.

[29] Fischer 1976, 5-9. For the most recent discussion on the location of Retjennu see Kopetzky, Bietak 2016.

[30] Ward 1961, 22-27; Schulman 1982, 180-181; Bietak 2007, 420; Jansen-Winkeln 2010, 296; Vogel 2004, 50-54; Lange-Athinodorou 2021, 258-260.

[31] pPetersburg116A, verso 8,1-8,2 and 8,8-8,10: Quack 1992, 48-53; Parkinson 1997, 222-223; Parkinson 2002, 315-316; Lange-Athinodorou 2021(a), 261-262.

[32] Dorner, Bietak 1998, 19; Czerny 2015.

[33] Adams 2007; Redford 2010, 17-43.

[34] Redford 2010, 45-57.

[35] Friedman 1992, 200-205; Adams 2007, 97; Adams 2009, 175-200; Adams 2020, 56-57.

[36] Redford 1999/2000, 18; Adams 2007, 96, 358-359. Redford 2010, 32, however, dates these tombs in the time of Pepi II. See also Redford 2010, 51. Adams 2020, 68, Table 3.6 again suggests a late First Intermediate Period date.

4. The seat of governors: Bubastis in the Middle Kingdom

At the end of the Third millennium, around 2080 BCE[1], the rulers of the Theban nome began a campaign of territorial expansion. Antef I, the founder of what the Egyptian priest Manetho of the Third century BCE would later count as the Eleventh Dynasty, was the first to take on a royal Horus name. In doing so, he challenged the claim of the titular kings of Egypt, at that time residing at Herakleopolis. His name "*Horus: He who pacifies the Two Lands*", also declared his far-reaching ambitions. Consequently, Antef I conquered land south of Thebes, overthrowing the nomarchs of the Upper Egyptian nomes of Hierakonpolis and Edfu. Their earlier lineage includes Ankhtifi, a nomarch of the Ninth Dynasty, whose famous detailed biography preserved in his tomb at Mo'alla (*Hefat*) describes Ankhtifi's activities to mitigate the results of famine, civil war, and social unrest as well as his military actions against the Fourth and Fifth Upper Egyptian nomes, possibly as an ally of the Herakleopolitan Kings (see Chapter 3).[2]

The descendants of Antef I continued his policy of expansion. Antef II shifted the borders of the territory controlled by the Thebans further north, at first to Thinis, the capital of the Eighth Upper Egyptian nome. Despite a counter-attack by the Herakleopolitan King Khety and the nomarch of Assiut, Antef II went on to conquer the land up to the Tenth Upper Egyptian nome. He was the first Theban ruler to call himself "*The Dual King, son of Ra*", openly claiming royal supremacy.[3] His successors continued the war against the north until Mentuhotep II finally defeated the Herakleopolitan Kings and reunited all Egypt under his rule, sometime before his thirty-ninth regal year.[4] For a short time, Thebes, the hometown of the Eleventh Dynasty, became the royal residence. However, his successor Amenemhet I moved the residence away from Thebes, leaving behind his ancestral home and even an unfinished royal tomb.[5] He probably settled in Memphis, the time-honoured capital of the Old Kingdom,[6] for a period of unclear length, before finally founding a new capital at Lisht, around 30 km south of the entrance to the Fayum. The residence had the programmatic name "*(It is) Amenemhet who seizes the Two Lands*" (*jmn-m-ḥȝ.t jt-tȝ.wy*), in literature mostly shortened to 'Itj-Tawy'.

The Fayum is the largest of Egypt's oases and became the focal point of an intensive residence-administered agricultural development in the later Twelfth Dynasty. Therefore, scholars have argued that the proximity of the Fayum oasis was a decisive factor in choosing *Itj-Tawy* as the location of the new capital. However, Judith Bunbury has recently shown that *Itj-Tawy* was located at the Delta apex due to the southward migration of the Delta head in response to sea-level changes at that time. The favourable geographical position of *Itj-Tawy* was therefore twofold.[7] At any rate, in Egyptological terms, the relocation of the capital to the north truly marks the beginning of the Middle Kingdom, as it was a decisive break with the traditions of the Eleventh Dynasty.[8]

One of the main reasons to move to the north was certainly the need to gain full control over the Delta, a region that had slipped before from the grip of the Herakleopolitans. At a time when Libyans and Asiatics roamed and may even have manned fortresses in the Delta[9], the new royal Dynasty could not stay back in the southern Nile valley. The position of *Itj-Tawy* at the Delta apex guaranteed quick access to all the main Nile branches flowing through the Western, Central, and Eastern Delta. Thus, supply routes to the troubled areas were as short as possible, not only for military manoeuvres to win back the territory, but also for the erection of buildings to defend the entry points to the Delta. Accordingly, the above-discussed literary text 'The Words of Neferti' (see Chapter 3) describes that the foremost action of the promised new King Ameni (Amenemhet I) was to build a fortress or chain of fortresses, named 'Walls-of-the-ruler' to protect the Delta against the intruders:

> "The Asiatics will fall by his slaughtering; the Libyans will fall by his flame. The rebels belong to his wrath, the indignant to his authority. The uraeus on his forehead calms the indignant. The Walls-of-the-ruler, life, prosperity, health, will be built, no Asiatics will be allowed to come down to Egypt anymore."[10]

Archaeological remains of this fortress have either not survived the tides of time or have yet to be identified. However, another literary text of the Middle Kingdom helps to pinpoint its probable location. A passage in another literary work of the Middle Kingdom, the 'Tale of Sinuhe'[11] shows that the 'Walls-of-the-ruler' was situated near Tell Retaba in the Wadi Tumilat. The main protagonist of the story, Sinuhe, an official in the court of Amenemhet I, had fled Egypt after overhearing a message to the son and successor Senwosret I, informing him of the death of his father, probably as the result of an assassination:

> "The nobles of the royal council sent [to] the Western (Delta) to let the prince know about the situation that occurred in the audience hall."[12]

From somewhere in the Western Delta, where he accompanied a military expedition of the crown prince against Libyan tribes, Sinuhe turned south. Under cover of night, he passed the Nile in the region of Memphis and headed towards the Northeastern Delta[13]:

> (After) I forced my legs to move northwards, I reached the Walls-of-the-ruler, made to repel the Asiatics and to trample down the Bedouins. (...) I made my way at nighttime; at daybreak, I reached Peten. I had settled down on the island of 'The great black' when I was struck by thirst.[14]

Other textual sources suggest that 'The great black' (km-wr) was either the designation of the Timsah-lake or of a fortress in this area, thus making a location of the 'Walls-of-the-ruler' around 40 km to the west at Tell Retaba possible.[15] Amenemhet I had fortresses erected in the western Delta as well. AHMED FAKHRY discovered one of these installations at Kom el-Fahm (Wadi Natrun)[16].

To secure the Delta, the king also initiated state-planned settlements. The best example is Tell el-Dab'a in the Northeastern Delta. As said above people who settled there played a key role in the consolidation, control, and protection of the Eastern Delta and the routes for military and quarrying expeditions to the Sinai and beyond.[17]

It is only logical to assume that in this formative period, already powerful cities such as Bubastis would have played a similar role. The location of Bubastis close to the entrance to the Wadi Tumilat, a major route to the Sinai, but also the importance of the cult of Bastet are reasons enough for close royal attention. Consequently, there is evidence for building activities of Amenemhet I in the temple of Bastet: A block of pink granite with his royal titles, carrying the inscription:

"*He made his monuments for his mother Bastet: A doorway [...]*".[18]

A fragment of a false door of pink granite discovered by the mission of the University Potsdam in 1997 bears the titles of queen Khenemet-Nefer-Hedjet-Weret, royal spouse of Senusret II:

"*[Prieste]ss of Khnum, King's wife, she who is joined to the beauty of the White Crown, the Older, possessor of reverence.*"[19]

However, as there are no royal tombs at Bubastis from the Middle Kingdom, the false door was most probably brought from somewhere else in the Libyan period and reused (see Chapter 7).

Of uncertain origin are the heads and broken parts of two seated statues of granodiorite of a king of the Twelfth Dynasty, most possibly Amenemhet III, discovered by NAVILLE in the temple, which he thought to have stood at the entrance. Given that the inscriptions on the side of the thrones of the statues were altered to show the titles of Osorkon II (see Chapter 7.2.), they might have brought here in the Libyan period as well.[20]

Fig. 18: *Inscribed false-door fragment of Queen Khenemet-Nefer-Hedjet-Weret at the temple of Bastet. (UNIVERSITY POTSDAM MISSION 1997)*

4.1 The palace of the governors

As one of the most important cities of the Middle Kingdom Nile Delta, Bubastis was administered by governors residing in a large palace on the Northern Kom of the site. This building is to date the only archaeologically preserved palace of the Middle Kingdom in all of Egypt. Due to the fact that the available archaeological evidence on palaces mostly derives from the New Kingdom, the palace at Bubastis is not only important for our understanding of the history of the city, but also for the study of the evolution of Egyptian palace architecture in general.[21]

At Bubastis, the function of the palace function was probably not limited to the housing of the governors of the city. Its layout, size and the discovery of a doorframe

Fig. 19: *Southeastern part of the governor's palace with magazines to the south and the wȝḥy-hall to the north. (TELL BASTA PROJECT 2014)*

of limestone decorated with Sed-festival episodes of King Amenemhet III point to the fact that the palace might have had a double nature. On the one hand, it was the seat of the governors of Bubastis, on the other hand, it could serve as a royal mooring palace, i. e. a royal rest house, where the king and his officials would find temporary yet appropriate accommodation when visiting the city, for instance, to take part in religious festivals such as the festival of Bastet (see Chapter 8).

SHAFIK FARID discovered the palace in 1961 while conducting archaeological excavations on the Northern Kom of Bubastis. According to his account at that time, the tell was still mostly undisturbed:

> *"The site was comparatively high and difficult to dig."*[22]

In the following years, EL-SAWI (1970-71) and BAKR (1978-80) conducted excavations on the Northern Kom as well.[23] Their excavations revealed a huge north-south oriented mud-brick building, measuring 134 by 128m. The palace was once even larger, but modern buildings have cut off the northernmost part where presumably the main entrance was once situated.[24] Another entrance close to the southeastern corner leads through a transverse portico where limestone bases of a double row of six columns each are still visible. Proceeding to the north, a large court with a colonnade on its western side followed, providing access to a

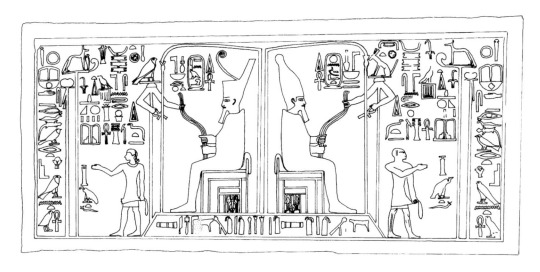

Fig. 20: *Amenemhet III celebrating the Sed-festival. Relief on a limestone lintel from the northeastern corner of the governor's palace. Line drawing based on* Van Siclen *1996, Fig. 11 (*Lange-Athinodorou *2004)*

large colonnaded hall with nine columns on its long side and a porticus on its northern side, consisting of a double row of four columns each. An opening in the middle of the eastern wall leads to the residential quarters of the palace; a small six-columned hall to the northeast of the colonnaded hall is accessible through an opening in the northern part of its eastern wall.[25]

Leaning against the western wall of the great colonnaded hall, FARID discovered three statues of governors of Bubastis from the Middle Kingdom: a seated and a cubic statue of limestone and a scribe statue of quartzite. Of them, only the latter is inscribed, identifying the represented official as governor of Bubastis, Khakaura-Seneb (see below). The statues might once have stood in an integrated *ka*-chapel of the governors.[26]

The portico in the north of the large colonnaded hall offers a slight off-axis transition into the so-called throne hall. The room obviously marks the centre of the eastern palace wing. Framed by remarkably thick walls and equipped with a double row of three monumental columns along both sides of the central axis, the hall has an opening in the centre of the northern wall leading into the now destroyed part of the palace where the main entrance once was. Small passageways on the north- and southeastern corners of the hall connect it with further rooms of uncertain function. It is interesting to note that the northeastern corner of the palace was the findspot of fragments of a monumental doorframe of limestone, i.e. a lintel and two further fragments belonging to the right and left doorframe. The lintel is decorated with a symmetrical emblematic scene showing Amenemhet III celebrating his first Sed-festival, enthroned in the festival chapel and wearing the Red Crown of Lower Egypt and the White Crown of Upper Egypt, accompanied by the deities of these geographical regions: Horus of Buto and Seth of Coptos. The fragments from the doorframe show the beginning of the royal titles under the wings of the deity Nekhbet. The door might have belonged to a chapel for the veneration of the king, possibly identified with the room to the northeast of the throne hall.[27]

It is obvious that the eastern wing of the palace had representational functions. The actual residences of the governors of the city were in the central and western parts of the building.

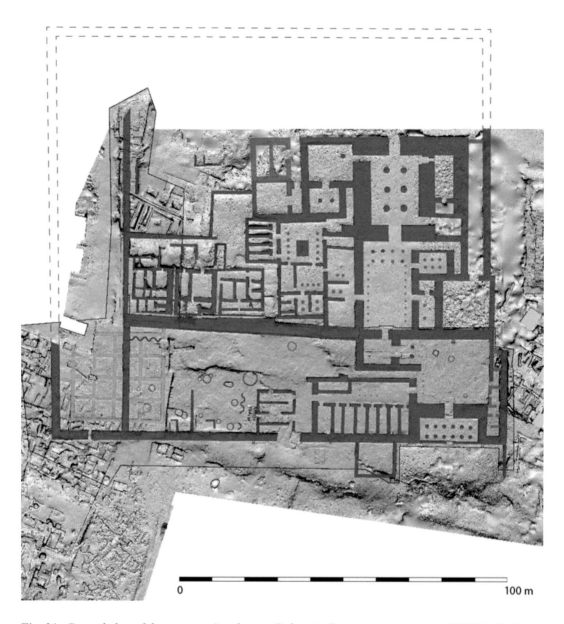

Fig. 21: *Ground plan of the governor's palace at Bubastis. (LANGE-ATHINODOROU 2018(a), Fig.2a)*

The largest of these apartments is close to the west of the large colonnaded hall, with a direct connection to some bureaus connected to the large colonnaded hall. The southern and eastern sectors of the palace consist of magazines and food processing areas with ovens.

Besides archaeology, Egyptian texts grant us the fascinating opportunity to reconstruct those once grandiose, splendid palaces, at least in a virtual way. To do so, we have to look for written sources, which provide terms for specific parts of palatial architecture and set them into a functional context. Three terms are most frequently mentioned: The '*great dual portal*' (*rw.tj wr.tj*), the '*colonnaded hall*' (*wꜣḫy*) and the '*audience room*' (*ꜥ-ḫn.wtj*).[28]

The '*great dual portal*' of the palace was a true liminal area, setting the inner sphere of the palace apart from the outside world and offering protection by controlling access to the building. For instance, the '*Tale of Sinuhe*' opens with a vivid description of how the palace went into lockdown after the king's death, referring to the great double portal now closed:

> "*The residence was in silence, the hearts were in sorrow, the great dual portal was sealed.*"[29]

Many years later however, his royal successor Senwosret I promises Sinuhe a warm welcome at the very same portal as he urges him in a letter:

> "*Return to Egypt! You will see the residence where you grew up. You will kiss the earth at the great dual portal, you will join the companions (courtiers) (...)*"[30]

When we compare the information from those texts with the archaeologically attested ground plan of the palace at Tell Basta, we can identify the great dual portal: it was probably located in the now lost northern part, leading to the six-columned '*audience hall*'. The entrance in the southeastern corner of the palace probably had a double portal as well.

According to the texts, the *wꜣḥy*-hall designates a spacious place where a large number of people gathered for audiences, banquets, and ceremonies. The etymology of the word is unclear, yet the textual references highlight its obvious multi-functional character. In the '*Tale of the Court of King Cheops*'[31] it is the location where the king meets the magician Djedi to watch him magically revive a headless goose:

> "*His majesty then proceeded to the wꜣḥy-hall of the palace, life, health, prosperity. (…) Then the goose was placed at the west side of the wꜣḥy-hall, its head at the east side of the wꜣḥy-hall. Then, Djedi uttered what he said as magic. The goose rose waddling and her head did likewise.*"[32]

A non-fictional text recording a daily list of accounts and expenditures of the palace at Thebes in the Thirteenth Dynasty mentions a banquet in the *wꜣḥy*-hall as a reward for sixty officials.[33]

At Bubastis, the *wꜣḥy*-hall is most likely the large colonnaded hall with the double porticus in front of the six-columned audience hall. Texts such as the '*Tale of Sinuhe*' corroborate this identification: Sinuhe describes his way through the palace to the royal audience granted to him as he returned from foreign lands:

> "*The companions who usher to the wꜣḥy-hall were showing me the way to the audience room. I found his majesty on the great throne in the recess of electrum.*"[34]

According to the text, the audience room, called ꜥ-ẖn.wtj, literally the '*inner part (of the palace)*' was directly connected to the *wꜣḥy*-hall. The ꜥ-ẖn.wtj was a reception room with a more private character than the *wȝḫy*-hall and more restricted access. It belonged to the secluded section of the palace. Apart from royal palaces, the residences of high officials, such as viziers and nomarchs, also contained their own private audience room. Not every palace official could enter, only an inner circle of trusted individuals. Access to it was a privilege that had to be earned. Thus, the official Sobekemhat boasts in a graffiti at the Hatnub quarries recalling his career under the nomarch of the Fifteenth Nome of Upper Egypt:

"*As I was a child, I was (already) a companion, a man of the ͨ-ḥn.wtj.*"[35]

In the Middle Kingdom, the title '*overseer of the ͨ-ḥn.wtj*', also translated as '*chamberlain*', which is unknown in earlier times, appears frequently. Biographies of such officials reveal that their duties included ensuring a strict protocol for visitors meeting the king or lord of the estate. Accordingly, the chamberlain Remeny-ankh describes himself as follows:

"*The one, who gives instructions to the companions regarding standing and sitting, the one who hears, what is (meant to be) heard alone (i.e., secret matters), the chamberlain of the hall of the sealbearer, Remeny-ankh (...).*"[36]

At Bubastis, the thick-walled six-columned hall in the innermost part of the palace, to the immediate north of the *wȝḫy*-hall, is a good candidate for what an Egyptian text would designate as the (private) audience hall *ͨ-ḥn.wtj*.[37]

4.2 The cemetery of the governors

In the course of excavating the governor's palace in 1961, FARID discovered the cemetery of the governors close to the eastern outer wall of the palace (Cemetery E).[38] This place is a rare example of an elite cemetery of the Middle Kingdom in the Delta and reveals the existence of a specific Deltaic funerary tradition that has no direct parallel elsewhere in Egypt: the custom of burying the governors of a city in the immediate vicinity of the place where they held office during their lifetime.[39] Within an area of 40 by 30 m, FARID excavated a massive enclosure wall of mud-brick, around 3.0 m thick, with an entrance in the middle of the northern side. Within the enclosed area were a number of heavily robbed vaulted tombs, also built of mud-brick, some of which had burial chambers lined with limestone, much like the tombs of the Old Kingdom cemeteries in Bubastis (see Chapter 2).[40] It remains unclear whether this was a cemetery within an enclosed area or a single large mastaba with multiple burial chambers, i.e. a mastaba of the so-called '*tombe-en-four*' type.[41]

The largest tomb (no. 1)[42] is located at the centre. It consists of a burial chamber of 6.0 by 4.10 m, made of large polished limestone blocks. Remains of the surrounding mud-brick structure are still visible, but the roofing seems to have disappeared already more or less entirely at the time of its discovery. Like all other tombs of cemetery E, tomb no. 1 is oriented north. According to FARID's drawing, a kind of long passageway connected its burial chamber entrance with the main passage through the northern enclosure wall. If this seeming passageway was in reality a sloping shaft, it would corroborate the view that cemetery D was really a single mastaba or at least started out as one.

Two limestone blocks closed the entrance of tomb no 1. Shafts and blockages like this

Fig. 22: *The governor's cemetery (Cemetery E) at Bubastis. View to the northwest.* (TELL BASTA-PROJECT *2016)*

Fig. 23: *The governor's cemetery (Cemetery E), tomb no 5. View to the north.* (TELL BASTA-PROJECT *2016)*

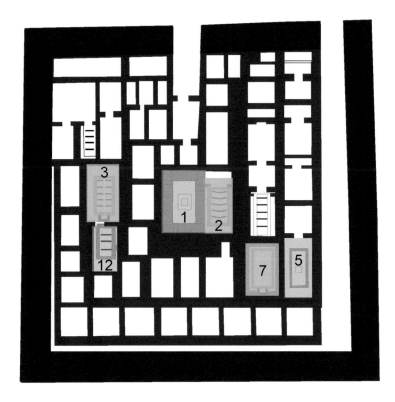

Fig. 24: *Ground plan of Cemetery E. Chronological pattern of use after VAN SICLEN's suggestion. Orange: stage 1 (earlier period), green: stage 2 (later period). (LANGE-ATHINODOROU 2015, Fig. 2)*

are typical features of the limestone-chambered tombs in the Old Kingdom Cemetery C at Bubastis (see Chapter 2.2.3), and the Middle Kingdom tombs at El-Qatta in the Southwestern Delta.[43]

Six grooves for wooden beams, which once served to keep the wooden coffin from any direct contact with the floor of the chamber, were carved into the limestone flooring. A canopic niche was sunk in the centre of the floor. FARID discovered a limestone offering table of a Rens(eneb), governor of Bubastis, in close proximity to the tomb, which may identify its owner (see below).

Tomb no. 2, directly to the east, is of smaller dimensions (4.5 by 2.5 m). Based on FARID's unpublished field notes, CHARLES VAN SICLEN produced a schematic ground plan of the tomb, with a canopic niche at the centre of the southern wall and five beam-grooves on the floor. The unpublished find of an inscribed jamb and offering table close by led him to the assumption that tomb no. 2 once belonged to the Lady Nefret, spouse of Rens(eneb).[44]

Four other tombs had limestone burial chambers. Two of them (no. 3 and no. 12), lie to the west of the central tomb, the other two (no. 5 and no. 7) to the southeast. At the time of its discovery, the now vanished remains of painted inscriptions on the limestone walls of tomb no. 3 identified its owner, the governor Maheshotep, son of Sithathor. His burial chamber of 3.50 by 2.60 m has a canopic niche in the centre of the southern side, framed by two additional niches. More niches are located in the northeastern and northwestern corners of the long sides of the chamber. The floor shows ten beam-grooves.[45] Tomb no. 12 to the immediate south is of smaller dimensions (2.90 by 1.40 m). Its canopic niche is set in the southeastern corner of the chamber and only four beam-grooves were cut in the floor. Based on the fragment of an inscribed stela found in front of the tomb, VAN SICLEN assigned this tomb to a son of Ren(seneb) and Nefret, whose name, however, is lost.[46]

Tomb no. 5 in the southeastern corner of the cemetery had some inscriptions preserved, identifying the governor Antef as its owner.[47] The burial chamber of 4.15 by 1.90 m has a canopic niche in the centre of the floor, but no beam-grooves. Tomb no. 7 to the immediate west has a slightly larger burial chamber (3.50 by 1.80 m) and five beam-grooves. Again, the canopic niche is set in the centre of the southern wall. The owner of the tomb is unknown.

There are about 20 more burial chambers in the cemetery[48], but none of them has a limestone chamber. Given the brief publication, the chronological timeframe of usage is as difficult to ascertain as the original number of burials. However, a closer analysis of inscribed objects coming from the area, presented in the next chapter, leads to some useful observations on the matter.

4.3 A dynasty of governors of Bubastis

During the excavation of the palace and the nearby tombs of the governors, FARID unearthed scattered funerary objects such as offering tables, stelae, and statues. Their inscriptions provide some insights into the identity of the tomb owners[49]:

Object	Inscriptions	Owner
Offering table B 1	Symmetrical running offering formula: ⸢An offering⸣ that ⸢the king⸣ gives and Bastet, lady of Bubastis […]Ma'at(iu)ᵇ (?), Ren⸢s⸣(eneb) […] Right column: The Revered One with ⸢Osiris⸣ […][…] User […]	**Ren(seneb)**
Offering table B 1503	Right side: [An offering that the king gives] and Anubis […], ⸢who presides over the Divine Booth⸣[…] ⸢Bastet⸣, Mistress of the Two Lands, that she (?) may give bread, beer, ⸢cattle and fowl⸣ […][for the Ka of] […] Khem, born of Menkh(et) […]. The Revered One with Osiris, Sat-Im, born of Khem […] Left side: [An offering that the king gives] [….] (and all) the gods. An invocation offering (consisting of) bread, beer, cattle, fowl for the beautification (?) […] the Revered One with Osiris […] may give ⸢thousands⸣of bread and beer, cattle and fowl, alabaster and clothing and thousands of offerings, thousands of provisions […] [for] ⸢the Ka of⸣ Khemet, born of Men[khet] […]. The Revered One with Osiris, Sat-Im, born of Khemet, justified.	**Khemet Sat-Im**

Object	Inscriptions	Owner
Offering table	Right side:	**Khety**
B 1511	*An offering that the king gives and Osiris, the foremost of the Westerners, lord of Abydos, (that he may give) an invocation offering, consisting of bread [...] at the [...] festival, ⸢fowl⸣ [...],*	**Tjebu**
		Antef-Akhu(?)
		Antef (I+II?)
	The governor, overseer of the priests, overseer of the production place, Khety, born of Mer(et)-Jj.t.	**Meket**
	The governor, (overseer of the priests, overseer of the production place), Tjebu, son of Antef, justified. The nomarch Antef-Akhu(?).	
	Left side:	
	An offering that the king ⸢gives⸣ and Anubis, who is upon his mountain, the Imi-ut, lord of the sacred land, (that he may give) his beautiful burial in the western desert of the necropolis⸢ [...].	
	[The governor], overseer of the priests, overseer of the production place, Antef-Akhu(?). The governor, (overseer of the priests, overseer of the production place), Antef, son of Ma'atju. The governor, (overseer of the priests, overseer of the production place), Meket, son of User.	
Statue of a cross-legged seated official	On the lap:	**Khakaura-Seneb**
	An offering that the king gives and Re-Horakhty, the son of Geb, Osiris, the Great Ennead, the row of Upper and Lower Egyptian chapels, and Bastet, lady of Bubastis, (that they may give) an invocation offering, (consisting of) bread, beer, pure cattle and fowl, incense, unguent, for the Ka of the jr.j-p^c.t, governor, spokesman of Nekheb in the Per-wer, overseer, of the priest(s) of Bastet, Khakaura-Seneb, begotten of Mut.	
	On the base: *The jrj-p^c.t, governor, overseer of the priest(s) of Bastet, Khakaura-Seneb, begotten of Mut, justified.*	
	On the dorsal pillar: *The jrj-p^c.t, governor, overseer of the priests of Bastet, Khakaura-Seneb, begotten of Mut, justified.*	

Object	Inscriptions	Owner
Base of a statue	Left side: *[...] [every good thing] on which a god lives, for the Ka of the jrj-pᶜ.t, Maheshotep. Maheshotep, possessor of reverence.*	**Maheshotep**
Base of a statue	*[...] the lady of the house, Kheret-ib [...].*	

Table 1: *Inscribed objects from cemetery E.*

Further information comes from painted inscriptions in some of the limestone-chambered tombs. FARID reported the name of Maheshotep, with the filiation "*son of Sathathor*", preserved on the walls of tomb no. 3. An inscription on the base of his statue, discovered in the governor's palace (see Table 1), informs us that he held the high-ranking title of a *jrj-pᶜ.t* (lit.: "*He, who belongs to the pᶜ.t-people*"). As mentioned above, tomb no. 5 also preserved the name of its owner Antef at the time of FARID's excavation. The following table lists all available information on each individual mentioned in the inscriptions.[50]

Name	Title	Related Individual	Source
Antef	*ḥꜣtj-ᶜ (?)* - Governor (?)		Wall inscription from tomb no. 5.
Antef	*ḥꜣtj-ᶜ* - Governor	Nefret (daughter)	Door jamb B 8 and offering table B 9 close to tomb no. 1.
Antef	*ḥꜣtj-ᶜ (j)m(y)-r(ꜣ) ḥm.w- nṯr (j)m(y)-r(ꜣ) gs-pr -* Governor, overseer of the priests, overseer of the production place[51]	Tjebu (son)	Offering table B 1511 from the debris of the eastern part of the palace.
Antef	*ḥꜣtj-ᶜ* - Governor	Ma'atju (father)	Offering table B 1511 from the debris of the eastern part of the palace.
Antef-Akhu(?)	*ḥꜣtj-ᶜ (j)m(y)-r(ꜣ) ḥm.w-nṯr (j)m(y)-r(ꜣ) gs-pr* - Governor, overseer of the priests, overseer of the production place		Offering table B 1511 from the debris of the eastern part of the palace.
Khety	*ḥꜣtj-ᶜ (j)m(y)-r(ꜣ) ḥm.w-nṯr (j)m(y)-r(ꜣ) gs-pr* - Governor, overseer of the priests, overseer of the production place	Meret-Jjt (mother)	Offering table B 1511 from the debris of the eastern part of the palace.

Name	Title	Related Individual	Source
Ma'atju	*ḥȝtj-ᶜ (?)* *rḫ nsw.t (?)* - Governor, king's acquaintance (?)	Antef (son)	Offering table B 1511 from the debris of the eastern part of the palace and offering table B 1 found near tomb no. 1.
Meket	*ḥȝtj-ᶜ* - Governor	User (father)	Offering table B 1511 from the debris of the eastern part of the palace.
User	*ḥȝtj-ᶜ (?)* - Governor (?)	Meket (son)	Offering table B 1511 from the debris of the eastern part of the palace and offering table B 1 found near tomb no. 1.
Tjebu	*ḥȝtj-ᶜ (j)m(y)-r(ȝ) ḥm.w-nṯr (j)m(y)-r(ȝ) gs-pr* - Governor, overseer of the priests, overseer of the production place	Antef (father)	Offering table B 1511 from the debris of the eastern part of the palace.
Khakaura-Seneb	*jrj-pᶜ.t ḥȝtj-ᶜ ḥrj-tp nḫb m pr-wr (j)m(y)-r(ȝ) ḥm.w-nṯr n(y) bȝst.t - jrj-pᶜ.t*, governor, spokesman of Nekheb in the Per-wer, overseer of the priest(s) of Bastet	Mut (mother)	Statue B 96 found in the colonnaded hall of the palace.
Maheshotep	*ḥȝtj-ᶜ* - governor	Sithathor (mother)	Wall inscription from tomb no. 3 and base of a statue found in the palace.
Sat-Jm	/	Khemet (mother); Menhet (grandmother)	Offering table B 1503 from the debris of the eastern part of the palace.
Khemet	/	Menhet (mother)	Offering table B 1503 from the debris of the eastern part of the palace.
Menhet	/	Khemet (daughter) Sat-Jm (granddaughter)	Offering table B 1503 from the debris of the eastern part of the palace.
Kheret-ib	*nb.t-pr* - Lady of the house		Base of statue B 663 found in the debris of the eastern palace.[52]
Mut	/	Khakaura-Seneb (son)	Statue B 96 found in the colonnaded hall of the palace.

Name	Title	Related Individual	Source
Sithathor	/	Maheshotep (son)	Wall inscription at tomb no. 3.
Nefret	/	Antef (father)	Fragmentary stela B 12,
		NN (son)	door jamb B 8 and
			offering table B 9.

Table 2: *The governors of Bubastis and their family members.*

The titles of the governors show, that they held important offices within the provincial administration of the Nile Delta in the Middle Kingdom and allow insights into the administrative network of the time. However, not all of the titles reflect specific functions but have to be understood as ranking titles, i.e., honorary titles such as, for example, the title *jrj-pᶜ.t* of Khakaura-Seneb. This is the highest-ranking title and well-attested since the Old Kingdom. It designates an official who could perform royal duties at various ceremonial events and on other occasions. In title strings of high officials, *jrj-pᶜ.t* is usually followed by another ranking title: *ḥȝtj-ᶜ* (lit: "*He, who is foremost of arm*") which is held by all governors of Bubastis. As said in Chapter 2, in this local context however, *ḥȝtj-ᶜ* is a function title, best translated as "*governor*".

As mentioned above, Khakauraseneb was also "*overseer of the priests of Bastet*". The combination of titles of offices of secular and religious power is typical for the provincial administration of the Middle Kingdom, and means that the official presided over the administration of the city and the local main temple.[53] Antef (I/II), Antef-Akhu(?), Tjebu and Khety also held this title. The same individuals were "*overseer of the production place*", which means they administered the artisans and products of a centre of workshops probably connected to the palace of the governors and likewise the temple of Bastet.[54]

Still, the genealogical and chronological sequence of the governors remains difficult to establish. For any attempt to do so, the starting point has to be Khakaura-Seneb. He bears a basilophoric name, including the throne name of Senwosret III, which indicates that his lifetime coincided with the reign of this king, at least partly. Although it must remain unclear whether he took this name to express his loyalty to the reigning king at a specific point in his career at the court, thereby changing his birth name, or if Khakaura-Seneb was already his birth name, the general time frame is clear. The facial features of the statue of Khakaura-Seneb are reminiscent of key features found on statues of Senwosret III, a well-known phenomenon of ancient Egyptian culture in which officials imitated certain portrait-like features in the images of kings in order to demonstrate their loyalty to the ruler.[55]

The offering formula on his statue reveals further information about his persona. The formula invokes Heliopolitan gods before mentioning the main deity of Bubastis, Bastet, although Khakauraseneb held the office of the main priest of the goddess. Does this mean that Khakauraseneb hailed originally from Heliopolis and had started his career there? On the other hand, in later sources, Bastet frequently carries the epithet '*Eye of Ra*' and '*privy to the secrets of Atum*'. The sun-god Ra is of course the main Heliopolitan deity together with Atum, with whom he oftentimes forms a union. Atum is also part of the divine triad,

Bastet-Atum-Mahes/Hor-Hekenu, at Bubastis (see Chapter 1). In the reliefs discovered at the location of the so-called '*Temple of Hermes*' of the time of the Libyan kings, Bastet appears in the sun barque together with the Heliopolitan triad Atum, Shu and Tefnut (see Chapter 7.4). There is ample possibility that the strong connection of Bastet with Heliopolitan deities in such later sources dates back much further. Therefore, the offering formula on the statue of Khakaura-Seneb could very well refer to a cult of Heliopolitan deities at Bubastis in the Middle Kingdom.[56]

Coming back to the issue of the chronology of the governors of Bubastis in the Middle Kingdom, we can safely assume that Khakaura-Seneb and his mother Mut, also mentioned in the inscription on his statue, date into the middle of the Twelfth Dynasty. Other than that, we can only sum up general information on the genealogy of the governors given in table no. 2 and try to combine them with clues as to the dating of inscribed objects, such as, for instance, the typology of the offering tables which generally fits into the second part of the Twelfth Dynasty.[57] However, this is not enough to build a definite chronology. To complicate matters further, some of the personal names attested for the governors, such as Antef and Khety, are very typical for the Middle Kingdom[58] and it is possible that several governors of Bubastis bore these names. For instance, according to the filiation given on the right side of offering table B1511, the governor Antef, owner of tomb no. 5, might also have been the father of governor Tjebu, while the inscription on the left side of the same offering table, mentioning an Antef "*son of Ma'atju*" might refer to another individual. Thus, there could have been an Antef I and II as governors of the city.

The offering table mentions Antef-Akhu(?) in the same line as the governor Khety, yet without any further indications about their relationship. Khety is the son of a woman called Meret-Jj.t[59], whereas there is no obvious filiation for Antef-Akhu. He, however, could have been the father of Khety, because he appears on the same line with his full title string.

On the lower part of the right side of the offering table B 1511 appears the governor Meket, "*son of User*". Both are also mentioned on offering table B 1. If the sequence with Antef-Akhu (?) and Antef on the left side of the offering table can be understood as a filiation, we can guess that Antef-Akhu(?) and Tjebu were brothers. Tjebu could be an older brother, succeeded first by his younger brother Antef-Akhu(?) and then by his nephew Khety. Following these presuppositions, the following hypothetical genealogy emerges:

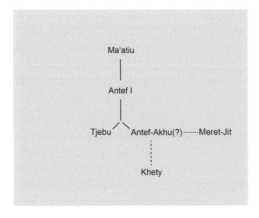

At any rate, the connection between the governors Khakaura-Seneb, and Maheshotep, who are attested on other objects (see table 1), remains uncertain.

Offering table B 1503 names several women of the families of the governors albeit without any titles. These are Sat-Im, her mother Khem, and her grandmother Menkhet. We only have further knowledge of Sithathor, the mother of Maheshotep, Mut, the mother of Khakaura-Seneb, and Nefret, the daughter of Antef. The relation of Sat-Im, Khemet, and Menkhet to any of the attested governors is unclear.[60] In addition, the base of a statue listed in table no. 1 mentions a "*lady of the house*" Kheret-ib, who must have been an otherwise unattested relative of a governor.

The existence of a huge provincial palace and a cemetery for the governors of Bubastis is testimony to the fact that in the Middle Kingdom Bubastis was a vital seat of great administrative power. It was here that products of the rural hinterland and goods coming from expeditions passing through the Wadi Tumilat were registered, processed, and sent to other places, especially to the capital and the royal court at *Itj-Tawy*. On the other hand, according to the geographical list on the White Chapel of Senwosret I at Karnak, Bubastis was not the capital of a nome itself at that time but belonged to the Heliopolitan nome of Lower Egypt.[61] At any rate, the list at Karnak depicts Isis and Bubastis' main goddess Bastet as the main deities of the Heliopolitan nome, proving the great importance of the city of Bubastis as a regional government authority of the Middle Kingdom in the Southeastern Delta.

Endnotes

[1] Hornung et al. 2006, 482.
[2] Vandier 1950; Schenkel 1965, 45-57.
[3] Sabbahy 2021, 120-22.
[4] Willems 2010, 87-89.
[5] Arnold 1991, 5-21; Arnold, Jánosi 2015, 54.
[6] Lorand 2016, 35; Silverman 2009, 72-74.
[7] Bunbury 2013, 63, 65.
[8] Vogel 2004, 97-98, Arnold, Jánosi 2015, 55; Lorand 2016, 31-48. Papyrus Petersburg 111B verso 63-64; Gestermann 1987, 109-11.
[9] Lange-Athinodorou 2021(a), 258-60.
[10] pPetersburg 111B verso 63-6z; Gestermann 1987, 109-111.
[11] Parkinson 2002, 297-298.
[12] pBerlin 10499 (verso), line 17-19: Koch 1990, R17-19.
[13] See Bunbury 2019, 69 Fig. 5.3.
[14] pBerlin 10499 (verso), line 41-47: Koch 1990, R41-47.
[15] Gomaà 1987, 130.
[16] Fakhry 1940, 845-848; Fakhry 1973, 210; Vogel 2004, 92; Arnold, Jánosi 2015, 55.
[17] Czerny 1999; Habachi 2001, 158-163, 174, Taf. 8-9.
[18] Naville 1891, Pl. XXXIIIA.
[19] Lange 2007.
[20] Naville 1891, 26 and Pl. X-XI. One of the heads is nowadays in the British Museum: EA 1063.
[21] Lange-Athinodorou 2018(a), 40-43.
[22] Farid 1964, 85.
[23] El-Sawi 1979; Bakr 1979.
[24] Lange-Athinodorou 2018(a), 46 Fig. 1a.
[25] Bietak, Lange 2014.
[26] Bakr et al. 2010, 8-10.
[27] Bietak 2014-15, 54.
[28] Lange-Athinodorou 2018 (a).
[29] pBerlin 10499, line 8-9: Koch 1990, R7-9.
[30] pBerlin 3022, line 188-189: Koch 1990, B188-189.
[31] Parkinson 2002, 295-296.
[32] pWestcar, 8.9-8.10 and 8.18-8.20: Blackman 1988, 10 .
[33] pBoulaq 18: Scharff 1922, pl. 10** (36), pl. 18** (36); Quirke 1990, 40.
[34] pBerlin 10499, line 250-251: Koch 1990, B250-251.
[35] Anthes 1964, Gr. 22.2-3 (pl. 22), 48.
[36] Gardiner, 1947, I, *44; Gauthier 1918, 169; Landgráfová 2011, 236.
[37] Lange-Athinodorou 2018(a).
[38] Farid 1964.
[39] Lange 2015; Lange-Athinodorou 2018(b).
[40] Farid, 1964, 85.
[41] Jequier 1929; Seidlmayer 1990, 382; Alexanian 2016, 243, 252.
[42] The numbering of the tombs follows Farid 1964, 87, Fig. 1.
[43] Lange 2015, 187-189.
[44] Van Siclen 1991(b)(b), 190-192.
[45] Van Siclen 1991(b), 190-192.

[46] Van Siclen 1991(b), 190, 191, Fig. 2.

[47] Van Siclen 1991(b), 190, 192.

[48] Some of the chambers marked as burials on the plan Farid 1964, 87, Fig. 1 may actually have been shafts.

[49] Lange 2015, 190-195.

[50] Lange 2015, 190-195.

[51] Lange 2015, 198-199.

[52] Van Siclen 1991(b), 193; Bakr et al., 2010, Fig. 13.

[53] Ward 1982, 35. 259; Grajetzki 2009, 110; Selve 1993, 73-81.

[54] Helck 1958, 107, 386, 509; Fischer, 1966, 66-67; Ward 1982, 52.411; Grajetzki 2000, 201-202; Grajetzki 2013, 254.

[55] Bakr et al. 2014, 10-11.

[56] Habachi 1957, 119-120; Lange-Athinodorou 2019(a).

[57] Cf. Hölzl 2002.

[58] Ranke 1935, 34.1 and 277.26.

[59] Cf. Ranke 1935, 161.14.

[60] Van Siclen 1991(b), 190-192.

[61] Helck 1974, 183, 195-196; Lacau, Chevrier 1956-1961, 235, pl. 26, 42.

5. Bastet and Seth: Bubastis in the time of the Hyksos Kings

From a general point of view, the end of the Middle Kingdom somehow mirrors the end of the Old Kingdom, albeit the underlying reasons differ. While extreme palaeo-climatic events were a main factor at the end of the Old Kingdom, it is the establishment of dynasties of foreign origin in the Delta that brought about the end of the Middle Kingdom. The outcome, however, is comparable: a time of short-lived kings and territorial fragmentation that ended in military conflicts.

The Twelfth Dynasty concluded with the reign of Nefrusobek, a daughter of an apparently heirless Amenemhet III. She filled the place on the throne after the death of his successor, Amenemhet IV, who himself might have been adopted by Amenemhet III from the ranks of high officials. As Amenemhet IV actually had sons, who later founded the Thirteenth Dynasty, Nefrusobek's accession to the throne was one of usurpation. These events indicate internal struggles amongst the members of the royal family, whether blood-tied or adopted.[1]

At any rate, the end of Nefrusobek's short reign of about four years (1763-1759 BCE) marks the end of the uninterrupted rule of the house of the political descendants of the Theban nomarchs and warlords who had united Egypt around 240 years before. In the following period many kings ruled for a short period of time, a typical feature of periods when the dissolution of central power occurred. Important discoveries at Tell el-Dab'a, Abydos, Thebes, El-Kab, Tell Edfu and Elephantine have recently shed new light on these events.[2]

From the Turin king list, we know that the Thirteenth Dynasty encompassed around 57 kings from different backgrounds, including common families, ruling for around 150 years. Most are not attested by any surviving monuments. Ample evidence on the social elite and the administrative system comes, however, from inscribed stelae of high-ranking officials, especially from their cenotaphs built at the terrace of the temple of Osiris at Abydos.[3]

Judging by the archaeological record, King Sobekhotep III and his successors Neferhotep I, Sahathor, Sobekhotep IV and Sobekhotep V were the most eminent rulers of this dynasty. The lack of large monuments is a result of the loss of control over the Delta and with it a large proportion of revenues for the royal court going instead to migrants coming from the Levant and their newly evolving independent fiefdoms, a process which started at the end of the Twelfth Dynasty. The royal residence *Itj-Tawy* (Lisht, see Chapter 4) was abandoned within the last 30 years of the Thirteenth Dynasty in favour of a return to Thebes. From a modern point of view, this action bears a certain historical irony: the retreat to the south is exactly the reverse of the northern expansion of their predecessors at the start of the Twelfth Dynasty. Moreover, in the same way as the move north once marked the beginning of the Middle Kingdom, the move south was its closure.[4]

As said above, the developments in the Delta were a decisive factor of these events. During the time of the Thirteenth Dynasty, the Delta was already divided into several fiefdoms and out of reach of the kings residing at *Itj-Tawy*, a situation that recalls the state of affairs in the First Intermediate Period. Delta rulers of foreign origin formed the Fourteenth Dynasty.[5] Of these, Nehesi, son of a Delta king named Sheshi, is the only one for whom we have a fair amount of detailed knowledge, thanks to the intensified archaeological exploration of the Northeastern Delta. The discovery of architectural remains, possibly of a temple of Seth, inscribed with his name and titles at Tell el-Dab'a, show that he chose the city of Avaris, the famous capital of the later Hyksos kings, as his residence. Judging by the territorial distribution of monuments of Nehesi, his realm stretched from Tell Hebua at the Northeastern Delta edge to Bubastis in the southeast.[6] These two locations were of imminent strategic importance. Tell Hebua is the site of the fortress Tjaru (archaeologically attested since the New Kingdom) at the Isthmus of Qantara, which had long since protected the start of the so-called '*Way(s) of Horus*', the main overland route to the Sinai and the Syro-Palestinian area.[7] Bubastis, at the entrance of the Wadi Tumilat, another important overland route, served as the entry point into the actual heartland of Egypt (see Chapter 1.1).

Excavations of the Austrian Archaeological Institute at Tell el-Dab'a, directed by MANFRED BIETAK and IRENE FORSTNER-MÜLLER, brought to light a rich archaeological record for this crucial period. The material culture coming from settlements and tombs revealed that a large number of people of Syro-Palestinian background had already settled at Tell el-Dab'a in the later part of the Middle Kingdom. Especially noteworthy in this respect is a palatial mansion with Near Eastern-influenced architecture of the early Thirteenth Dynasty, built over an older edifice whose ground plan was that of a typical Syrian middle-room house, which may have served as the residence of a ruler or high official of Near Eastern origin. Connected to the building was a cemetery in a garden-like setting. The mud-brick tombs with vaulted and other types of roofs were mostly robbed. The remaining grave goods, however, show that the tomb owners belonged to the local elite of a mixed Egyptian and Levantine background. The discovery of donkey burials in front of the tombs' entrances corroborate this assumption, as this is a typical custom of Syro-Palestinian culture of the Middle Bronze Age. In Egypt, the custom of donkey burials seems to be restricted to the Eastern Delta of Egypt and is so far attested in Avaris, Bubastis, Tell el-Maskhuta, Tell el-Yahudiya, and Inshas.[8]

These and other finds attest to the fact that at the time of the late Thirteenth Dynasty, a population of Levantine origin with the cultural background of the Syrian Middle Bronze Age (MB II A) had settled at Avaris/Tell el-Dab'a, living side by side with the Egyptian population. An Egyptian-Levantine mixed culture emerged, spreading into the Eastern Delta. Material remains of this culture were also uncovered at Farasha, Tell el-Maskhuta, and Bubastis.

During the reign of Nehesi, another wave of migrants from the northern Levant arrived at Avaris. Their grave goods contained several kinds of weapons (i.e., daggers and axes) pointing to their particularly martial background. Within the period of their assimilation, the city tripled in size. From the ranks of these newcomers came the rulers who followed Nehesi on the throne of Avaris. Not much is known of these kings, besides the listing of their names in the Turin Canon and a large number of seals discovered at a multitude of sites in Egypt, Nubia and the Levant.[9]

The kings of the succeeding Fifteenth Dynasty (of unclear relation to the Fourteenth Dynasty) called themselves ḥqꜣ-ḫꜣs.wt (Greek: *Hyksos*), literally "*Lord of foreign lands*", a designation adopted in Egyptian textual sources.[10] Among these, Khayan and Apepi are best attested. Their chronological setting, as well as the possible chronological overlapping of rulers of the Thirteenth-Sixteenth Dynasties, recently became the subject of discussion as new finds emerged at Tell el-Dab'a, Tell Edfu, and other sites.[11]

The remains of a large mud-brick palace of the Hyksos Period, which underwent at least two building stages, were excavated in recent years at Tell el-Dab'a. According to the seals discovered in offering and fire pits, the palace dates mainly to the time of Khayan.[12] The excavations of the Oriental Institute Chicago Expedition at Tell Edfu under the direction of NADINE MOELLER led to the discovery of a large number of discarded sealings of Khayan within an administrative building, indicating close contact to the royal residence of the Hyksos rulers at Avaris.[13]

Apepi, on the other hand, figures very prominently as the military opponent in the victory report of Kamose, the last Theban king of the Seventeenth Dynasty, who waged war against the Hyksos (see Chapter 6). Apepi usurped older royal statues from all over Egypt and had them brought to Avaris.[14] Famous examples are the so-called '*Hyksos monuments*', a group of statues of Amenemhet III of the Twelfth Dynasty discovered in Tanis, Fayum, Elkab and also Bubastis, where they were brought in later periods after the expulsion of the Hyksos (see below).[15]

The Hyksos, residing in Avaris in the Northeastern Delta, attempted to control the whole of Egypt, but in a very different way than the former Egyptian kings. Instead of establishing an absolute central authority based on an elaborate wide-ranging provincial administration, the Hyksos ruled the country by means of a feudal system. Several distinct military bases and fortresses, like Neferusi and Gebelein, served for observing and controlling the elongated Nile Valley.[16] This system could not prevent the existence of local dynasties, which rose up against the Hyksos dominion. The most important of these were the Theban Sixteenth and Seventeenth Dynasty, which will be discussed in the next chapter. Recently, the discovery of a royal cemetery at South Abydos with the tomb of a local king Seneb-Kay, who had died during combat, proved an older theory of the existence of a short-lived dynasty at Abydos. Three kings of this dynasty are listed in a now fragmented column of the Turin Canon, while the cemetery at South Abydos contains eight tombs.[17] The latest research shows that their rule could coincide with the time frame dating from the end of the Thirteenth to the Theban Sixteenth Dynasty (1650-1600 BCE).

It is evident that kingship in the Second Intermediate Period was not reliant on the unchallenged dynastic bloodline of a single royal house, but could be claimed by several lineages holding power over different geographical parts of Egypt. Although there might have been treaties and cooperation, it eventually led to frequent territorial conflicts between the regional kings. In addition, the situation here was not a simple South-against-the-North-affair, but one driven by a multitude of local agents and factors of which we have little knowledge. The death of the above-mentioned king Seneb-Kay from Abydos, who seems to have died in a battle with the Thebans during their military conquest of the fragmented southern Egypt at the beginning of the Seventeenth Dynasty, is a telling example of these multi-layered historical events.[18]

5.1. Burials of the Second Intermediate Period at Bubastis

The core region of the Hyksos realm was the Eastern Nile Delta, where Bubastis is situated. Does the archaeological record of Bubastis reflect this fact? In other words: Are there traces of the above-mentioned Egyptian-Levantine mixed culture to be found at Bubastis?

Up to now, the only archaeological contexts uncovered at Bubastis with Late Middle Kingdom and Second Intermediate Period material are burials, situated in close proximity to the governor's palace (s. Chapter 4.1). These finds, are, however, only very briefly published.

BAKR mentions a number of donkey burials around the Middle Kingdom palace; one of them was discovered inside a silo, the others contained the head of a donkey and some pottery. Another indicator is the presence of a certain type of pottery, the so-called '*Tell el-Yahudiya Ware*', excavated during field seasons conducted by FARID, EL-SAWI and BAKR as grave goods within some burials from one of the levels that covered the governor's cemetery of the Twelfth Dynasty and the Middle Kingdom palace.[19] The term '*Tell el-Yahudiya Ware*' designates a specific type of pottery, i.e. small jugs with a black or brown polished surface and decoration in the form of small punctures, sometimes filled with a white paste. It has been discovered all over the Mediterranean in archaeological horizons dating to the beginning of the Second millennium BCE and, while it first appears in the northern Levant, its mass production in Egypt started just before the beginning of the Fifteenth Dynasty. The Tell el-Yahudiya Ware from the tombs at Bubastis belong to types that date into the time span from around 1630-1550 BCE, i.e., in the late Second Intermediate Period, the time of the Hyksos kings.[20]

Within those burials were a number of scarabs of possible Palestinian origin dating to the later Middle Bronze Age (MB IIB). For example: a scarab from EL-SAWIS' excavations shows a lion and hieroglyphs forming the phrase ⸙ *nṯr nfr*-"*perfect god*", a common part of the Egyptian royal titulary. The motif of the lion is rare on scarabs of Egyptian provenance from the Late Middle Kingdom and the Second Intermediate Period, but appears frequently on scarabs of Palestinian origin.[21] Other scarabs show motifs of the so-called '*anra*'-formula, named after the typical appearance of the group of the single consonant signs ⸺ (*n*) and ⸦ (*r*). This design first appears in Palestine, and is often associated with pseudo-hieroglyphs.[22] The same is true for a scarab with a central cross and convoluted coils. Examples of this type found in Egypt come from Second Intermediate Period contexts in the Eastern Delta.[23]

In Palestine, locally produced scarabs occur for the first time in contexts of the Late Middle Bronze Age Period (MBIIA and MBIIB) as grave goods, most probably in imitation of Egyptian funerary culture. The timing of their appearance coincides with the final phase of the Late Middle Kingdom and the beginning of the Second Intermediate Period. Considering the associated pottery in well-stratified deposits at Tell el-Dab'a, these scarabs can be dated to the late Eighteenth or early Seventeenth century BCE. Their motifs imitate Egyptian motifs of the Middle Kingdom but with the addition of pseudo-hieroglyphs and other misunderstood signs, which do not occur on the Egyptian prototypes. Therefore, we can conclude that local workshops produced Egyptianizing scarabs, created indigenous motifs, and formed a new typological corpus. The Palestinian scarabs then found their way back to northern Egypt, where they seem to have been used by members of a group with mixed Egyptian-Levantine cultural background. Thus, the presence of Palestinian scarabs and Tell el-Yahudiya Ware in Second Intermediate Period tombs at Bubastis points to the possible existence of such a social stratum there as well.[24]

5.2 Hyksos Kings in the temple of Bastet?

Attestations of rulers of the Thirteenth Dynasty come from the temple of Bastet, where, in 1888, NAVILLE discovered two inscribed blocks and a statue, all bearing royal titles. An architrave block of pink granite has the prenomen: "*The Mighty One, Ra, Protector of the Two Lands*".[25] Two kings of the Thirteenth Dynasty bear this prenomen: Sobekhotep I, the first ruler of the 13th Dynasty and another king dating to the middle of the Thirteenth Dynasty, whose nomen is unknown.[26]

The Hyksos Kings themselves appear in the temple of Bastet as well. A part of a monumental doorframe of pink granite shows two columns of a building inscription of Apepi, reading:

> "[...] the son of Ra: (Apepi)|, given life [...] he [made] many flagpoles (and) a door consisting of copper for this god [...]".[27]

Another block, also of pink granite, bears the beginning of the Horus name of the same king, accompanied by the depiction and name of the goddess Nekhbet (see fig. 25). The lower part of a seated statue of Khyan is also preserved in the temple. The statue, made of dark granite, originally belonged to a king of the Twelfth Dynasty before it was usurped by Khyan who had his royal titles: *"Horus: He, who embraces the Two Lands; the son of Ra: Khyan"* and the epithet *"Beloved of his Ka"* added.[28]

Fig. 25: *Block with an inscription of Hyksos King Apepi from the temple of Bastet.* (TELL BASTA PROJECT 2011)

In 1944, while excavating the area declared as the temple of Mahes, an annex temple to the immediate north of the sanctuary of the temple of Bastet, HABACHI found the lower part of a dyad of sphinxes. Although the statue is not inscribed, its stylistic characteristics reveal that it belongs to the corpus of the '*Hyksos Monuments*' mentioned above.[29]

There is, however, an element of great uncertainty: The temple was renovated during the time of the Libyan kings, especially Osorkon I (924-889 BCE) and Osorkon II (874-

850 BCE) of the Twenty-second Dynasty (see Chapter 7.2), who brought stone blocks and statues from temples and other buildings in the Eastern Delta and Memphite area for their building projects in the temple of Bastet. Older inscriptions were not always removed in the process; instead, the stone was simply turned in a way that the original decorated side was hidden. Thus, as Bastet is not mentioned in the surviving inscriptions on the above-discussed monuments, we have no means to decide if these stone elements really are the remains of monuments of the kings of the Second Intermediate Period at Bubastis or originate from other places nearby. These would most probably be Avaris and Piramesse, the two subsequent capitals of Egypt, which were abandoned at the time of the Twenty-second Dynasty.

At any rate, the geographical position of Bubastis in the vicinity of Avaris makes it possible to assume a certain level of building activities by the kings of the Late Middle Kingdom and the Hyksos Period in the main temple of Bubastis. The dedication inscription of Apepi is intriguing as it mentions the copper door of a temple of a male deity. If the inscription really originates from Bubastis, we can only speculate whether he dedicated this prestigious object to a male deity and companion of Bastet, like Atum, Mahes or Hor-Hekenu, who are attested in inscriptions of later times, or if there was actually a temple of a Hyksos god, i.e. Seth-Baal, in Bubastis at that time.

Endnotes

[1] Ryholt 1997, 209-210, 294.

[2] Moeller, Forstner-Müller 2018.

[3] Franke 1995, 746; Ryholt 1997, 9-31, 69-74; Schneider 2006, 175-181.

[4] Franke 1995, 746-747; Willems 2010, 98-99; Priglinger 2021, 87-90. Critical is Ryholt 1997, 79-80.

[5] Ryholt 1997, 94-97, 298-301.

[6] Bietak 1984; Bietak 1996, 39 Fig. 33.

[7] GDG IV, 67; Bietak 1975, 133-134; Bietak 1984, 61; Hoffmeier, Abd el-Maksoud 2003, 171-172; Abd el-Maksoud, Valbelle 2011.

[8] Bietak 1991; Eigner 1996; Bietak et al. 1994, 39, 45, Fig. 32, 47-48; Forstner-Müller 2008, 45; Schiestl 2009, 33-62; 180-182; Prell 2021, 21-100.

[9] Ryholt 1997, 103-117.

[10] Bietak 1996, 9-54; Eigner 1996, 73-80, Fig. 1; Ryholt 1997, 118-150; Schiestl 2009, 24-182; Bietak 2010, 19-20; Prell 2021, 135-143.

[11] Moeller, Forstner-Müller 2018

[12] Bietak, Forstner-Müller 2009; Forstner-Müller 2011; Bietak et al. 2012/2013; Moeller, Forstner-Müller 2018, 7-8.

[13] Moeller, Marouard 2018.

[14] Ryholt 1997, 134 no. 1471.

[15] Habachi 1978; Ryholt 1997, 133 no. 468; Verbovsek 2006.

[16] Priglinger 2021, 93-95.

[17] Ryholt 1997, 19-31; Wegner, Cahail 2021.

[18] Wegner, Cahail 2021, 356-374.

[19] El-Sawi 1979, Fig. 16-19; Ashmawy 2016.

[20] Ryholt 1997, 301, 410; Aston, Bietak 2012; Ashmawy 2016, 148, 155.

[21] El-Sawi 1979, Fig. 64 (no. 1695); Ben-Tor 2007, 27, 97 and Pl. 99-100.

[22] El-Sawi 1979, Fig. 64, 127 (no. 1734 and no. 1898); Ben-Tor 2007, 83 and Pl. 55-57.

[23] El-Sawi 1979, Fig. 124 (no. 1855); Ben-Tor 2007, 170 and Pl. 89.

[24] Ben-Tor 2007, 117, 191-192.

[25] London BM EA 1100: Naville 1891, Pl. XXX.I.

[26] Franke 1988, 252-254; Ryholt 1997, 71 Fig. 10, 73, 408; Schneider 1996, 405-406.

[27] London BM EA 1101: Naville 1891, pl. XXXV.C; Budge 1914, pl.18.

[28] Naville 1891, pl. XXX.A-C.

[29] Cairo JE 87082: Habachi 1978; Verbovsek 2006, 25-26.

6. The '*Field-of-the-God*': Bubastis in the New Kingdom

In the middle of the Sixteenth century BCE, a dynasty of nomarchs from Thebes brought the reign of the Hyksos dynasty to an end, victoriously raging war against the foreign rulers. While their ancestors, a number of kings now considered to form the Sixteenth Dynasty[1], seemed to have accepted the dominion of the Hyksos over Egypt, the rulers of the following Seventeenth Dynasty sought to reunite the country. As recent research has shown, Antef V (Nubkheperre, 1625-1622 BCE), already commanded a viable realm in the Southern Nile Valley with its own infrastructure stretching from Edfu to Abydos. The following rulers consolidated what their predecessors had achieved. Based on their success in creating a well-functioning and independent small state in the Southern Nile Valley, the last rulers of this dynasty mustered the strength to reclaim Egypt. The military conflict between Thebes and Avaris, probably having seethed under the surface for long, started in the later part of the reign of Apepi (~1581-1541 BCE), the most prominent king of the Hyksos Dynasty.[2] In the temple of Amun at Thebes (Karnak), Kamose (1554-1549 BCE), the last king of the Seventeenth Dynasty, had three stelae erected with accounts of the events of that time. They describe the initial throne room session of the king and his council, where he decides to no longer rule as a mere chieftain under the supremacy of the Hyksos King Apepi, and so ensues the Theban conquest of the territories north of Thebes with his military ships until the siege of Avaris.[3]

In fact, military actions must have started earlier, because the mummy of Seqenenre (1558-1554 BCE), Kamose's immediate predecessor, shows several head wounds, indicating that he died in battle. As investigations have demonstrated, his traumatic injuries were inflicted by a chisel-shaped battle axe of Syrian-Palestinian type, a typical weapon of the Hyksos, thus showing that Seqenenre's death occurred during the war against the Hyksos and their allies[4], which lasted altogether around 15 years. It was Ahmose (1549/39-1524/14 BCE)[5], Kamose's successor and probably a son of Seqenenre, who achieved the final victory and captured Avaris, thus repelling the Hyksos and reuniting Egypt under his rule around 1520 BCE.

The defeat of the Hyksos is the founding event of the New Kingdom, an era that is commonly perceived as the most glorious one in the history of ancient Egypt. During the following centuries, the kings of Egypt created a Late Bronze Age empire, pushing the borders of Egyptian-controlled territories far into Nubia to the south and Syria-Palestine to the northeast. An extensive diplomatic network with the Aegean and Levantine world provided not only an influx of goods and products in addition to the booty of war and taxes from the now overthrown cities, but also cultural, religious and scientific ideas and concepts, which enriched the Egyptian world.[6]

The kings of this epoch erected a multitude of great temples, tombs and monuments; literature and art flourished. Thebes, with its huge temple complex for Amun, the god of the victorious Theban Dynasty now considered to be the king of all gods of Egypt, served as the capital for the new rulers until the reign of Amenhotep IV/Akhenaten (1353-1336 BCE), who built a new capital at Amarna in Middle Egypt. His later successor Tutankhamun (1332-1323 BCE) left Amarna but did not return to Thebes; he chose the ancient capital of Memphis as the new seat of the royal court.[7]

Around 40 years later, Ramses II (1279-1213 BCE), the third ruler of the Nineteenth Dynasty, founded a new royal residence in the Northeastern Delta, at the site of Avaris, the old capital of the Hyksos kings, renamed *"House of Ramses"* (*pr-rꜥw-ms-sw*, Pi-Ramesse). Thebes continued to be the religious centre of Egypt, but the political situation of the Late Bronze Age raised the importance of militarily securing Egypt's territories in the Syrian-Palestine region. Having a capital in the Northeastern Delta close to the Pelusiac Nile branch and the *'Ways of Horus'*, an overland route and an area with fortresses of great strategic importance to protect Egypt's northeastern border, guaranteed much faster access to those regions than Thebes, located far-distant in the Southern Nile Valley. Consequently, the focus of royal interests shifted to the Nile Delta, which would become the location of several capitals in the following centuries.[8]

While we have no textual or archaeological evidence regarding the fate of Bubastis during the years of war against the Hyksos, its key location on the Pelusiac branch, the same branch on which Avaris was located further downstream, has to be considered. Bubastis was a strategic check-point on the river, controlled by the Hyksos and later by the Thebans, as their war fleet needed to pass by during military actions. It probably served as a main military outpost of the Thebans during the war as well.

A multitude of structures and objects of the New Kingdom have been unearthed at Bubastis. Judging from the evidence described in detail below, the importance of the city reached its heights during the middle of the Eigthteenth Dynasty (the reign of Amenhotep III: 1390-1353 BCE), the first half of the Nineteenth Dynasty (until the reign of Merenptah: 1213-1204 BCE) and then again in the early Twentieth Dynasty (Ramses III: 1187-1156 BCE). In view of this evidence, it is no coincidence that Bubastis became the capital of the southern *'royal child'*-nome (*jm.t*), the Eighteenth nome of Lower Egypt in Ramesside times.[9] Thanks to its strategic position commanding important waterways and overland routes, the city had not only reclaimed its position amongst the central places of the Eastern Nile Delta after the turmoil of the Second Intermediate Period, it had also developed into a major metropolis of the region.

6.1 The temple of Bastet: royal and private monuments

Many of the stone blocks, architraves, door lintels, and statues that form the remains of the temple of Bastet we can see today, date from the New Kingdom. A great number of them are, however, reused objects, brought from other places in the time of the Libyan Kings, who rebuilt the temple on a grand scale. Even so, some stone objects bear inscriptions specifically mentioning Bastet as *'Lady of Bubastis'*, thus revealing that in fact they do originate from the New Kingdom temple of Bastet. Unfortunately, we have no knowledge of the ground plan or layout of the temple at that time, but we can glean some interesting information on the cult of the lioness goddess from these objects. The following description and discussion of selected stone elements from the temple of Bastet from varying places of origin will illustrate their informative value on different issues of research. Most of the objects discussed in the next chapter were found by Naville during his excavations in the temple in 1887 and 1888, but important discoveries have also been made since then.[10]

The earliest object dating back to the New Kingdom is a door lintel of pink granite from

Fig. 26: *Fragment of a papyrus column in the hypostyle hall of the temple with cartouches of Ramses II, usurped by Osorkon II. (TELL BASTA PROJECT 2021)*

the western part of the temple of Bastet close to the remains of the sanctuary erected by Nectanebo II (360-343 BCE, see Chapter 8). The lintel bears two symmetrically arranged scenes showing Amenhotep II (1426-1400 BCE) offering to the god Amun-Ra, who is labelled as *"dwelling in Peru-Nefer"* and as *"the foremost of Peru-Nefer"*. Two columns of hieroglyphs in the centre of the lintel bear the titulary of a king. Surprisingly, it is not the titulary of Amenhotep II, but of Seti I (1290-1279 BCE), a king who ruled Egypt more than a century later. The unfinished inscription reads: *"He renewed the monument for [...]"*.[11] Obviously, Seti I restored a building of Amenhotep II, of which the door lintel formed a part, and declared his restoration work by adding his own titles to its decoration. The original location of this lintel was most likely at Peru-Nefer, the toponym mentioned in the inscription referring to Amun. For a long time, scholars identified Peru-Nefer with the harbour of Memphis, however, an identification with the harbour of Avaris (Tell el-Dab'a), has been suggested more recently as well.[12]

Evidence for the activities of Thutmose III (1479-1426 BCE) at the temple of Bastet come from another source: in his biographical inscription, Minmose, the *"overseer of work in the temples of the gods of Upper and Lower Egypt"* presents a list of temples where he conducted work on the orders of Thutmose III. Amongst those temples is that of Bastet at Bubastis. Unfortunately, the text does not reveal the nature of Minmose's task there.[13]

Part of a pink granite stela of a ruler of the New Kingdom, probably Amenhotep III,[14] contains 13 columns with the description of a military campaign in Nubia. If there really were annals of this king inscribed on the walls of the temple of Bastet as JAMES HENRY BREASTED suggests,[15] is hard to say because there is no mention of the goddess or the city in the preserved part of the inscription. Therefore, the block could have been brought from somewhere else in later times. On the other hand, there are some monuments of this king at Bubastis with a clear connection to it, surely attesting to the vital interest this ruler had in the city and its goddess. In addition, a number statues of high officials from the time of Amenhotep III were found at the temple (see below).

A slab of pink granite, dating back in the first part of the reign of Amenhotep IV/Akhenaten shows two cartouches with the earlier version of the name of the god Aton. It was reused by Ramses II, as can be deduced by two cartouches of this king inscribed on the top side of the slab.[16] The objects was thus usurped two times: first by Ramses II and later by Osorkon I (924-889 BCE) or Osorkon II (874-850 BCE), and had made at least two journeys, first from its unknown original location to Pi-Ramesse (today: Qantir), the capital of Ramses II, and then to Bubastis (see Chapter 7). However, on the available information, its original provenance remains impossible to determine.

Quite famous are NAVILLE's discoveries of two headless statues of the vizier Amenhotep, who served in the reign of Amenhotep III. After their discovery in 1888, one of the statues was transferred to the British Museum in London, and the other to the Egyptian Museum in Cairo. The statue now in Cairo[17] represents Amenhotep in the typical posture of a scribe: sitting cross-legged on the ground with a half-unrolled papyrus on his lap bearing eight columns of hieroglyphs. He wears the official clothing of a vizier: a long gown enveloping the legs, affixed by two straps tied behind the neck. The point where the straps meet forms a kind of badge, decorated with the throne name of Amenhotep III. A cartouche incised on the right shoulder holds a shorter version of the same name. The garment is almost transparent, revealing the anatomical details of the individual depicted, namely the folds of fat around his stomach. Amenhotep bears his scribal equipment: an ink palette hanging down from his left shoulder, and a bowl for water resting on his left knee. The inscription on the papyrus roll reads:

> "To perform the law and to let justice endure, to assign the directive to the companions (courtiers) by the jrj.-p^c.t ḥ₃.tj-^{c}, the great companion, the Beloved One of his lord, the overseer of all royal work (in) the nomes of Upper and Lower Egypt[18], sealer of the king of Lower Egypt, mayor and vizier, the noble Amenhotep, possessor of veneration."

The statue of Amenhotep in the British Museum in London represents him in a similar manner: sitting cross-legged on the ground, dressed in the vizier's official clothing with a badge bearing the throne name of Amenhotep III. The left hand rests on the left leg, the right hand holds a kind of handkerchief. The head, shoulders and left arm are missing.
A vertical inscription on his front says:

> "The hereditary prince, custodian of the stations of the broad courtyard, count, guardian of Nekhen, pleasant of strides in the Tabu-land, the mayor, the vizier, the noble Amenhotep, he who may repeat life".[19]

The persona and career of the vizier Amenhotep are relatively well known. He held the position of vizier together with Ramose during the last part of the reign of Amenhotep III. The sources (among them the statues of Amenhotep at Bubastis) are not explicit enough to answer the still-debated question as to which of the two, Amenhotep or Ramose, was the vizier of the north, and who was the vizier of the south. Either way, as a high-ranking official, Amenhotep was responsible for accomplishing special duties, for example, directing the building of a number of shrines for Amenhotep III dedicated to Amun and Sobek at Silsileh.[20]

As we learn from a letter in a cache of documents containing international correspondence found at the palace archive of Akhenaten at Tell el-Amarna, the vizier Amenhotep also seems to have been sent to Byblos to meet the Syrian ruler Rib-Adda. The letter, written by Rib-Adda and addressed to the vizier, praises him as follows:

> *"Behold, thou art a wise man who knows the king, and because of thy wisdom, the king sent thee as commissioner".*[21]

To be sent on a mission to Syria could explain his presence at Bubastis, the city which served as the starting point for expeditions and journeys to the Near East. He would have spent some time here and had the opportunity to dedicate statues to the temple of Bastet.[22]

Another well-known official from the reign of Amenhotep III, Kheruef, the steward of queen Teje, is attested at the temple of Bastet, where NAVILLE discovered the inscribed base of a seated statue of this official made of dark granite. The inscription mentions Kheruef's titles *"royal scribe"* and *"director of the palace"*. HABACHI has suggested that the erection of the statue of Kheruef in the temple of Bastet was connected to his duties in the organization of the Sed-festival of Amenhotep III, which included the building of a Sed-festival chapel at Bubastis (see also Chapter 6.4).[23]

Other officials from the reign of Amenhotep III who dedicated a statue at the temple of Bastet are the steward and cup-bearer of the king Sennefer[24] and the *wab*-priest Iun-Ka. The upper part of the block statue of the latter was found during the excavation of a Roman well in the northern part of the hypostyle hall of the temple by the mission of the University Potsdam in 1994. The offering formula on the front and on the dorsal pillar of the statue addresses the deities Amun-Ra, Sekhmet, Amun '*the Primeval One*', Horakhty, and Ptah. Unfortunately, it is unclear if these gods and goddesses had a cult at Bubastis or were just named due to the duties of Iun-Ka at other temples. The inscription on the right part of the statue however mentions the institution of the *pr-ꜥnḫ* of Bubastis. The *pr-ꜥnḫ*, translatable as *"House of Life"* was a temple-institution, i.e., a library where religious, medical and scientific texts were kept and priests performed rituals (see Chapter 6.3). Iun-Ka's inscription also provides the earliest hitherto known evidence of the festival of the goddess Bastet which became most famous in Late Dynastic and Ptolemaic times (Chapter 8), when he states that the king performed the festival[25]:

> *"The wab-priest of Sekhmet, Iun-Ka, he says: "[...] I followed the perfect god [...] of the disorder of the 'House of Life'. I was given [...] in the praise of the lady of Bubastis, all rewards [...] he raised the Red Crown to perform the festival of Bastet and [he] supplied [...] of his ka very much. He put me [...] he appeared on his throne to perform (the festival) of Bastet and he supplied for her cattle [...] he offered 71 perfect bulls, bread and cake 20 [...]".*

Another offering formula stating *"All what comes forth on the altar of Bastet for the Ka of the dignitary Iun-Ka"* is written as an enigmatic text in two short columns on the right shoulder.[26]

In 2013, excavations of the TELL BASTA PROJECT in the area of the dromos - the ancient

Fig. 27: *The block statue of Bebi from Area A east of the temple of Bastet. (TELL BASTA PROJECT 2016)*

processional street leading to the temple of Bastet - brought to light the fragment of a block statue made of quartzite (26 by 17.1 by 14.8 cm). According to the style and palaeography of the inscription, the statue depicts an official of the Nineteenth Dynasty. The partly damaged inscription on the front of the statue reads:

> "*An offering that the kings gives and Bastet, lady of Bubastis, Sekhmet, lady of the Two Lands, Horakhty, Osiris, ruler of eternity and the gods and goddesses who reside in Bubastis, the lords of the Field-of-the-god. So that they may give everything that comes forth on their altars (i.e.) a thousand of [bread], a thou-*

sand of [beer], a thousand of cattle and fowl, a thousand of linen and alabaster, a thousand of incense and oil, a thousand of all good and pure things, what the sky gives and the earth creates and what the inundation brings [...] in each festival for [...] Bebi [...]".

HABACHI's sondages to the south of the temple of Bastet, i.e. somewhere around its sanctuary, brought to light three statues. One of them, the statue of an official named Horkhui dates to the Twenty-sixth Dynasty and will be discussed in Chapter 8.2. The others date to the New Kingdom. One is the lower part of a seated dyad of a husband and wife, made of gray granite and most probably dating to the reign of Amenhotep III.[27] The inscriptions running down the centre front of each person informs us of their names and titles. On the man's garment, we read:

"All that goes forth on the altar of Bastet, lady of Bubastis, for the Ka of the supervisor of the foreign countries, petitioner at the first Sed-festival of his majesty, Khamewaset, the Revered One."

The woman's garment has:

"All that goes forth on the altar of Bastet, lady of Bubastis, what is given every day for the Ka of the lady of the house, the chantress of Sekhmet, the Great One of the troupe of singer- dancers[28] of Bastet, lady of Bubastis, Khebyanenes, the Revered One."

The titles of Khebyanenes confirms that in the New Kingdom the temple of Bastet had its own professional singers and dancers, overseen by the wives of high officials such as Khebyanenes, who also served as a chantress in the cult of Sekhmet, which was active at Bubastis as well. Also informative, are the texts on the side of Khaemwaset's seat:

"An offering that the king gives and Horakhty-Atum the truly Praised One and the Ennead residing in Bubastis, so they may give the existence on earth in the king's graces, the heart's satisfaction with all good (things), to receive food that comes forth on the altar of the lords of offerings. He shall be called in front of the Justified Ones who are with Wennefer, he shall approach in front of the sacred seat, he shall be made to ascend the noble stairway for the Ka of the jrj-pᶜ.t and ẖȝ.tj-ᶜ, the great companion of (all) companions, the beloved of his lord every day, the Excellent One, master of rectitude of heart, the Kind One, cool to anger, free of falsehood, (already) favoured by the king as a child (and until) the reaching of old age, with his enduring praise, the chief of the archers, the supervisor of the foreign countries and petitioner at the first Sed-festival, Khaemwaset".

The inscription on the side of the seat of Khebyanenes is much worn and the published photograph does not allow for a clear reading. However, according to Habachi's translation, the offering formula mentions the goddesses Sekhmet, Bastet, Wadjet and Shesemtet of Bubastis and their temples.[29]

The second is a naophorous-type statue fragment with a shrine containing the depiction of a standing official with the head of a lioness. The remaining part of the dorsal pillar has the titles but not the name of the owner of the statue preserved: *"jrj-pᶜ.t and ḥꜣ.tj-ᶜ, the sealer of the king of Lower Egypt, the sole companion"*. The front part of the naos is inscribed with two symmetrically arranged offering formulae:

> *"An offering that the king gives and Bastet, the Great One, lady of Bubastis, so they may give food and all things, what the sky gives and the earth creates and what the inundation brings from its cave for the Ka of the Venerated One with Bastet [...]. An offering that the king gives and the gods of Bubastis, so they may give food, everything that comes forth on the altar in the third time of the ritual for the Ka of the Revered One with the gods [of Bubastis] [...]."*[30]

Of the royal objects that can be assigned with certainty to the New Kingdom temple of Bastet at Bubastis, the lower part of an enthroned statue made of dark granite (Cairo Museum CG 34509) is most remarkable. It bears a eulogy of Ramses II, which reads:

> *"(1) [...] [the Dual King:] (powerful of Ma'at, Ra, chosen by Ra)|; son of Ra: (Ramses, beloved of Amun)|, the founder of Egypt, given life (2) [...] lord of the nine bows, sistrum player of Bastet, the child of Sekhmet (3) [...] the founder of Egypt, given life, nursling of Wadjet, suckling of Shesemtet. Bubastis (sic) has deployed their protection for you (4) [...] his [...] for Egypt like Nefertem. Mut, Eye of Ra, has decreed for him life, stability and dominion (to) his two nostrils. Those who reside in (5) [...] their protection is united with his body. The Dual King: (powerful of Ma'at, Ra, chosen by Ra)|; the son of Ra: (Ramses, beloved of Amun)|, the founder of Egypt, given life. (6) [...] excellent monuments in front of her (as) she appears and she is content in all her festivals because of the exaltation he has made forever. (7) [...] [the son of Ra:] (Ramses, beloved of Amun)|, the founder of Egypt, given life. 'I have taken up the tambourine rejoicing since you have appeared (because) you have doubled for me benefactions millions of times. (8) [...] I [...] to provision my altars daily. My staircase is renewed with excellent things by what you have done; all sweet freshness is before me. You gave (9) [...] to eternity like Ra. I am on your brow.' The Dual King: (powerful of Ma'at, Ra, chosen by Ra)|, the son of Ra (Ramses, beloved of Amun)|, the founder of Egypt, given life (10) [...] resting inside it together with her son. The divine assembly, which is inside, moves about in joy."*[31]

The specific mentioning of Bastet in the inscription indicates that the temple of Bastet is the original place of the statue. Moreover, the text also informs us on other lioness goddesses who received a cult in that same temple: Sekhmet, Wadjet and Shesemtet (see Chapter 1).[32]

In addition, the text provides us with information about the cult of Bastet in Bubastis. Line 6 explicitly calls attention to the religious festivals of the goddess, which became most famous in Egypt and in the wider Mediterranean world in the Late Period and Ptolemaic and Roman times (see Chapter 8). Together with a text on a private statue from the time of Amenhotep III (see above), this is one of the earliest attestations of the annual festivals of Bastet.

Intriguingly, the text allows Bastet herself to speak about her temple when she addresses the king (line 7-8):

> "*I have taken up the tambourine rejoicing since you have appeared (because) you have doubled for me benefactions millions of times. [...] I [...] to provision my altars daily. My staircase is renewed with excellent things by what you have done.*"

What part of the temple was the "*staircase*" mentioned in the inscription? In ancient Egyptian, the word is ⌐ *rwd*, a term that can also be translated as "*terrace*".[33] A most famous *rwd*-terrace was connected to the temple of Osiris at Abydos, and was called "*the terrace of the great god*" and has been identified with the northern cemetery of the late Middle Kingdom adjacent to the enclosure wall of the temple, thus actually belonging to the surrounding topography.[34] In the case of Bubastis however, things are different: The *rwd* of the temple of Bastet cannot have designated an area around the temple, because the text points out very clearly that the king has renewed the *rwd* of the goddess, indicating building activity and the allocation of offerings. Therefore, the translation "*staircase*" is more fitting and designates either the staircase to the sanctuary or the staircase-like base of the chapel of Bastet in the sanctuary (see Chapter 8.1). A related word is ⌐ *ḥnd(w)* covering a similar semantic field (staircase, throne-platform). It appears as early as in the beginning of the Fourth Dynasty in the title of an official named Akhtyhotep, who is a "*priest of Bastet on her staircase*", and in some epitheta of Bastet as well, probably designating the same structure as *rwd* (see Chapter 1 and 8). In any case, the eulogy of Ramses II attests to the existence of the temple of Bastet in the Nineteenth Dynasty, equipped with a naos for the goddess, obviously standing in the inner sanctuary, and of the royal interest in the goddess and her cult in that time.

A block statue of Montuherkhepeshef, the fifth son of Ramses II, demonstrates that not only the king, but also members of the royal family had an interest in commemorating monuments to the temple of Bastet, probably connected to the building activities of Ramses II. The statue was obviously usurped: the individual depicted originally sported a round wig, which was altered at the right side of the head into a side lock, the typical iconography of young members of the elite. Also, the inscription on the front and back might be a later addition. The original owner of the statue is unknown. The inscription on the dorsal pillar reads:

> "*An offering that the king gives and Bastet, lady of Bubastis, so that she gives life, wellbeing, and health for the Ka of the first charioteer of his father, the son of the king, Montuherkhepeshef. An offering that the king gives and Wadjet, lady of Bubastis, so that she gives life, wellbeing, and health for the royal scribe, the overseer of the horses, the son of the king, Montuherkhepeshef.*"

The mention of Bastet as lady of Bubastis confirms that the statue once stood in the temple of Bastet to participate in her cult offerings. Moreover, the mention of Wadjet in the second offering formula provides further evidence for a cult of Wadjet in the temple of Bastet. The

Fig. 28a: *Seated statue of Ramses IV from the temple of Bastet. (TELL BASTA PROJECT 2022)*

lines of the inscription on the front are partly damaged; however, what remains makes clear that several deities residing at Bubastis are also invoked. Here, Bubastis is called the "*Field-of-the-god*" (*sḫ.t nṯr*).[35]

The Egyptian Antiquities Service excavations around the temple of Bastet in 2003 brought to light the block statue of Kakaru, an official from the time of Ramses II, which mentions the temple cult of Isis at Bubastis. According to the inscription, Kakaru held a position in a temple dedicated to Amun-Ra that was built by Ramses II. Whether or not this temple was located at Bubastis or at Pi-Ramesse has to remain an open question for the time being.[36] In any case, the discovery of an inscribed libation statue of Sen-Mut, from the time of Amenhotep III, who bore the title "*overseer of the house of Amun*" and whose offering formula mentions "*Amun the Primeval One*", the exact same hypostase of the god Amun that the offering formula of Iun-Ka (see above) also refers to, makes the existence of a cult of Amun at Bubastis a distinct possibility.[37]

The remains of the temple of Bastet include a large number of fragments of monumental royal statues, mostly belonging to Ramses II. Many of them were reused in the temple

Fig. 28b: *Seated statue of Ramses IV from the temple of Bastet. (TELL BASTA PROJECT 2022)*

building of the Libyan Kings Osorkon I and II who had the flat undersides of their bases decorated and used as part of walls. Again, we face the problem that if the original inscription (if preserved at all) does not mention Bastet or Bubastis, it is impossible to decide whether the statues were originally erected in the temple or brought from Pi-Ramesse.[38] The same is true for other statues, such as a seated statue of Ramses VI made of granodiorite from the northern part of the temple[39], and the monumental statue of a queen consort of Ramses II, either Nefertari or Meritamun, which was reused for Karomama, the main queen consort of Osorkon II (see Chapter 7.2).

6.2 The '*House of Life*' at the temple of Bastet

Connected to the temple of Bastet was the institution of the *pr-ꜥnḫ*, the "*House of Life*", in which priests of Sekhmet and Bastet were in attendance. Its earliest attestation so far comes from the above-mentioned inscription on the statue of Iun-ka, but there is later evidence for its existence as well. HABACHI describes the chance find in 1949 of part of a door lintel from the Twentieth Dynasty at Bubastis depicting Ay, the *"chief royal scribe in the House of Life, wab-priest of Sekhmet"*, and son of the vizier Juti (see below), who is worshipping the cartouches of a king, possibly Ramses III.[40] The door lintel might once have belonged to the entrance of the residence of Ay at Bubastis.

At Qantir, the site of Pi-Ramesse, a number of inscribed limestone door panels were uncovered during the expansion of the Sama'ana canal at 1945/46 and some agricultural work. HABACHI recorded those objects, amongst them an inscribed door lintel and fragments of the door panels of Iyroy, the *"royal scribe, the overseer of the wab-priests of Sekhmet at Bubastis"*. Iyroy was thus connected to the *'House of Life'* as well, especially as this institution is mentioned in the offering formula, where the god Atum is designated as the *"lord of the House of Life"* and the goddess Sekhmet-Bastet as *"lady of the house of papyrus books"* (*pr-mḏȝ.t*).

Iyroy also holds a very interesting string of titles: *"who foretells the festivals, who carries and embraces the Wedjat-Eye, who is pure at both his arms for Weseret"*.[41] Those titles probably refer to the festivals of Bastet at Bubastis, a subject we will discuss in detail in Chapter 8. Habachi and Ghalioungui have argued that this Iyroy is the same as the *wab*-Priest of Sekhmet Iyroy, who was accused of having taken part in the conspiracy against Ramses III and listed amongst the criminals in the Juridical Papyrus Turin.[42]

It is a well-established fact that priests of Sekhmet were learned individuals of healing as well as physicians.[43] One of those was the high official Yuni, son of the chief physician Amenhotep, who lived during the early Ramesside period. We know about him from his naophorous statue which was found at Deir Durunka in Middle Egypt, the elite necropolis of Assiut. His titles include the rank of *'overseer of the wab-priests of Sekhmet'* and, more importantly, he is called *"who knows the secret of the chest (hn) of Bubastis"*.[44] This *hn*-chest is also mentioned in a paragraph of the Chapter on Bubastis in Papyrus Brooklyn 47.218.84, a compendium of local religious traditions of Delta cities that dates into the second half of the Seventh century BCE. There, it refers to a chest where the divine child of Osiris and Bastet, mutilated by a wild cat, was deposited and became Horus-Hekenu. The chest was thus believed to have divine healing powers, and knowing its secrets would therefore be most fitting for a physician. In addition, the so-called monographies on the nomes of Egypt in the Ptolemaic soubassement-reliefs in the temple of Horus at Edfu give the name of the chest as *"the secret chest of the Secret One"*; it is the chest where the leg of Osiris is kept as a sacred relic of the Bubastite nome. According to the inscriptions from Edfu as well as other sources, the goddess Bastet used herbs from the *'Field-of-the-god'* at Bubastis contained in the chest to produce a protective ointment.[45]

6.3 The tombs of the viceroys of Kush and other New Kingdom elite burials

The Northern Kom of Bubastis, around 150m north of the temple of Bastet, was the funerary zone of the city, with cemeteries dating from the Old Kingdom to the Late Dynastic period. In 1925, during the construction of the Egyptian railway, the mud-brick tomb of the viceroy of Kush, Hori (II), was discovered by accident in the southwestern part of this area. HENRI GAUTHIER, who published a short report on the structure and its discovery, gives a rather vague description on the tomb's location, stating that it was situated around 220m to the southwest of the Coptic cemetery.[46] Therefore, it is difficult to pinpoint the tomb's location

Fig. 29a: *The western wall of the tomb of viceroy Hori I. (*Tell Basta Project *2022)*

with any precision on a modern sitemap. When measuring the distance from the estimated location of the cat cemetery as given on Habachi's map[47], one arrives at an area that is over-built today by the modern road that separates the Western Kom of the site from the Central and Eastern one (see fig. 3).

The tomb was built of mud-bricks and had a vaulted roof. The walls were sitting on a base level of burnt bricks (see fig. 29a), a construction that is quite rare in New Kingdom architecture. The burnt bricks served as protection against environmental damage to the construction, such as rain or rising damp.

Of the subterranean chapel, remains of the plastered floor might have been preserved as well. The inner structure of the tomb consisted of three chambers; judging from the sketch in the published report, they might have been set parallel to the tombs east-western (?) central axis.[48]

The westernmost chamber was empty, but each of the next two rooms contained a sarcophagus. The anthropoid sarcophagus of the central chamber was made of pink granite, measuring 2.95 by 1.10 m with a height of 2.0 m. An inscription running across the length of the lid gives the name and titles of the deceased:

> *"The Osiris, viceroy of Kush, the overseer of the southern foreign countries, fan-bearer to the right of the king, royal scribe Hori, the Venerated One, son of the viceroy of Kush Hori, the Venerated One."*[49]

The short sides at the head and feet of the sarcophagus show the goddesses Isis and Nephthys and an inscription with their names and epithets as well as the titles of Hori. An ushabti from the burial of Hori had been in private possession from before the tomb's discovery.[50] At that time, the viceroy of Kush Hori II, who served in the reign of Ramses IV, was already known

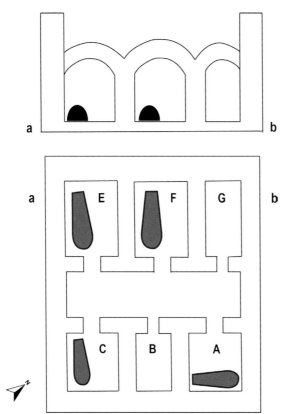

Fig 29b: *Ground plan and section of the tomb of viceroy Hori I. (LANGE-ATHINODOROU 2024, slightly simplified version of HABACHI 1957, Fig. 27).*

from a number of other monuments.[51]

Almost twenty years later, in 1944, HABACHI started excavations on the southern part of the Northern Kom, around 80 m to the southeast of the tomb of Hori II.[52] After removing four meters of later occupation levels, he encountered a large vaulted mud-brick tomb with six chambers, three of which branched off to the east and west of the central passage, measuring 7.50 by 2.20 m. As was the case in the tomb of Hori II, the lower parts of the walls consisted of rows of burnt bricks. The tomb had been heavily robbed but four of the chambers still contained a sarcophagus. The first, found in the southeastern chamber C, was made of pink granite and had no decoration. The second sarcophagus in chamber A, made of limestone, was of anthropoid shape with the depicted figure holding the signs for protection (*s3*) and endurance (*ḏd*) in its hands. Of the three chambers on the western side, chambers E and F contained anthropoid sarcophagi as well.

While all sarcophagi are without inscriptions, the find of a box of ushabtis in the southern wall of chamber E and a number of ushabtis lying at the base of the northern wall of room F identify the main owner of the tomb as Hori (I), the viceroy of Kush and father of Hori (II) whose tomb lies not far to the northwest. The discovery of ushabtis of "*Khayit, the chantress of Mehit*" in chamber F identified his wife as the person buried with him.

In the passage of the tomb, a limestone sphinx of Amenhotep III was discovered as well. Its inscriptions show that Bubastis was its original place because it calls the king: "*beloved of Bastet, lady of Bubastis*".[53] It is not known how the sphinx ended up in the tomb of Hori I, but it seems very probable that it once belonged to the temple of Bastet.

Possibly only a few metres to the west of the tomb of Hori II, FARID discovered the large multi-chambered mud-brick tomb of the vizier Juti of the Twentieth Dynasty in 1964.[54] Although the results of this excavations were never published, creating uncertainties about the exact location of the tomb, several objects from his burial were identified and presented in detail in a recent publication.[55] The son of Juti, the *"chief royal scribe in the House of Life, wab-priest of Sekhmet"* Ay, whose door lintel has been discussed above, might have been buried in the same tomb or nearby. Of his funerary equipment, a canopic jar of alabaster has come to light, listing his additional titles: *"supervisor of the priests of Bastet in Bubastis, privy to the secrets in the Field-of-the-god".*[56]

Nothing was left of the superstructure of the tombs of the viceroys of Kush at Bubastis, including their cult chapel, but as WOLFRAM GRAJETZKI has pointed out, we might find parallels at Esna in the Nile Valley, where tombs of comparable type and date are preserved, in one case with the original superstructure in the form of a mastaba. There, a staircase starting from the northern side of a single central room in the centre of the above-ground part of the superstructure leads to an underground system of five chambers.[57] At any rate, the fact that Hori I and Hori II were buried at Bubastis, surely their hometown, underlines the importance the city held in the late New Kingdom.

HABACHI also reports the surface find of a small funerary stela made of limestone close to the tomb of Hori II. It shows the owner of the stela Tameret, the *"chantress of Bastet, lady of Bubastis"*, and her grandson Thutmose, the *"wab-priest of Sekhmet, the god's father of Bastet, lady of Bubastis"* in front of Osiris and Isis. The offering formula in the lines on the base of the stela mentions *"Osiris Atef-Wer"*, thus connecting him to his cult at Heliopolis.[58]

From 1978 to 1979, BAKR continued the investigation of the southern part of the Northern Kom, to the northwest of the tomb of Hori I. Here, he discovered a two-chambered vaulted tomb with a central passage, built of mud-bricks. The floor of the eastern burial chamber had a pavement of limestone slabs and still contained an amphora and three ushabtis. One bore the name and title of Maj, the *"singer of Osiris."* Another vaulted single-chambered tomb to the east had two burials in slipper-coffins. Both burials were equipped with jars of uninscribed ushabtis as well.[59]

Apart from the single tombs just described, the burial site of the New Kingdom stretched much further to the north and west, with simple pit-burials or burials of slipper coffins interred into a rectangle laid out by a single course of mud-bricks and sometimes provided with jars filled with ushabtis. Already in 1964, FARID had discovered New Kingdom burials in the layers above the level of the governor's palace. Some were interred directly into the massive enclosure wall of the building. During his excavations on the Western Kom, EL-SAWI revealed a large number of mostly simple burials dating to the New Kingdom as well (see fig. 3).[60]

6.4 The so-called chapel of Amenhotep III and the dyad of Khaemwaset and Menena

During his excavations on the Western Kom in 1948, HABACHI discovered a mud-brick structure around 150 m to the south of the Ka-temple of Pepi I. The right jamb of a limestone doorway inscribed with titles of Amenhotep III was found nearby. Due to the ongoing work of the erection of a hospital in the vicinity at that time, there was no possibility for extensive excavations and HABACHI was not able to reconstruct the ground plan of the temple. He assumed that it was generally a rather small, simple building.[61] Whether the chapel was devoted to a deity of Bubastis or a *ka*-chapel of the king remains unknown. As there is no certainty as to the place of origin of the inscribed limestone jamb which was not found in situ but just lying on the surface somewhere in the vicinity, we cannot exclude the possibility that, contra HABACHI's interpretation, the building was not a temple or a chapel but served an entirely different purpose, and the door jamb belonged to a different structure, perhaps even brought there from the temple of Bastet for the purpose of reuse.

Near the walls of the building, a statue came to light of an official from the reign of Amenhotep III, Khaemwaset, of whom we have discussed above another double statue. This one, however, shows him with his (second?) wife, Menena. Rather unusually, the statue, made of steatite, rests on a pedestal of limestone.

The dyad is a perfect example of the fine workmanship of the Eighteenth Dynasty. Khaemwaset is shown in a striding position, both arms beside his body. He wears an elaborate dress, consisting of a tunic with short sleeves and a long pleated kilt with a sash. His face, framed by the curls of his luxurious wig, has suffered severe damage which may have been intentional, considering the otherwise almost perfect state of preservation of the object. Cartouches of Amenhotep III are written on the right part of the chest and on the right sleeve of the tunic.

Menena, standing on Khaemwaset's left side, is dressed in a long tight skirt. Her left arm, covered by a pleated shawl, holds a so-called '*Menit*', an instrument consisting of several strings of pearls and a pendant, that was used in the cult of gods and was particularly connected to Hathor. Bracelets, a broad collar and a heavy, long wig with a wreath of lotus flowers complete her luxurious attire. The back pillar of the dyad has six columns of inscription. The columns behind Khaemwaset read:

> "*An offering which the king gives and Renenutet, mistress of the good provision, the good snake of this house, that they may give food, provision and sustenance, offerings and affluence of fowl and fish every day, a prospering granary, that, what was given (to) this house in festival without interruption, anointed with myrrh, clothed with linen, the spending of a joyful day, for the Ka of the jrj-pᶜ.t and ḥȝtj-ᶜ, praised and beloved of the Lord of the Two Lands, the truly Silent One who is well-tempered, the master of rightness, lucky of hours, the chief of the archers, the overseer of all northern foreign lands, Khaemwaset, justified.*"

The columns behind Menena read:

> "*An offering which the king gives and Sekhmet, beloved of Ptah, that she may give a perfect lifetime, devoid of evil, (with) joyful heart, happiness, rejoice, together with what is praised by the orders of her Ka, enjoyment in singing and dancing, a good life, together with health, a joyful heart, united with love, the going in and out of her temple with a satisfied heart because of all the good things for the Ka of the mistress of the house, the chantress of Bastet, Menena, justified.*"

The inscription between the feet of the couple reads: "*Thousands of bread and beer, thou-*

sands of oxen and birds, thousands of linen and alabaster vessels, thousands of incense and anointments for your Kas. Purified two times."

It remains an open question if the statue of Khaemwaset and Menena and the deities mentioned in the inscription, i.e. Renenutet, Sekhmet and Bastet, had any connection to the mud-brick building HABACHI thought to be a chapel or temple built by Amenhotep III. The serpent-shaped goddess Renenutet was a deity of welfare and agriculture, closely related to grain and all other kinds of field crops. Therefore, her numerous epithets are connected to general topics of food, prosperity and nursing, as alluded to in the inscription on the statue of Khaemwaset.

The mention of Bastet in Menena's title *"chantress of Bastet"* is self-explanatory, as she is the main deity of the city, enjoying the daily ritual in her temple which included musical performances. Sekhmet, on the other hand, was also worshipped at Bubastis, as was discussed above. The close relation of Bastet and Sekhmet is well attested throughout the religious history of ancient Egypt. In fact, the similarities of these two goddesses are so striking that they seem to have sometimes been understood as mere aspects of each other. Still, the common Egyptological interpretation of Bastet as nothing more than the peaceful side of Sekhmet ignores a large number of sources which show Bastet as a similarly protective, dangerous and martial lioness goddess (cf. Chapter 1).

6.5 The *"Tell Basta Treasure"*

On 22 September 1906, during the construction of the Egyptian state railways through the Nile Delta, workmen dug up a part of the Western Kom. There they found the first of two treasure hoards, consisting of heaps of metal vessels and jewelry. CAMPBELL COWAN EDGAR, the Chief Inspector of the Antiquities Service in the Nile Delta at that time, described the discovery as follows:

> *"It happened on that day, that some of the workmen, levelling the ground beside the temporary railway, suddenly caught sight of a buried treasure."*[62]

In the following days, a complete silver pitcher with a handle in the shape of a male goat, inscribed for the *"royal cup-bearer Atumemtaneb"* (vessel A)[63], fragments of a pitcher of the same type and material (vessel B)[64], and a golden lotus-form goblet with the cartouche of Queen Tawosret on the stem[65] were retrieved from the workers. Later on, more objects from the first hoard found their way to antiquities dealers. They were purchased by the Egyptian Museum of Cairo, the Ägyptisches Museum and Papyrussammlung Berlin, and the Metropolitan Museum of Art, New York. These included a situla and a strainer of electrum with the cartouches of Tawosret[66], vessel B of Atumemtaneb, and a silver vessel for the *"chantress of Bastet, Meriptah"*, who is shown rattling a sistrum in front of the seated lioness-headed goddess, designated as *"Lady of Bubastis"*.[67] The cartouche of Tawosret provides a *terminus post quem* (Nineteenth Dynasty, 1191-1181 BCE) for the deposition of the hoard.[68]

A year after the chance discovery of the first hoard, EDGAR conducted his own excavations and found the second treasure, which he describes as being close to the findspot of the first. Still, his description of the findspot is not very conclusive:

Fig. 30: *Vessels from the Tell Basta Treasure at the Metropolitan Museum. (Metropolitan Museum, Open Access)*

> *"The spot where the second treasure lay was quite close to the place where the first is supposed to have been found. But the two hoards must have been at least several metres distant from each other, for at the time when the first was discovered, the mound under which the second lay buried had not yet been cut away. The first treasure must have lay a little closer to the temple. (…) The spot where the treasure was found lies west of the temple, 160 m from the west corner of the ruins and 100 m from the more north-westerly of the two circular chambers in the Roman building"*.[69]

While the term *"temple"* obviously means the temple of Bastet, the passage *"western corner of the temple"* is puzzling; because of the general east-west orientation of the temple, there is a western side of the temple, but not a western corner. Therefore, it should be either the northwestern or the southwestern corner. Another of EDGAR's remarks referring to the work preceding the discovery suggests that it may have really been the northwestern corner:

> *"For several weeks (...) I kept a few of our workmen employed in the neighborhood of the places where the finds have been made. They were engaged for the most part in clearing out some peculiar buildings of Roman date close to the northwest end of the temple"*.[70]

As the *"Roman building"* with the *"two circular chambers"* he refers to is nowhere mentioned before and cannot be identified, it is therefore useless as a clue for pinpointing the findspot on the site map. On HABACHI's map, however, the find spots are placed to the southwest of the western part of the temple, contradicting the information in EDGAR's report.[71] A new study by KACPAR LAUBE on the other hand again argues that the two hoards should have

94

been located in the northwest.[72]

We will never really know where exactly the treasure was found or if there was an archae-ological context attached. Even though Edgar states that he did not see any walls or struc-tures, the special difficulties of Delta archaeology, especially when it comes to excavating mud-brick architecture, provokes doubts about that statement. In any case, there may or may not have been structures, we simply cannot say. Still, it might be possible that the treasures were deposited within or close to the precinct of the temple of Bastet, close to its northwest-ern corner, under the ruins of one of the tower houses of the Ptolemaic and Roman periods, resembling the ones located to the east of the temple (see Chapter 8). Remarkably, a block of limestone came to light in the vicinity of the second hoard with only a partly preserved inscription that does mention the goddess Neith.[73]

The second hoard contained vessels and jewellery of precious metals and stones, includ-ing gold bracelets inlaid with lapis lazuli bearing the cartouches of Ramses II[74], gold studs[75], gold granulated beads and carnelian pendants[76], and two gold jars with ring handle and incised decoration.[77] As CHRISTINE LILYQUIST has pointed out, the jewellery is doubtless of royal origin and was probably part of an official donation to the temple treasury.[78] The hoard also included non-royal objects, such as a silver patera with golden handles and incised dec-oration showing desert and papyrus marsh scenes. The inscription on the outer rim of a dish shows that the bowl was dedicated to the *"chantress of the goddess Neith, Amy"* (see below).

The two hoards probably represent the deposit of the contents of the treasury of the temple of Bastet. Moreover, the analysis of their decoration and typology of some of the objects are also evidence to the fact that the late New Kingdom elite of Bubastis saw themselves not only as part of Egypt but of the wider Mediterranean region which, at that time, formed the *koiné* of the so-called '*International Style*'. The term was invented by HELENE KANTOR in 1960 and later changed by MARIANNE FELDMAN into '*Hybrid Imagery*'.[79] It refers to specific luxury goods in the Mediterranean region of the late Second and First millennium BCE, that display very distinctive features of a mixed Egyptian-Phoenician style. The most significant features of the *International Style* are combative groups (hunting scenes or animal combat), and balanced scenes with paired animals and geometric or floral motifs. The decoration often runs as narrow bands around the contours of the object. Some objects from the two treasure hoards of Bubastis belong to this kind of material culture, especially the vessels of Atumemtaneb and Amy which will therefore be discussed in more detail.

The silver pitcher of Atumemtaneb from the first treasure find (vessel A), is doubtless one of the most prominent object of the two hoards. The material is silver, except for the golden handle in the shape of a he-goat, i.e. the Egyptian domesticated form of the wild goat *capra aegagrus*. The small figurine is hollow cast with hammered-in details. A strip of beaten gold is laid over the rim of the pitcher. The body of the vessel shows ornaments of overlapping pointed scales, imitating pinecones. Three registers with engraved decoration run around the upper shoulder and the neck of the vessel. The upper two registers are purely ornamental and in the uppermost one we find the typical elements of the *International Style*: pairs of animals led by an Aegean-styled griffin between composite volute palmettes of Near Eastern origin. Four of the five scenes show combative groups: a lion and cheetah attacking antelopes and calves, a griffin attacking a lion and a dog or cheetah attacking a lion. One scene, however, shows the mating of two Dorcas gazelles. In the second register are scenes of fishing and fowling in the marshes of pure Egyptian style. The inscription in the third register reads:

"May [live] your ka and your face be with life (and) well-being (as) one who achieves eternity with life and well-being! For the ka of the royal cup-bearer Atumemtaneb, with well-being and life."[80]

Another fragmentary pitcher from the same deposit, known as vessel B, is fashioned in the same style as vessel A. It also has an animal-shaped handle, this time in the shape of an aurochs (*Bos primigenus africanus*). The neck of the pitcher has two incised bands, showing a scene of two horses in the papyrus marshes in the upper register and a floral band in the lower one. A dedicatory inscription is on the shoulder of the vessel:

"May live your ka and your face with life (and) well-being, may you achieve millions of years [...] first royal cup-bearer of the lord of the Two Lands, Atumemtaneb. For the ka of the excellent and righteous [...] royal envoy to all foreign countries, who pleases his lord [...]."[81]

Both vessels show a separate votive scene depicting Atumemtaneb in front of a goddess. On pitcher A, the goddess sports a very distinctive hairstyle, which makes clear that she is not a typical Egyptian deity: she wears a crown with three strands of hair visible on top of it. In addition, the sceptre she holds in her right hand, a papyrus staff with a small bird, is not part of the usual Egyptian iconography of female deities. On vessel B, a similar scene occurs, with the goddess wearing the same crown as on vessel A, yet carrying a spear and a shield. The hair strands on top of the crown and on her shoulders are clearly visible. There is little doubt that this goddess is Astarte, a Canaanite war goddess, whose cult became popular in Egypt in the time of Ramses II.[82]

The silver patera of Amy has two concentric bands running around the centre of the inside of the vessel. The inner one shows a Nilotic scene: a ferryman with a calf, and two naked females swimming side by side. One is depicted in the typical Egyptian style of the naked swimming girl we know from another category of object, the so-called '*cosmetic spoon*'[83], and the other figure sports the special "*Astartian*" hairdo described above. Fishes, ducks and lotus flowers complete the Nilotic setting. The outer frieze takes us into a completely different world: a desert-like landscape with pairs and groups of animals in combat and in balanced scenes, separated from each other by composited voluted palmettes. A pair of female winged sphinxes show the same distinctive hairstyle as the swimming girl and the goddess on the vessels of Atumemtaneb. This might be another depiction of Astarte.

As on the two pitchers of Atumemtaneb, the inscription on the outside of the bowl contains a toast to its owner, who bore the title "*chantress of the goddess Neith*". Remarkably, the toast refers to the "*open courtyard of the temple of Neith*", where the alcoholic contents of the bowl should be consumed, and provides evidence as to the actual use of the vessel:

"(For) your ka and your face! One wipes away the years (?), lasting in joy. May your lifetime be multiplied in health and life. May your stride extend (when) the morning comes, may favors and riches arise for you as food and provisions. May you be drunk with wine and pomegranate juice in the open courtyard (of the temple) of Neith; mistress of the house, chantress of Neith, Amy."

Given the prominence of the goddess Neith in this context, the discovery of the above-mentioned inscribed block mentioning Neith at the find spot of the second hoard where the silver patera of Amy comes from, is remarkable. Could we see this as evidence of the former existence of a temple of this goddess at Bubastis? It might even be that the mention of drunkenness in the temple of Neith at Bubastis is connected to the religious festivals of Bastet.

There has long been a debate in scholarly literature about the precise dating of the two hoard finds. However, the technique, style and motifs of the different objects, and the royal cartouches are strong evidence for dating most of the objects in the later Ramesside Period, at the very end of the Second millennium BCE. The two vessels discussed here certainly date to that time, as we can see from the type of dress Atumemtaneb is wearing as well as his titles, which fit well into this time span. The patera of Amy bears a close resemblance both to the style and motifs of the decoration, especially the *International Style*, as well as to the palaeography, design and lexicography of the inscriptions of the vessels of Atumemtaneb, and should therefore date to the same period. Of course, the date of the deposition might not necessarily be identical with this.

In her studies about the *International Style* and the *koiné*, FELDMAN has stressed the role of such luxury objects as the materialisation of high-level diplomacy to maintain a balance of power between greater and lesser kings of the Levant and Egypt. However, Atumemtaneb and Amy, the owners of the vessels discussed here, demonstrate very clearly that recipients of the international exchange are not only rulers but also members of an urban elite, which developed especially in the cultural contact zones such as the Eastern Nile Delta. Atumemtaneb was a high member of the court, as "*first royal cup-bearer*" in close contact to the king. In Ramesside times, royal cup-bearers were often of foreign origin. This was probably true for Atumemtaneb as well: the inscription on the vignette on vessel B has his personal name Iry, with the determinative of a throw- stick and the mountain range 〰〡, decoded as the semantic field meaning "foreign land", with his name possibly referring to a city named Arri or Arra in Northern Syria. Pointing even more in this direction, is the title of Atumemtaneb: "*envoy of the king in all foreign countries*". The title means that he was a direct agent of the Egyptian King in the Eastern Mediterranean, in close contact with the regions where luxury goods of the *International Style* flourished. His own name, Atumemtaneb, which translates as "*Atum is in all countries*", hints to the foreign origin of this individual as well, for this kind of loyalist name is quite usual for foreigners who rose to high offices at the Egyptian court.[84] Furthermore, the goddess he worships is Astarte, a famous and illustrious Levantine deity who may have enjoyed her own temple cult at Bubastis.

Atumemtaneb was a professional diplomat in the Levantine countries and city-states, reporting to the king in his capital at Pi-Ramesse. He himself might have been living in Bubastis or was at least visiting the temple, so the centre of his life in Egypt would be the Eastern Delta which we can consider a part of the *koiné* of the *International Style*. He also belonged to the social elite of that time, being of foreign origin himself – a very good example of the people who used luxury objects of the *International Style* as a way of expressing themselves as educated and high members not only of a city but of a greater, truly international region.

Although the inscription on the patera of the "*chantress of Neith*" Amy does not reveal as much of a foreign background for her as in the case of Atumemtaneb, the combination of Astarte and Neith by means of the decoration and inscription on the vessel is telling.

What is more, the depiction of Astarte on the vessels of Atumemtaneb and Amy reaches beyond the sphere of a shared aesthetic representation of rulership, as proposed by FELD-MAN.[85] There is an obvious connection between Astarte, Neith, and Bastet and her festival. The latter, however, is nothing other than a local variant of the many festivals all over Egypt for certain goddesses such as Mut, Sekhmet, Neith, and Hathor, which centre on rituals of drunkenness and sexual activities, understood as a celebration of the fertile aspects of the goddess as well as the pacification of her feared ferocity.

The grouping of Sekhmet, Bastet, Neith and Astarte at Bubastis is very meaningful, showing that the *International Style* is much more than just an eclectic representation of royal iconography of different regions in the Levant, it is a kind of *language by decorum*. The elite members of the cities of the Eastern Delta took it much further, by integrating Astarte into the theology and festivals for the goddesses of Egypt, i.e. into cultic activity, experienced by many, which goes far beyond the language of diplomacy between rulers alone.

6.6 The deities of Bubastis in the New Kingdom

In comparison to earlier periods, the richer textual material of the New Kingdom allows us to reconstruct the Bubastite pantheon at that time. At its top was of course the goddess Bastet, oftentimes designated as "*Lady of Bubastis*" (*nb.t bȝs.t*), and also as "*the Great One*" (*ȝ.t*). Other deities accompanied her, first of all Sekhmet, with whom Bastet shared her distinctive lioness character and appearance. Sekhmet and Bubastis were believed to bring illness to people by sending out arrows but at the same time, they were also considered to possess divine healing powers. Accordingly, Bastet and Sekhmet presided over the temple institution of the '*House of Life*' at Bubastis, where priests kept manuscripts of a medical and theological nature. Furthermore, inscriptions on the double statue of Khaemwaset and Khebyanes inform us about the existence of singer-dancers of Bastet and chantresses of Sekhmet. Given the fact that dancing and singing was an essential part of the cult of the goddesses, in particular during their festivals (see Chapter 8), these artists were a key element of the cult personnel of the temple of Bastet which was led by the High-priest of Bastet at Bubastis, i.e. individuals such as Ay, the son of the vizier Juti of the Twentieth Dynasty and the "*god's father*" Thutmose of the same era.

Further goddesses were attached to the cult of Bastet and Sekhmet of which the most important ones are: Shesemtet, a lioness goddess of the Eastern Delta whose close connection to Bastet and Sekhmet is attested since the Old Kingdom (see Chapter 1)[86]; Wadjet, the cobra goddess of Buto, who embodied the Red Crown of Lower Egypt; Neith, an anthropomorphic goddess of deltaic origins and the main deity of Sais.[87] Their connecting element is a specific theology which revolves around these deities imagined as mighty and protective yet fearsome in their ambivalent nature, who might turn against humans in an unpredictable way, especially in their connection to the Heliopolitan-based theology of the so-called solar-eye goddess. In the late New Kingdom, the foreign goddess Astarte was integrated into this circle of dangerous goddesses at Bubastis as well.

Male deities are less frequently mentioned. At any rate, we find Osiris, especially in his Heliopolitan aspect as Osiris Atef-Wer and the gods Atum and Nefertem who, in later periods, act as the divine consort and son of Bastet respectively. There also might have been a cult of Amun at Bubastis in the New Kingdom, but the textual references still leave room for other interpretations.

Endnotes

[1] Ryholt 1997, 151-159. For the dynasty of Abydos see Ryholt 1997, 163-166 und Wegner, Cahail 2021.

[2] Polz 2018; Polz 2022. For the regnal years see Ryholt 1997, 201-204.

[3] Habachi 1972.

[4] Bietak, Strouhal 1974.

[5] Cf. Ryholt 1997, 201-204; Hornung et al. 2006, 198, 492.

[6] Morris 2018, 117-186.

[7] Bryan 2000; van Dijk 2000.

[8] Pusch, Herold 1999.

[9] Helck 1974, 184, 195-196.

[10] If the circumstances of the discovery of an object are not specified in the text, they were found by NAVILLE during his seasons from 1887 to 1889.

[11] London BM EA 1103: Naville 1891, pl. XXXV.D.

[12] Bietak 2017, 2018. Against this identification: Forstner-Müller 2021.

[13] Urk. IV, 1443.

[14] Naville 1891, pl. XXXIV.A. Breasted 1906, 337-340, §846-850, dates the inscription into the reign of Amenhotep III for palaeographic and historical reasons.

[15] Breasted 1906, 337, §846.

[16] Naville 1891, pl. XXXV.I.

[17] Cairo CG 590: Naville 1891, pl. XIII left, XXXV.F'.

[18] Following Helck 1961, 280.1840; HABACHI (1957, 106, 121) unconvincingly translates the unusual sign-group for the writing of *sp3.wt šmʿ mḥw* ("*the nomes of Upper and Lower Egypt*") as an otherwise unattested toponym "*Shobak*".

[19] London BM EA 1068: Naville 1891, pl. XIII right, pl. XXXV.E; PM IV, 31; Edwards 1939, pl. 11; Wiese 2001, No. 1068.

[20] Caminos 1987.

[21] Albright, 1946, 12.

[22] Helck 1958, 302-305; Gordon 1989.

[23] Cairo CG 897: Naville 1891, pl. XXXV.H, H'; Habachi 1957, 106-107; Habachi 1971, 69. Cf. Urk IV, 1840.

[24] Berlin SMPK 21595: Schulz 1992, 80-81.

[25] Bakr et al. 2010, 176-179, no 53.

[26] Gabolde 2016, 90-91.

[27] Habachi 1957, 96-97, Pl. XXVIII–XXIX.

[28] Ward, 1986, 69-80.

[29] Habachi 1957, 96-97, Pl. XXIXB.

[30] Habachi 1957, 95, Pl. XXVII A-B.

[31] Cairo CG 34509: Naville 1891, pl. XXXVIII.B; RITA II, 140-142, §88.

[32] For their connection with Bastet see Chapter 1.

[33] WB II, 409.9-15.

[34] Snape 2019.

[35] Boston MFA 88.748: Naville 1891, pl. XXXVIII.C'; RITA II, 585-586, § 355; Schulz 1992, 88-89.

[36] Gomaà et al. 2006, 100-104.

[37] Cairo JE 38996: Bernhauer 2010, 279-280.

[38] Some of the statues of Ramses II at Bubastis originally belonged to Sesostris I: Sourouzian 1988, 231.

39 Naville 1891, pl. XXXVIII.I, I'; Loth 2003, 146-151.

40 Habach, Ghalioungui 1971, 68.

41 Habachi, Ghalioungui 1971, 61-62; Habachi 2001, 199-200.

42 Habach, Ghalioungui 1971, 63-67.

43 v. Känel 1984.

44 Habachi, Ghalioungui 1971, 69-70; Allen 2005, 66-68, no. 57.

45 Meeks 2006, 22; Leitz 2014, 344-347. See also Chapter 8.

46 Gauthier 1928.

47 Habachi 1957, pl. I.

48 Gauthier 1928, 129, Fig. 1.

49 Cairo JE 49612: Gauthier 1928, 131.

50 Cairo JE 52005: Gauthier 1928, 133.

51 Gauthier 1928, 134-136.

52 Habachi 1957, plan; see also the suggested location in Auenmüller 2021, 26, Fig. 10.

53 Cairo JE 88634: Habachi 1957, 97-101.

54 Leclant 1966, 133 §9a; Habachi, Ghalioungui 1971, 69; Bakr 1982, 157.

55 Auenmüller 2021.

56 Habachi, Ghalioungui 1971, 69; Bakr, Brandl 2014, 150-151.

57 Grajetzki 2003, 91; Downes 1974, 18-24

58 Habachi 1957, 101-102, Habachi, Ghalioungui 1971, 67-68; Bakr, Brandl 2014, 152-153 (no 29).

59 Bakr 1982, 157-163. For further ushabti finds of New Kingdom burials see Bakr 1992, 133-153.

60 Farid 1964, 95-96; El-Sawi 1979, 13-63, 81-98.

61 Habachi 1957, 102-103.

62 Edgar 1904, 93.

63 Cairo JE 38705, 39867, CG 53262, SR 1/6609: Edgar 1907, pl. XLIII; Lilyquist 2012, 12, Fig. 5.

64 Cairo JE 38720, 39868, CG 53258, SR 1/6623: Edgar 1907, pl. XLIV; Lilyquist 2012, 13, Fig. 6.

65 Cairo JE 38708, 39872, CG 53260, SR 1/6622: Edgar 1907, pl. XLIV; Lilyquist 2012, 12, Fig. 4.

66 Berlin SMPK ÄM 20104, 19736: Lilyquist 2012, 13, Fig. 8.

67 New York MMA 07.228.19: Simpson 1959, 30, 34-35; Lilyquist 2012, 9-10, 33, Fig. 48.

68 Edgar 1907, 93-94; Lilyquist 2012, 9-10.

69 Edgar 1907, 95-96.

70 Edgar 1907, 95.

71 Habachi 1957, 6-7, pl. 1.

72 Laube 2023.

73 Edgar 1907, 97.

74 Cairo JE 38710, 39873, CG 52575-76, SR 1/6620: Lilyquist 2012, 15, Fig. 14.

75 Cairo JE 38712a-b: Edgar 1907, pl. LIII ; Lilyquist 2012, 15, Fig. 15.

76 Cairo JE 38713, 39875, CG 53184, SR 1/6611: Edgar 1907, pl. LII; Lilyquist 2012, 15, Fig. 16.

77 Cairo JE 38706-07, 39870-71, CG 53259, 53261, SR 1/6621, 1/6624: Edgar 1907, pl. XLVIII; Lilyquist 2012, 15, Fig. 12-13.

78 Lilyquist 2012, 14-15.

79 Kantor 1956; Kantor 1960; Feldman 2006.

80 Edgar 1907, 98.

81 Edgar 1907, 100.

82 Lilyquist 2012, 20-22.

83 Phillips 1941, 173-175.

84 Lilyquist 2012, 22-35.

85 Feldman 2006.

86 Lange 2016.

87 Wilson 2006, 2-3; Wilson 2011, 186-187.

7. The Secret Capital of Egypt: Bubastis in the time of the Libyan Kings

In the Nineteenth Dynasty, the royal court moved to the Delta, where Ramses II had founded a new capital in the early years of his reign. The city, called Pi-Ramesse (see Chapter 2), was however not built on virgin ground but had integrated structures of the nearby earlier capital Avaris, where other kings of the New Kingdom, namely Thutmose III and Seti I, had palaces built after the victory of Ahmose over the Hyksos.[1] Pi-Ramesse was a magnificent city with palaces, temples, stables, domestic and industrial areas, and docks, stretching for over several kilometres along the Pelusiac Nile branch. While settlement activities continued until the Twenty-second Dynasty, the capital was nonetheless moved to the city of Tanis on the Tanitic Nile branch around 30 km north during the reigns of the last Ramesside kings (1130-1076 BCE). It seems that over time fluvial-driven processes, possibly the gradual silting-up of the Pelusiac Nile branch, had diminished the very favourable geographical conditions of Pi-Ramesse, but other factors might have contributed to this development as well. At any rate, the Tanitic branch obviously offered a stable and navigable river, the existence of which was a *conditio sine qua non* for the functionality of any major city, even more so for the capital of Egypt.[2]

The new capital of Tanis (San el-Haggar) was a planned city like Pi-Ramesse, and, like its predecessor, it made use of earlier settlement structures as well. So far, archaeological remains discovered at the site of San el-Haggar do not date back before the middle of the Twenty-first Dynasty, however, the name of the settlement ($ḏˤn.t$) appears already in the written records of the Nineteenth Dynasty, attesting to its earlier existence.[3] A literary text known as the '*Report of Wenamun*', composed in the transitional time between the New Kingdom and Third Intermediate Period, explicitly names Tanis as the residence of Smendes (*Nesibanebdjedet*, 1069-1043 BCE), the first king of the Twenty-first Dynasty, and his wife Tentamun (*Tanetimen*): "*Day of my arrival at Tanis, where Nisubanebdjedet and Tanetimen are*"[4]; thus indicating that Tanis had achieved its status as the capital of Egypt with the accession of Smendes to the throne after the death of Ramses XI (1105-1070 BCE).

The origins of Smendes lie more or less in the dark, as do the events that led to his rise to royal power. He might have been a son of Herihor, the High Priest of Amun at Thebes, and son-in-law of Ramses XI, the last ruler of the Twentieth Dynasty, and thereby a member of the extended royal family. The accounts narrated in the '*Report of Wenamun*' attest to his role as a de facto ruler of the north, a role that evidently gave him enough power to be the founder of a new dynasty.[5] Smendes was also the first king to abandon the Valley of the Kings as a funerary place. Instead, he founded a new tradition of royal burials by having his tomb built within the enclosure of the temple of Amun at Tanis (see Chapter 7.3).

At the same time, the High Priests of Amun at Thebes accumulated considerable power and were effectively leading a theocracy. These officials, originally rising from the military ranks, had created their own dynasties through the inheritance of the priestly office. Yet, even though the High Priests of Amun were de facto rulers of the Southern Nile Valley and, during the first part of the Twenty-first Dynasty, took on royal titles, they were by no means openly acting as adversaries of the king ruling from his capital in the north. Moreover, kings and high priests were often entangled by family relationships: As stated above, Smendes might have been a son of the High Priest of Amun, Herihor. Psusennes I, the third and most important ruler of the Twenty-first Dynasty (1040-992 BCE), was a son of the High Priest of Amun, Pinudjem I, and his brother Menkheperre followed Pinudem I in his office in Thebes, which led to the fact that they held their respective offices almost simultaneously (1038-990 BCE). Pinudjem II, the High Priest of Amun who held office in the later Twenty-first Dynasty was the father of Psusennes II, the last king of this dynasty (957-944 BCE).[6]

Following Psusennes II on the throne was Shoshenq I (945-924 BCE), the second king of Libyan origin. He was a former *"Great chief of the Ma(shwash)"*, an important Libyan tribe, an army commander and nephew of the Libyan King Osorchor (985-978 BCE), the fifth ruler of the preceding dynasty. Shoshenq might have been a co-regent of Psusennes II and linked his family further to the royal line by the marriage of his son Osorkon (later Osorkon I) to Maatkare, a daughter of Psusennes II.

Shoshenq I is nowadays widely known for his military campaigns into Palestine, ending a long period of inactivity of Egyptian rulers in that region. He is traditionally identified with the *"Shishak, king of Egypt"*, whom the Old Testament mentions as the Egyptian pharaoh who marched on Jerusalem in the fifth year of King Rehoboam and returned home with the treasures of the temple and palace of Salomon. This, however, remains much disputed, because the relief decoration on the gateway erected by Shoshenq I in his new peristyle court at Karnak, which lists the towns he had conquered during a military campaign into Palestine, does not mention Jerusalem.[7]

Shoshenq I established a dynasty of Libyan kings, of whom Osorkon I and Osorkon II in particular, undertook large-scale building activities in the temple of Bastet at Bubastis (see chapter 7.2). The importance of the city to the Twenty-second Dynasty kings was so evident that Manétho called them a *"dynasty of Bubastite kings"*[8]. Yet, does this mean that the Libyan kings did in fact hail from Bubastis? Unfortunately, hard evidence for this is still missing.

In their influential works on that historical period, KENNETH KITCHEN and ANTHONY LEAHY have argued that the favouring of the Eastern Delta and especially Bubastis by the Libyan rulers have their origins in major historical events at the end of the New Kingdom. According to this, after defeating the Libyans and their allies – the Sea-Peoples – who invaded the Western Delta, Ramesses III placed the captured Libyans in military settlements within Egyptian territory. Bubastis seems to have been one of the major settlements of this kind, subsequently establishing the base for the development of generations of a powerful Libyan elite. The founder of the Twenty-second Dynasty, Shoshenq I, could have been their descendant. However, other scholars have argued against such a view. As KARL JANSEN-WINKELN pointed out, there is no direct proof for the presence of Libyan rulers at Bubastis before the reign of Osorkon I. The origin of this dynasty might, in fact, be found at Herakleopolis south of the entrance to the Fayum.[9]

Be that as it may, the numerous remains of the temple of Bastet at Bubastis from the reign of Osorkon I and Osorkon II show beyond any doubt that, whatever their geographical point of origin, kings of the Libyan Dynasty had chosen the principal goddess of Bubastis, Bastet, as their main dynastic deity besides Amun. Accordingly, the city must have served as a royal residence or at least a fiefdom alongside the capital Tanis.

7. 1 Bastet and the Libyan Kings

From the time of Osorkon II, the kings of the Twenty-second Dynasty regularly adopted the epithet 's*on of Bastet*', highlighting their special relationship with the feline goddess.[10] Further illuminating on that topic is an inscribed block of pink granite discovered by the mission of the University of Potsdam in 2003 at the southwestern corner of the temple's entrance hall. The long inscription on side A of the block consisting of nine lines, dating to the reign of Osorkon I, sheds an interesting light on a new concept of legitimacy and kingship that blends both Egyptian and Libyan traditions. After a fragmented line of praise of the goddess, the king addresses Bastet:[11]

> "*[May] you grant [me] numerous Sed-festivals and health. The mistress of the slaughter and the mistress of the secret are to his sides, for the protection of the body of the god, which comes forth from thee. May you unite for me the forms of the lord of all and the belovedness of the son of Isis in the heart of the gods. May you weld my sweetness in the bodies of the people and my fame in the heart of the people of the sun-folk. May fire [burn] in those who rebel against me, may the victorious slaughter be mighty among the rebellious.*

> *May you increase my reputation throughout the land. May you summon (?) my relatives (?) in my time, (that of) the Dual King: (powerful of appearance, Ra, chosen by Ra)|; the son of Ra: (Osorkon, beloved of Amun)|, beloved by the Ennead, the lords, who let the field of Bubastis flourish.*

> *O how great is your ka as mistress of the two lands because of the tribute of the foreign countries, those with angry (?) hearts whom you have given to me - nothing like that has happened since primeval times. I have not spoken in impurity (?); the sun goddess is witness. Come and complete what you have done for me with might and strength: a great kingship and health, numerous Sed-festivals of Tatenen, while offerings are donated to your ka daily (and) while my heart is guiding me and my arms are acting.*

> *I know that you have put it in my arm to exalt my kingship, to let my son(s) appear on the throne of Horus (and as) High-Priest of Amun-Ra, the king of gods, (as) chiefs of the Ma(shwash), as Great Ones of the foreigners, as priests of Herishef, the Dual King, (and as) lords of all countries, whereby they descend, (each) after his brother without ceasing while thou art with them, being victorious in eternity because of doing what is beneficial for your house as I have done every time the shining one appears at the sky as well as the appearing one, enduring and lasting every day. Then posterity will say: "To act for you is useful, because you have rewarded the Dual King, the lord of the ritual: (powerful of appearance, Ra, chosen by Ra)|; the son of Ra, [lord of the diadems]: (Osorkon, beloved of Amun)|, according to what he did in the Neheh-eternity and Djet-eternity.*"

Given the location of the block, the goddess addressed in the main inscription is undoubtedly Bastet, even though her name does not appear in the preserved part of the text. The royal prayer to Bastet consists of two parts. First, an invocation and praise of the goddess with a

Fig 31: *Inscription of Osorkon I: White Light scan. (TRIGONART 2006)*

striking emphasis on the martial and dangerous aspects of Bastet, related to the two crown goddesses Nekhbet and Wadjet, and, second, a request for favours to be granted to the king, which makes up the largest part of the inscription. It is Osorkon himself who appears as the speaker. He pleads for the goddess's help in safeguarding his rule, i.e. a long and successful reign, his reputation to endure amongst gods and men, the subduing of foreign countries and the elimination of adversaries. While this part is well-rooted in Egyptian traditions, Osorkon I departs from established themes of royal ideology as he continues setting out his ideas for the preservation of his own dynasty. His successor on the Egyptian throne was to be one of his sons, while his other sons were to assume all other key positions in the country. This part of the text is very unusual. It reveals the ideological and pragmatic foundations of a kingship that are alien to Egyptian concepts but are rooted in Libyan traditions of rule. The priority was clearly to fill the most influential positions and offices in the country with the sons of the king, i.e. men who were not distinguished by their education, knowledge, and aptitude, but by family descent, and who were bound to each other and to the king by kinship. A very close parallel is offered by the so-called oracle-prayer on a stelophorous block of Osorkon II from Tanis.[12]

Two sides of the same granite block show columns of a dedicatory inscription. Judging from the palaeography of the hieroglyphs, this inscription also dates to the reign of Osorkon I or the time of his immediate successors. The preserved part of the text on side A.1 of the block mentions:

"[...] for me as king from the beginning of the Neheh-eternity, so that I will complete the Djet-eternity on the throne of Ra. [...] vessel: 20. Silver: 5 fire basins. Silver: 2 milk jars. Silver: 1 incense bowl. [...] his majesty. The great image of Bastet, the Great, lady of Bubastis [...]. [...] pure chased silver, each god in their stride like those who are in the nocturnal barque. 2 collars [...]."

Likewise on block side A.2:

"[...] 2 [...]. Silver: 1 splendid chapel. Silver: 1 offering table. [...] Gold: 1 collar. [...] hacked silver: 20000 deben. Silver: 1 fan (?) [...]. Gold, silver: 1 sḥ-vessel of the great majesty (?) [...]".[13]

These two lists of donations consist mostly of utensils for the cult made from gold or silver. It seems that the beneficiary was the temple of Bastet, as the donation of a cult statue of the goddess is also listed here, as well as silver statues of various deities, which remain unnamed and are only referred to as the crew of the nocturnal barque. These passages give an impression of the riches of the temple of Bastet.

Unfortunately, the name of the royal donor is lost, but a palaeographical comparison with the fragments of a large donation inscription of Osorkon I, also found at Bubastis, shows close parallels. The same is true for the layout and content of the donation list (see Chapter 7.4).

The distribution of the donation inscription on the two narrow sides of the block and the prayer to Bastet on the broad side makes it difficult to reconstruct an architectural context for the block which would allow each side to be viewed (such as a pillar construction or the like). It seems, therefore, more likely that the inscriptions do not date to the same time and that the block was reused after a rather short period of time, possibly even within the reign of Osorkon I.

7.2 The temple of Bastet

The city of Bubastis' growing importance was reflected in the rise of its goddess, whom the Libyan Kings chose as a principal divine protector and source of legitimacy for their new dynasty (see Chapter 7.2). Therefore, the new rulers, especially Osorkon I and Osorkon II, took great interest in the temple of Bubastis and had it enlarged and renovated. Around three-quarters of the preserved remains of the temple date from their time.

In his famous *Histories*, the ancient Greek historian HERODOTUS gave a description of the city of Bubastis and the temple of Bastet (whose name is identical to the name of the city in Greek) in his time (ca. 450 BCE, second half of the Twenty-seventh Dynasty), providing us with some very useful information that will also be discussed in detail in a later section of this book (see Chapters 7.4, 8.1 and 8.2):

"In this city, there is a sanctuary of Bubastis, which is very remarkable; for there are other larger and more costly sanctuaries, but none that is more delightful to the eye. Bubastis is, in the Greek language, Artemis. This is her temple: Except for the entrance, the rest is an island. The canals, which come from the Nile, are not joining one another,

Fig. 32: *The temple of Bastet at Bubastis. View to the south.* (*TELL BASTA-PROJECT 2022*)

but each one extends to the entrance of the temple; one surrounds one side, the other the other side, and each one is 100 feet wide and shadowed by trees.

The propylaeum has a height of ten fathoms and is adorned with notable reliefs six cubits high. The temple is in the midst of the city, the whole circuit of which commands a view down into it; for the city's level has been raised by embankments, but that of the temple has been left as it was from the first, so that it can be seen into from without. Around it runs a wall in which reliefs have been carved, and inside is a grove of mighty trees planted around a great sanctuary wherein is the image of the goddess.

The temple is a square, each side measuring a furlong. A road, paved with stone, of about three furlongs in length leads to the entrance, running eastward through the marketplace, towards the temple of Hermes; this road is about four hundred feet wide, and bordered by trees reaching to heaven. Such is the temple."[14]

However, due to the severe destruction of the architecture of the temple in later times, especially with the parts built in limestone completely gone, we can only offer a very basic reconstruction of the ground plan of the building.

The temple was oriented along an east-west axis, with the entrance in the east. The area covered today by its remains indicates a length of around 170 m and a width of 70 m. HERODOTUS' account however, points to larger dimensions: depending on what exact type of furlong he refers to (see Chapter 7.4), the temple would have measured at least around 176 by 176 m.[15] This, however, cannot refer to the dimension of the temple building alone but must include parts of the sacred landscape.

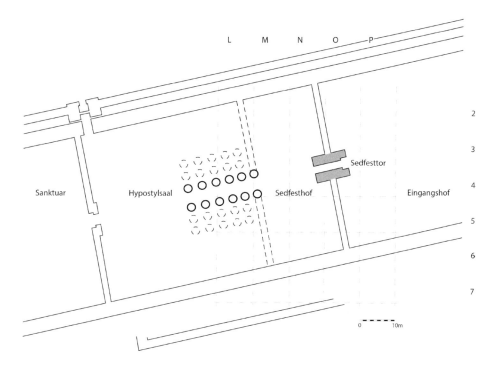

Fig. 33: *Reconstruction of the ground plan of the temple of Bastet. (Lange-Athinodorou 2019 (a), Abb. 2)*

Although it would be quite unusual for a temple of that time, there is a possibility that it never had an enclosure wall. Not only have no remains of one been detected so far, but also the specific landscape in which the temple was situated, with two sacred canals surrounding the building only a short distance from it (see Chapter 8.1), makes the reconstruction of a massive large enclosure wall rather improbable. An essential part of the so-called '*formal*' layout of temples since the New Kingdom are pylons, monumental gateways marking the passage from one court to the next. Unfortunately, none are preserved at Bubastis, including the first pylon that would have formed the entrance to the whole temple. However, we know from other examples that colossal statues used to flank pylons along the processional route inside the temple.[16] Therefore, the find of a monumental statue of a queen in the northern part of the first courtyard of the temple at Bubastis points to the fact that pylons must once have existed here too (see fig. 34).

The queen's statue was discovered by the mission of the University of Potsdam in 2003. Once towering more than 10 m high, it was found broken into two pieces. It shows a queen wearing a heavy tripartite wig partly covered by a vulture cap, flanked by two uraei, and a *modius*, a cylindrical crown, on top. The latter has a rectangular opening in the centre to accommodate a crown attachment, such as the double plumes or the sun disc between the horns of a cow, representing the goddess Hathor. The attachment is, however, lost. Her left hand holds a flywhisk in the shape of a lotus flower. The small figure of a princess holds onto her right leg. The back pillar displays two columns and at the lower part three lines of inscription. The two columns have the royal titles of Osorkon II:

Fig. 34: *Restored statue of Queen Karomama at Bubastis. (LANGE-ATHINODOROU 2022)*

"Horus: Mighty bull, beloved of Ma'at, whom Ra has appointed as king of the Two Lands. The Dual King, the lord of the Two Lands: (powerful of Ma'at of Ra, chosen by Amun)|; the son of Ra, lord of the diadems: (Osorkon, beloved of Amun, son of Bastet)|, lord of all living beings, eternally. The Golden Horus: Great of strength, who strikes back the Asiatics, rich of dominion and respect in all countries (powerful of Ma'at of Ra, chosen by Amun)|; the son of Ra, lord of the diadems: (Osorkon, beloved of Amun, son of Bastet)|, all life, duration and dominion like Ra."

However, the irregular stone surface on some parts of the inscription proves that the statue originally bore the names of another king, which were erased and overwritten. A closer inspection of the royal titles that were changed and those left unaltered reveal that the original titles were most probably those of Ramses II.

The base of the statue has three additional lines of inscription giving the titles and the name of the depicted queen. It reads:

"The jrj.t-pᶜt, Great of praise, lady of Upper and Lower Egypt, lady of graciousness, the Beloved One who pleases Horus-in-his-palace, who creates rejoice, who is pleasant of scent, who appears as the Beloved One of the perfect god, king's daughter and king's great wife, first of his majesty [...] (Karomama)|, she may live."

Queen Karomama was the principal wife of Osorkon II. It is clear, that the statue was usurped to rededicate it to her, but for whom it was originally made is not so obvious. Of course, it must have been a great royal wife of Ramses II and, based on their importance, either Nefertari or his daughter-wife Meritamun. From other statues, we know that the iconography and depiction of facial features of statues of both queens are almost identical and so offer no hint as to its identification. As there are no clear traces of whatever name was written before in the cartouche, the question on the former identity of the depicted queen remains unanswered for now.

Monumental statues of Osorkon II once stood at the first and second pylon as well, yet only fragments remain. The lower part of one of his two seated statues, originally belonging to Amenemhet III (see Chapter 4) are re-inscribed with the titles of Osorkon II, who added the epithet "*son of Bastet*" to his proper name (fig. 35).

Passing through the temple from east to west, the visitor would have first entered an open courtyard, measuring around 47 by 45 m. The discovery of broken parts of columns and two palm leaf capitals suggest

Fig. 35: *Throne of a seated statue of Amenemhet III, usurped by Osokon II in the temple of Bastet (Tell Basta-Project 2014)*

that one or two rows of columns might have stood along its walls. Most of the surviving material from the first courtyard are blocks of pink granite, decorated with reliefs showing Osorkon I offering to Bastet, Amun and Hor-Hekenu. There is also a number of blocks and fragments of statues inscribed with the titles of Ramses II, revealing the well-known custom of re-using earlier architecture and statues, originating from Bubastis and other places.

The second court was of smaller dimensions, measuring around 21 by 45 m. Its dominating element was a monumental gateway of 10 m length and 11.50 m height. The gateway, which served as a passageway to the following pronaos of the temple, was decorated with episodes from the Sed-festival of Osorkon II.

Pictorial and textual sources on the royal ritual of the Sed-festival (ḥb-sd) span almost three millennia, beginning with Early Dynastic period up to the time of the Ptolemies. However, not all sources offer a complete corpus of the elaborate ritual. In most cases, the depiction of the Sed-festival is just limited to the display of an icon-like depiction of the king enthroned

Fig. 36a: *Relief from the entrance hall: Osorkon I offering a an Udjat-Eye to Bastet. (TELL BASTA-PROJECT 2011)*

Fig. 36b: *Relief from the entrance hall: Osorkon I and Hor-Hekenu. (TELL BASTA-PROJECT 2011)*

in a kiosk, dressed in a tight, knee-long cloak-like garment. Therefore, the decoration of the gateway of Osorkon II in the temple of Bubastis with its extensive depictions of a variety of episodes of the ritual is of exceptional importance for understanding the Sed-festival.[17]

Because the relief blocks were scattered over the area of the second courtyard, the

Fig. 37: *Naville's Reconstruction of the Sed-festival gateway. (Naville 1892, frontispiz)*

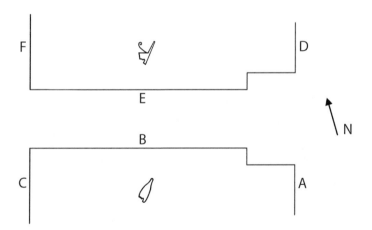

Fig. 38: *Location and orientation of the walls of the Sed-festival gateway. (Lange-Athinodorou 2019(a), Abb. 3)*

reconstruction of some parts of the gateway and its relief decoration have been speculative until now.[18] Although in many cases the joints between relief blocks are obvious and were already noticed and published by Naville, the sequence of episodes and their location on the sides of the gateway were not as evident as one would wish. The fact that several parts are missing complicates this task even more. At any rate, due to a new documentation of all reliefs in the temple, the author of this monograph was able to develop a sequence of episodes that would fit better with the available evidence on the architecture of the gateway, as follows[19]:

The episodes start in the lowest register on sides A and D. These were the front sides of

Fig. 39a: *Relief from the Sed-festival gateway of Osorkon II, showing musicians and the royal princesses. (TELL BASTA-PROJECT 2022)*

the gateway a visitor would see first when walking through the temple from east to west, i.e. from the entrance towards the sanctuary (see fig. 38).

The first episode shows several deities welcoming the king. The episode already bears references to the topic of the Sed-festival: Thoth and Bastet present a palm panicle combined with the hieroglyph for *ḥb-sd* to the king, alluding to the theme of the Sed-festival as a unit of time, comparable to the well-known *"millions of years"* given to the king.[20] Bastet addresses the topic further, greeting the king with the words:

> *"(I) give you life and dominion to your nose, (I) give you the years of Ra. I give you Sed-festivals [...] on the throne of Horus".*

Thoth says:

> *"I write down for you the Sed-festivals of Ra and the years of Atum".*

The episode appears on both front walls of the gateway, which means that the depictions refer

Fig. 39b: *Relief from the Sed-festival gateway of Osorkon II, showing chapels of deities. (TELL BASTA-PROJECT 2022)*

to each other. The same is true for all the following episodes shown on these walls.

Fig. 39c: *Head of a royal statue reused for the Sed-festival gateway of Osorkon II. The relief on the back side shows a procession of princesses (see Fig. 39d). (TELL BASTA-PROJECT 2022)*

Fig. 39d: *Relief from the Sed-festival gateway of Osorkon II, showing a procession of princesses. (Tell Basta-Project 2022)*

The second episode marks the beginning of the Sed-festival. The king appears in the chapels of the two crown goddesses, Nekhbet and Wadjet, where he offers them the so-called '*clepsydra*', a rather enigmatic object used for the measurement of time, and he receives the crowns of Upper and Lower Egypt in return. The movement to the next station of the ritual, the festival hall, is shown as a procession that is preceded by the standard bearers of the god Wepwawet. The festival hall is obviously the place where the full coronation of the king took place, conducted by several pairs of deities, as is shown in the next episode.

As the rituals and actions involving the king are shown on wall A, the corresponding processions of officiants of the festival, always moving towards the king, are displayed on wall D. Here we have a multitude of royal daughters, priests, officials, dancers, envoys, and the like, celebrating and welcoming the approaching king.

After a further procession, the king appears in a throne pavilion, obviously indicating the end of the first stage of the festival. The episodes continue further on wall B, the southern inner wall of the gateway, starting with some very fragmented episodes. The main episodes, however, are the offerings made by the king to the numerous chapels of gods, apparently representing the pantheon of Egypt and all districts of the country, as well as the decree issued by the king in favour of Amun. Some of these episodes extend onto wall C, where the king is depicted entering the shrine of the Heliopolitan deities, thus emphasizing his role as heir of the creator god Atum. The sequence of episodes on the southern part of the gateway ends with the arrival of the king at the palace, obviously marking another temporary end of the celebrations.

Except for side D, the episodes on the northern part of the gateway clearly follow other themes and topics. Walls E and F have several episodes that centre on the enthroned king in the Sed-festival chapel, accompanied by officiants presenting objects or performing rituals that are often difficult to understand.[21] Of particular interest are processions of bearers of birds and fishes, presented in a list-like manner with additional inscriptions naming toponyms and names of deities and priests. They represent the remains of an onomasticon of unknown age and origin.[22] The final episodes are lost.

When comparing the episodes of the Sed-festival of Osorkon II with other monumental Sed-festival reliefs, the main sources available are the reliefs of Niuserre in the sun-temple at Abu Ghurob, the reliefs of Amenhotep III at the temple of Amun at Soleb, and the reliefs in the tomb of the official Kheruef of the time of Amenhotep III in the Assasif (TT 192). The detailed study of the relation between these corpora revealed that the southern part and wall D of the northern part of the gateway of Osorkon II at Bubastis was strongly influenced by the Sed-festival decoration of Amenhotep III at Soleb, or rather the '*pattern books*' compiled and used for that building. On the other hand, the northern part shows a strong resemblance to the Sed-festival reliefs of Niuserre at Abu Ghurob. However, the existence of an onomasticon and several other alterations may hint that another, otherwise unknown, source of Sed-festival reliefs from the Old Kingdom was used.[23]

An investigation of the episodes on the gateway of Osorkon II revealed that some rituals had a higher significance than others, which led to the identification of the following key episodes:

1. Clepsydra offering and receiving the crowns of Upper and Lower Egypt,
2. Coronation by Heliopolitan deities,
3. Presenting offerings to the gods of Egypt as confirmation of the legitimate accession to power,
4. Entering the shrine of the Heliopolitan ennead as the legitimate heir,
5. Throne episodes in the iconic Sed-festival chapel as the legitimate king.

These key episodes show that the rituals performed at the Sed-festival of Osorkon II focused on the renewed granting of the legitimacy of kingship by the gods and the acknowledgment of him as heir and ruler by his divine father Atum and the ennead of Heliopolis. They may be a repetition of the rituals and ceremonies performed during the first enthronement of the king. Contrary to general Egyptological opinion, the Sed-festival is not at all a ritual to magically rejuvenate the king. This is in fact an interpretation that is based on incorrect and unmethodical conclusions made by PETRIE in the early Twentieth century, who took his observations on tribes in the Sudan and projected them back to ancient Egypt. The available sources do not allow for such interpretations, however.[24]

After the second courtyard with the Sed-festival gateway, came the pronaos or hypostyle hall measuring approximately 50 by 45 m. Columns with papyrus-bud capitals flanked the central axis[25]. Excavations of the University of Potsdam in 1993 revealed the foundations of some of these columns, which must have stood at least two rows deep.[26]

The discovery of several beautiful capitals with the face of the goddess Hathor is evidence for the existence of at least ten to twelve pillars of a kiosk within the pronaos, probably in its western part. Such a feature was very fitting for the temple of Bastet, a goddess who had close connections with Hathor since the Old Kingdom. The best-preserved capitals, some bearing the cartouches of Osorkon I and Osorkon II, are nowadays in the Egyptian Museums of Berlin, Boston, Cairo, London, Paris, and Sydney.[27]

To the west of the pronaos was the sanctuary, where the statue of the goddess would have resided in a stone naos. The remains covering the area today however are all from a later period, i.e. the reign of Nectanebo II, who had this part of the temple completely renewed (see Chapter 8.1). As there have been no excavations in the sanctuary up to now, we do not know if remains of the sanctuary of the Third Intermediate Period are still preserved in deeper layers and what layout this phase of the sanctuary might have had.

Around sixty meters north of the sanctuary, NAVILLE noted fragments of pink granite columns with palm-leaf and papyrus-bud capitals, inscribed with the titles of Osorkon II and the epithet "*Beloved of Mahes*". This led HABACHI to excavate the area, which he thought to be a small temple for the lion-god Mahes, the son of Bastet. He succeeded in discovering further parts of columns and four column bases, which would be key for a basic reconstruction of the layout of the temple, but, unfortunately, he did not publish a plan of their locations. Some of the fragments HABACHI discovered also bore the titles of Osorkon II, again with epithets pointing to Mahes: "*Beloved of Mahes, lord of Bubastis*" and "*Beloved of Mahes, son of Bastet*". A block of pink granite found in the near vicinity must have come from the corner of a wall or a doorway of the building. It has two decorated sides, showing Osorkon II offering to Bastet: "*Privy to the secrets of Atum, mistress of heaven, mistress of the Two Lands*", and the falcon-headed god Hor-Hekenu called: "*Lord of protection*", who was also considered to be a son of Bastet.[28]

7.3 Royal tombs in the temple?

The Libyan period in Egypt witnessed the development of a new funerary custom: while kings and members of the royal family were buried before in the desert wadi now known as the Valley of the Kings in Western Thebes, they were now laid to rest in tombs within the enclosure of temples. The main reason for the change is still debated. Was it really the de facto division of the country into two spheres of power, with the former capital Thebes as the seat of the High-Priests of Amun in the south and the ruling dynasty of kings in Tanis in the north? The kings of the Ramesside period however, although already residing in the north at Pi-Ramesse, still had their large, decorated tombs constructed in the Valley of the Kings. The use of the southern burial ground ceased at the end of that period in the reign of Ramses X or XI.[29] Smendes, the first king of the Twenty-first Dynasty, had his tomb erected in the temple enclosure of Amun at Tanis. Several scholars have argued that the cause of the sudden change in funerary customs lies in the fact that the new rulers did not share the traditional Egyptian funerary beliefs in their fullest sense, due to their foreign background.[30]

However, a key concept of the New Kingdom royal funerary religion was kept alive: The kings of Tanis had a temple of Amun erected, which mirrored the grand complex at Karnak. And while the kings of the New Kingdom once built royal funeral temples on the western bank of Thebes to serve as places for the cult of the deceased ruler and Amun at the same time[31], the rulers of Tanis now placed their burials within the temple enclosure itself, following the same objective.

While excavating the remains of domestic houses in the southeastern part of the temple of Amun in 1939, French Egyptologist PIERRE MONTET discovered a complex of royal tombs of the Twenty-first and Twenty-second Dynasty, including the burials of Smendes, Psusennes I, Amenemopet (993-984 BCE), Siamun (978-959 BCE), Psusennes II, Shoshenq IIa (*Heqakheperre*, ~890 BCE), Takelothis I (885-874 BCE), Osorkon II, Takelothis II (850-825 BCE), Shoshenq III (825-773 BCE), Pamiu (773-767 BCE), and Shoshenk IV ('Quartus',

767-730 BCE).[32] However, tombs of several kings of these dynasties are still unaccounted for, i.e. Amenemnesu (1043-1039 BCE) and Osorchor of the Twenty-first Dynasty and Shoshenq I, Shoshenq IIb (*Tutkheperre*, regnal years unknown), Shoshenq IIc (*Maakheperre*, regnal years unknown)[33] Osorkon I, Shoshenq V (767-730 BCE), and Osorkon IV (730-715 BCE) of the Twenty-second Dynasty.

There is a possibility that these rulers were not buried at Tanis but in other temples of the Delta and the Northern Nile Valley, which played a very important role at that time. An example would be the temple of Ptah at Memphis, where Shoshenq I most probably had a mortuary temple erected, suggesting that he might also have been buried there.[34] As well, the temple area of Ptah was arguably hosting the burials of a side-line of the Twenty-second Dynasty. Close to the southwest corner of the temple enclosure wall and south of a sanctuary of Ramses II, the tomb of the eldest son of Osorkon II and High-Priest of Ptah at Memphis, Shoshenq D, together with the tombs of his son Takeloth B and his descendants were discovered.[35] The discovery of the tomb of a Queen Kama of the Twenty-second or Twenty-third Dynasty at Leontopolis (Tell Moqdam)[36], highlights the fact that major temples of the Delta besides the temple of Amun at Tanis were considered to be suitable burial places for royals as well.

Another possible burial ground for the kings of that period, especially of the Twenty-second Dynasty, would be Bubastis, a city that was only second to Tanis in the eyes of the kings of that time. As described above in detail, the temple of Bubastis saw a great deal of building activity in the reigns of Osorkon I and Osorkon II. And, as said above as well, while Osorkon II was certainly buried at Tanis, the locations of several tombs of other kings of that period are unknown. In this context, two recent discoveries at Bubastis are very intriguing. The first was made in front of the entrance of the temple of Bastet, in an area designated '*Area A*'. From 2008 to 2017, the TELL BASTA PROJECT excavated several casemate foundations here dating to the Ptolemaic Period, and a limestone-paved Roman open court (see Chapter 8.5).[37] Shortly after we had started to work in this area, in March 2009, we dug a small test trench in order to establish the stratigraphic sequences of the archaeological layers underneath the Roman court. Within an infill that was made in Ptolemaic times to level the surface before building houses, a lens with small pieces of polished limestone and fragments of faience came to light. Three of the faience fragments showed traces of decoration in the form of a royal cartouche with the name '*Shosh[enq], beloved of Amun*' (*šš[nq] mrj jmn*). According to the slightly curved surface, these fragments may have belonged to vessels or small statues, such as shabtis. The latter were funerary figurines, intended to act as a substitute for the deceased in the netherworld and oftentimes found in elite burials.

Since there were a number of kings with the prenomen Shoshenq and the epithet '*Beloved of Amun*' (*mrj jmn*), an identification of the owner of the faience objects is difficult. The preserved parts of the inscriptions could refer to: Shoshenq I, Shoshenq IIb, Shoshenq IIc, Shoshenq III, Shoshenq IV, and Shoshenq V from the Twenty-second Dynasty, and Shoshenq VI (793-787 BCE) from the Twenty-third Dynasty.[38]

Especially intriguing is the possibility that these titles refer to Shoshenq IIb, who was recently introduced into the king lists of the Third Intermediate Period, based on another fascinating discovery at Bubastis: in 1994, the mission of the University of Potsdam made the surface find of a fragment of an inscribed limestone block (H/3.9) in the western part of the hypostyle hall of the temple of Bastet. The relatively small fragment, measuring 0.32 by

Fig. 40: *Faience fragments X/2 TS KF 007, 001, 004 and 003 with the cartouche of Shoshenq Meriamun. (TELL BASTA PROJECT 2009)*

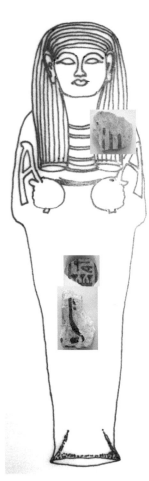

Fig. 41: *Suggested reconstruction of an ushabti of King Shoshenq Meriamun. (TELL BASTA PROJECT 2009)*

Fig. 42: *Inscription on block H/3.9 with the titles of King Tutkheperre Shoshenq Meriamun (LANGE 2004, Abb. 1-2)*

0.54 m, shows the upper part of a royal titulary. Of the original six symmetrically arranged columns five are preserved, reading: "*The Dual King: (Tutkheperre Setep[enre/amun])| [...]; the son of Ra: (Shoshe[nq] Meriamun)|*".

This block was the first evidence of the existence of a king of this name since EMILE AMÉLINEAU's publication of an ostracon with the titles of a king (*twt ḫpr rꜥw stp.n jmn)| (šš[nq] mrj jmn)|* he had found at Abydos in 1897. Interestingly, NAVILLE had also reported the discovery of a fragment of a limestone block with the lower part of the titles of a King Shoshenq, the throne name of whom included the element *ḫpr* but shows the epithet *mrj rꜥw*. Provided the latter was just a variation of the god's name in the epithet, which is not unusual for royal titles of the Twenty-second Dynasty, this fragment might belong to the same structure as fragment H/3.9.[39]

The block fragment is one of the very few pieces of limestone architecture to have survived in the temple of Bastet, but if it was once part of its architecture is not certain. It could also have come from a different building, for example, a burial chamber built of stone blocks, like the royal tombs at Tanis.

If we consider the hypothesis that kings or members of the royal family of the Libyan Dynasties were buried at Bubastis, the following questions arise: where exactly would a royal necropolis be located, what would it have looked like, and is there any chance that some of the tombs have survived? In order to find the answers, it is useful to look at the location of the royal tombs of that and later periods discovered at other temple sites. In a study published in 1971, RAINER STADELMANN conducted a comparative architectural analysis of tombs of the Twenty-sixth Dynasty in the temple of Neith at Sais, of the tombs of Harsiese and the God's Wives of Amun from the Twenty-second and Twenty-fifth Dynasties in the Amun-Temple

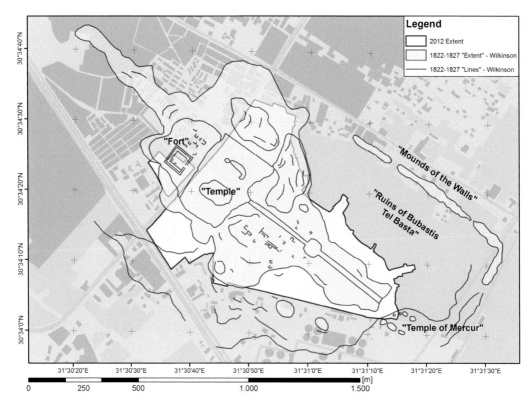

Fig.43: *Georeferenced map of the ruins of Bubastis c. 1827, based on J. G. WILKINSON. (LANGE et al. 2016, Fig. 5b)*

at Medinet Habu and the royal tombs of the Twenty-first and Twenty-second Dynasties at Tanis. In all three cases, the tombs are positioned inside the enclosure wall, in the immediate vicinity of the first pylon, and always south of the main axis of the temple to which they are connected. STADELMANN also pointed out that most of these tombs share main typological features: a sloping passageway, a small antechamber, and a burial chamber made of blocks of sandstone with a sarcophagus.[40] Interestingly, the same is true for the tombs at Memphis (see above).[41]

Another significant characteristic of the royal funeral culture of the Libyan period is the coffins and sarcophagi with falcon heads. They were already known since PIERRE MONTET discovered the burial of Shoshenq IIa at Tanis in 1939.[42] JEFFREY SPENCER added further material to the record with his discovery in 1998 of three tombs of the Twenty-second Dynasty within the enclosure wall of the temple of Amun at Tell el-Balamun in the Northern Delta. There, the mud-brick tombs were dug into the northeastern corner of the Ramesside enclosure wall, thus at the northern side of the main temple axis. They had several tomb chambers, lined and covered with limestone slabs. The finds of a falcon beak made of bronze and two pairs of bronze inlaid eyes with a male burial in a chamber in tomb no 3 is evidence that the deceased was once laid to rest in an assemblage comprising a wooden coffin and a full body cartonnage. SPENCER suggests that the outer one was a falcon-headed coffin that was almost entirely destroyed by the groundwater and salt penetrating the tomb. In another chamber of the same tomb was the burial of a four-year-old child. Also found here was a bronze hawk beak and a pair of bronze inlaid eyes from an exterior coffin and an inner mask.[43]

As falcon-headed coffins were confined to the sphere of the royal funerary culture of the Twenty-second Dynasty, the finds in these two burials at Tell el-Balamun suggest that the deceased must have belonged to the royal family and could have been High-Priests of Amun at Tell el-Balamun. Who they were is hard to say, however, because there were no inscribed objects found within the burials, except for a heart scarab and some ushabtis with the titles and name of the '*Vizier of the north*', Iken, dating to the reign of Osorkon I in tomb no. 1, who, however, did not possess a falcon mask.[44] Apart from that, the exact dating of the burials is not clear. The temple of Amun at Balamun already existed in the Ramesside period and was rebuilt under Shoshenq III. Therefore, the tombs date to somewhere in the first part of the Twenty-second Dynasty.[45]

Coming back to the possibility of royal tombs at Bubastis: judging from the parallels just presented, a probable location for them would be in the forefront of the temple entrance, south of the temple axis. Interestingly, the place where the inscribed faience fragments of Shoshenq Meriamun were found meets these specifications almost perfectly. However, we did not find any stone blocks or other remains of funerary architecture there. This, on the other hand, is not surprising given that the area was largely rebuilt in the Ptolemaic and Roman periods (see Chapter 8.5). However, covered by the debris of NAVILLE's excavations, there is a large unexcavated area further to the southwest of the find spot, where a royal or elite cemetery of the Third Intermediate Period could still lie undetected. What might be left of it? If everything has not been demolished and built over later, we might expect to find modest multi-chambered tombs made of reused stone blocks, such as at Tanis, or some simple mud-brick tombs with chambers lined with limestone as at Tell el- Balamun.

7. 4 The '*Temple of Hermes*'

In the above-cited description of the temple and city of Bubastis by the Greek historian HERODOTUS, the temple of Bastet served as the cardinal geographical point to whose location everything else is placed in relation. According to HERODOTUS, the main axis of the city was the east-west oriented dromos (the processional street) of the temple of Bubastis, lined with tall trees. The section in question reads:

> "*The temple is a square, each side measuring a furlong. A road, paved with stone, of about three furlongs in length leads to the entrance, running eastward through the market-place, towards the temple of Hermes; this road is about four hundred feet wide, and bordered by trees reaching to heaven. Such is the temple.*"[46]

Thus, HERODOTUS' account informs us that there was another important temple at Bubastis, a building he calls the "*Temple of Hermes*" (Ἑρμέω ἱερόν), at the eastern starting point of the dromos. Although this temple was of great significance for the city at that time, we know very little about it today. During his visit to Bubastis in the 1820s, JOHN GARDNER WILKINSON states that in order to find the temple he followed the apparently still visible track of the dromos for a distance of the three furlongs mentioned by HERODOTUS. At the end of this track, some 2250 feet long, he noted a handful of blocks of pink granite he thought to be the remains of the temple:

> "*This street, from the temple of Bubastis to that of Mercury, I found to measure 2250 feet, which exceeds the three stades of Herodotus; but the breadth, owing to the confused mass of fallen walls, could not be ascertained*".[47]

After a description of the badly preserved state of the temple of Bastet, he continues:

> "*The temple of Mercury is in a still more ruinous state: a few red granite blocks are all that remains of it, and one only presents a few imperfect hieroglyphics.*"[48]

Assuming that the granite blocks found by WILKINSON are indeed from the temple of Hermes, we can deduce from his account an approximate distance between the two temples of about 686 m. In HERODOTUS' own account, a furlong (stadion) is equivalent to 600 feet. However, neither the length of a stadion nor a foot was standardised in his time but varied: the '*Olympic*' stadion measured 176.40 m, the '*Babylonian-Persian*' stadion 196.10 m, and the '*Phoenician-Egyptian*' stadion 209.20 m. Since it is still disputed which one HERODOTUS used, and as it is also possible that he might even have used different stades, the length of the dromos can only be approximately determined.[49] Nevertheless, the information in WILKINSON'S work allows us to estimate that HERODOTUS referred to the '*Phoenician-Egyptian*' stadion of 209.20 m, which would result in a length of the dromos of 627.60 m. The difference to the 686 m given by WILKINSON can easily be explained by the fact that WILKINSON had found both temples in a very demolished state thus obscuring the start and end points of the dromos, despite his claims that he measured from one enclosure wall to the other.[50]

During his excavations at Bubastis from 1887-1889, EDOUARD NAVILLE also tried to locate the temple of Hermes, following the longitude given by HERODOTUS. It is clear that he was also able to recognise the course of the dromos at this time and stated the following:

> "*We hear from Herodotus that at a distance of three furlongs from the temple of Bast, at the end of a road which passed through the market-place, and which was lined by trees of an extraordinary height, was the temple of Hermes. The direction of the road is still traceable, although above its level there is an accumulation of several feet of earth. At the distance indicated by the Greek writer, the Tell ends, and we reach cultivated fields where, when I went there first, a few granite blocks were scattered. After long and difficult negotiations, I obtained from the owner, the sheikh of a neighbouring village, the permission to excavate in his field, with the condition that I should not carry away anything which I might discover. This excavation lasted a week. It brought to light a small heap of broken stones jumbled together, and which evidently were the remains of a building smaller than the Temple of Bast.*"[51]

NAVILLE discovered and published some blocks of pink granite showing reliefs and inscriptions dating to Osorkon I which, nevertheless, have attracted little attention in research to date, except for a long endowment of this king made to several temples and deities. That an account of this type was displayed in a temple of Bubastis once more underlines the high relevance of this city for the Libyan rulers. The best-preserved part of the account reads as follows[52]:

"[*Regnal year ... month] of the winter season, day 21. Beginning of the Neheh-eternity, receiving of the Djet-eternity [...]. [Mighty bull: Beloved of Ra, Atum has placed him on his throne to found the Two Lands; the Two Mistresses: He who makes the appearances great, rich in wonders; the Golden Horus: Victorious in strength, who repels the 'Nine-Bows', the ruler, who seizes all countries; the Dual King, [lord of crowns], lord of the Two Lands: (powerful of appearance, Ra, chosen by Ra)|; [the son of Ra: (Osorkon, beloved of Amun)|. [...] of the time of the kings of Lower Egypt because of the order of [his] majesty [...]. What [his majesty] has given [...]. Their forms are content in their places. (Regarding) all hearts: They are not against them (?) as in the years of rebellion since the time of the kings of Lower Egypt before. Never has there been the likeness of you before in this land. Each god endures on his throne, he unites with his sanctuary in joy. You will be introduced to [...] [his] majesty [...] what his majesty has given. Words spoken by his majesty: [...] their temples were built, their ḥnm-vessels of gold, silver and all precious stones were made numerous while his majesty was giving instructions for it in his form as first one of Heseret.*

List of the endowments made by the Dual King, lord of the Two Lands, [...] lord of the foreign countries: (powerful of appearance, Ra, chosen by Ra)|; [the son of Ra: (Osorkon, beloved of Amun)| [...] in regnal year 1 first month of the winter season, day 7 until regnal year 4, fourth month of the summer season, day 25, altogether: 3 years, 3 month and 16 days.

That what his majesty gave to the temple of his father, Ra-Horakhty: perfect hammered gold: 1 chapel for Atum-Khepri, the great one of Heliopolis. Perfect wrought gold: 1 Sphinx statue. Genuine Lapis lazuli: 10 Sphinx statues; a total of: perfect gold: 15345 deben, silver: 14150 deben, genuine lapis lazuli [...]. A total of perfect gold: braziers (?) 140 [+x] 4000 [+x]. Makes a total of deben: 100000.

Given in the presence of Ra-Horakhty-Atum, who begets his two children: 1 sḥn-vessel. Makes a total of perfect gold: 5010 deben, of silver: 30720 deben, of real lapislazuli: 1600 deben, of black copper: 5000 deben, 1 chapel. A total of 100000 deben.

Given in the presence of Hathor, lady of Hetepet in Hetepet: perfect gold, silver: 1 sḥn-vessel.

Given in the presence of Mut, who carries her sistrum: perfect gold, silver: 1 sḥn-vessel, hammered silver: 1 chapel.

Given in the presence of Herishef, the first of Heliopolis: perfect gold, silver: (1) sḥn-vessel.

Given in the presence of Thoth, the first of the house of the magistrate: perfect gold, silver: 1 sḥn-vessel.

Given in the presence of Bastet, the first of the house of the magistrate: perfect gold, silver: 1 sḥn-vessel.

Given in the presence of Thoth, in the midst of ḥw.t-ḥr: perfect gold, silver: [...].

That, what his majesty has given: [...] perfect gold [...] silver: 9000 deben, black copper 30000 deben, his revenues from the oases Bahariya and Kharga/Dakhla of wine, sweet wine, wine of Hamu and wine from Pelusium likewise, (and) to exempt his temple in accordance with the order to that effect.

That what his majesty gave to the temple of Ra and his ennead: silver: 3 fire basins on stands. Fine gold as sheet metal (?): 3. Silver: 3 ḏw-jars, 3 offering stands, 14 fire basins, 1 offering plate, 1 cartouche-vessel, 2 bowls, 10 ḫȝ-offering stands, 1 hin-jar, 1 washing basin, 1 wḏḥ-vessel. Perfect gold: 103 fire basins on stands, 1 wḏḥ-vessel, 2 baboon statues, 2 large arm-like censers, 6 ḫȝ-offering stands, 1 quadruple arm-like censer. Perfect gold: [...] lapislazuli: [...], sum: [...]. Genuine lapis lazuli: wȝ-vessel: 60 [+x] 332000 [+x] deben. Total: 594300 deben.

That what his majesty gave to the temple of Amun-Ra, the king of gods: his majesty created their arm-like censers after his appearance (?) from perfect gold and chased silver. Makes: perfect gold: 183 [+x] deben. Silver: 19000 [+x] deben. Black copper: [...] deben. Perfect Gold: [...] 1 arm-like censer. Perfect gold with (?) silver: [1] ḫȝ-offering stand, libation stone 40 [+x] [...].

Scholarly comments on this endowment list mostly focus on the considerable quantities of gold, silver, and copper units, the numerous objects made of precious metals and stones as well as their possible origin.[53] However, of greater interest here is the question to what deities and temples Osorkon I donated these riches and what links they might have had to Bubastis, where this inscription was displayed, and to its deities. In order to answer these questions, we need to take a closer look at the deities and sanctuaries, taking into consideration the fragmented parts of the list as well:

- Atum-Khepri, '*Great One of Heliopolis*'
- Ra-Horakhty-Atum
- Ra
- Hathor, '*Lady of Hetepet*'
- Mut
- Herishef, '*First of Heliopolis*'

- Thoth, '*First of the house of the magistrate*'
- Thoth, '*in the midst of ḥw.t-ḥr*'
- Bastet, '*First of the house of the magistrate*'
- Iusaas
- Horus
- Lady of the Two Lands
- Temple of Ra-Horakhty
- Temple of Ra and his ennead
- Temple of Amun-Ra, '*King of gods*'

As the compilation shows, the preserved list of endowments mentions deities who are either clearly located in Heliopolis or have a strong Heliopolitan aspect. Besides the obvious Atum-Khepri ('*Great One of Heliopolis*'), and the other solar deities, it is very interesting to note that Bastet and Thoth are designated as the '*First of the Magistrate*' (ḫntj ḥw.t-sr), with ḥw.t-sr being the name of the main temple of Heliopolis.[54] Likewise, female companions of the sun god and main deities of Heliopolis, Iusaas, and Hathor, the latter specified as '*Lady of Hetepet*', the name of the sanctuary of this goddess at Heliopolis,[55] appear on the list.

Thus, it becomes clear that the preserved part of the inscription is concerned with royal donations to the deities and temples of Heliopolis. There is, of course, the chance that other parts would have mentioned comparable endowments to other temples of Egypt as well but were simply not preserved or have yet to be discovered. At any rate, other sources attest to the close historical, geographical, and religious connection between Bubastis and Heliopolis as well. The main Heliopolitan solar god Atum was considered to be the spouse of Bastet, who usually bears the epithets '*Eye of Atum*', '*Eye of Ra*' and '*Privy to the secrets of Atum*' (see Chapter 1). It is fitting that the few remains of relief decoration on the blocks of the temple of Hermes discovered by Naville show Bastet with Atum and Shu and Tefnut in the sun-barque.[56]

In this context, another inscription from the same find spot has to be discussed. It is a very fragmented Bubastide temple monograph, presumably dating to the reign of Osorkon I. The text deals with the so-called '*Seven Arrows of Bastet*', each carrying a demonic name. In the text, the arrows are interlinked with seven mounds at Bubastis. Readable in the inscription are the names of the first arrow ("*Great of power*") and the fourth ("*His face is a flame, who scratches with his claw*"), as well as the names of the fifth mound ("*Divine child, south of its city*") and the seventh ("*Who creates the flame which endures*").

Such monographs, although attested from a later period, are well known for other female deities, i.e. Sekhmet, Neith, Wadjet, Nekhbet, and Mut, all of whom were goddesses considered to be dangerous and were thought to send disease, called "*annual plague*" (jȝd.t), amongst the human population of Egypt by shooting demonic arrows. Consequently, the annual plague, a hitherto unidentified infectious disease, or a number of different diseases, is also mentioned several times in the fragmented Bubastide version.[57] This suggests that the inscription might have been a royal hymn to Bastet (/Sekhmet) calling for protection against the disease-demons of the annual plague and was meant to appease the goddess who sent it. This kind of monograph was of course particularly effective in Bubastis, the main cult place of the goddess Bastet. There is even a possibility that this invocation was connected to the annual festival of Bastet.

In this specific context, it is also most intriguing to consider the dates given by the inscriptions from the temple of Hermes. These are: a month of the winter season, day 21 (number of the month lost) and the second month of the winter season day 10[+x][58]. The phrase *'winter season'* actually designates the Egyptian term *pr.t*, literally the *"coming forth"* or *"emergence"*, referring to the sprouting of new plants. This season spanned the months from November to March and followed the time of the inundation (*ȝḫ.t*). As CHRISTIAN LEITZ has shown, the time of the receding Nile flood, from the third month of inundation, day 20 until at least the first month of the winter season, day 19 or longer was the prime time of the outbreak of the annual plague. He argues that the disease could have been the bubonic plague, which was transferred by fleas of rodents, which would have shared spaces with humans that are more cramped at that time, making the spread of infection more likely.[59] More recent medical studies however attach far greater importance to transmission by human ectoparasites.[60] Due to the fact that the area around settlements were submerged for a considerable amount of time during the inundation, people were forced into more confined living spaces which would further the infection rate by human ectoparasites as well. It is therefore interesting to note that the time span in which the endowment to the temples and deities of Heliopolis (and other cities) was made, also starts in the first month of the winter season, but if there is a connection to the Bubastide monograph, remains unclear.

In the end, the inscriptions and depictions coming from the possible site of the temple of Hermes shed light on its real purpose since, in the time of the Libyan Kings, the temple would not have been dedicated to a Greek deity but an Egyptian one. To whom, then, was the so-called temple of Hermes at Bubastis dedicated? As described above, the dromos formed the connection between the temple of Bastet in the west and the temple of Hermes in the east. The inscriptions of the latter show that it was firmly integrated into the cult of the lioness goddess; here, Bastet appears as a member of a constellation of Heliopolitan deities. Her role as a dangerous, and equally protective and destructive goddess is clearly honoured by her portrayal as both a protector of the sun barque as well as the mistress of the dangerous demonic disease-carrying arrows. Yet, she might not have been the main goddess of that temple. HERODOTUS had attributed the temple to Hermes, which would be the Greek equivalent of the Egyptian god Thoth. NAVILLE had already argued that this could be explained by the mention of Thoth in the preserved part of the endowment list. Following HERODOTUS' interpretation, NAVILLE further claims the building was a *"treasury"* that had belonged to the god Thoth, and argued that HERODOTUS had seen statues of Thoth there, which are now destroyed.[61] HABACHI had also dwelled on the matter, referring to the relief depictions of Atum, concluding that the temple was dedicated to the Bubastide triad of Bastet, Atum and Mahes/Hor-Hekenu.[62]

At any rate, besides paying attention to the depictions and inscriptions, a hypothetical attribution of the temple has to include the local cult topography as well. The temple was without doubt an important part of the city, according to HERODOTUS even the starting point of a processional route that led from east to west, through the city centre to the main temple of Bubastis. The relief depictions show Bastet as a member of a Heliopolitan group of gods in the solar barque, perhaps the evening barque of Ra-Atum. The inscriptions with the list of endowments and the hymn to the dangerous lioness goddess in her capacity as protectress from the annual plague, a goddess whose festivals culminated in cultic barque rides on the sacred canals around her temple (see Chapter 8.1), could indicate that the temple of Hermes was in fact a stationary sanctuary of the barque of the goddess. This sanctuary could easily have been dedicated to Atum as well, thus entailing the cult of other Heliopolitan deities. In this capacity, the temple would have been the ideal place for Bastet to unite with her divine consort Atum and the crew of his evening barque.

Endnotes

[1] Bietak 2017, 62.

[2] Bietak 1975, 215-216; Bietak 2017, 63; Franzmeier 2022, 122.

[3] Poole 1999, 755; Leclère 2008, 393-403.

[4] pMoskau 120, Recto: Gardiner 1932, 61, 1,3-1,4; Schipper 2005, 4.

[5] Jansen-Winkeln 1992; Schneider 1996, 435; Kitchen 1986, 245.

[6] Jansen-Winkeln 1994, 2000, 2001; Römer 1994; Dodson 2012; Broekman 2018.

[7] Kitchen 1986; 248-361; Jansen-Winkeln 1994, 2000(a), 2001; Dodson 2012, 16-106.

[8] Waddell 1964, 158.

[9] Jansen-Winkeln 2001, 172; Sagrillo 2009.

[10] Poiron 2019.

[11] Lange 2008, 131-133.

[12] Jacquet-Gordon 1960, 12-23, Pl.VII-VIII; Jansen-Winkeln 2007, 108-109; Lange 2008, 138-141.

[13] Lange 2008, 134-135.

[14] Hd. II. 138.1-4; Wilson 2015, 208-209; Nesselrath 2017, 184.

[15] Lange-Athinodorou 2019(b), 549 n. 4.

[16] Spence 2007, 376. On the concept of the 'formal temple' see Kemp 2018, 145-158.

[17] Lange-Athinodorou 2019(a), 17-71.

[18] Barta 1978; Van Siclen 1991(a).

[19] Lange-Athinodorou 2019a.

[20] Hornung, Staehelin 2006, 41-46.

[21] Lange-Athinodorou 2019a, 80-290.

[22] Lange-Athinodorou 2019b.

[23] Lange-Athinodorou 2019a, 72-187.

[24] Lange-Athinodorou 2019a, 315-409.

[25] Cf. Arnold 1996. His hypothesis of the existence of an Old Kingdom temple of Bastet embellished with large columns of pink granite seems, however, unlikely.

[26] Tietze, Martin 1993, 64-92.

[27] Bernhauer 2005, 96-101.

[28] Habachi 1957, 46-55.

[29] Dodson 2016, 106.

[30] For instance Jansen-Winkeln 2017(a), 209-211.

[31] Ullmann 2002.

[32] Montet 1952; Stierlin, Ziegler 1987; Aston 2009, 39-61; Dodson 2016, 106-113.

[33] On the new numbering of the kings named Shoshenq see Broekman et al. 2009, 445.

[34] Sagrillo 2009; Dodson 2016, 110; Naunton 2018, 176.

[35] Fischer 1959; Aston 2009, 79-82; Dodson 2016, 113.

[36] Aston 2009, 64-65; Dodson 2016, 113.

[37] Lange-Athinodorou 2022.

[38] Lange 2010.

[39] Lange 2004; Lange 2010.

[40] Stadelmann 1971.

[41] Anthes 1959, Pl. 1.

[42] Montet 1952, 36-50.

[43] Spencer 2001, 18-19; Spencer 2003, 20-30.

[44] Spencer 2003, 20-23, 43-44; Broekman 2009, 72-74.

[45] Spencer 2003, 30; Broekman 2009, 77-80.

[46] Hist. II, 138.3-4: Wilson 2015, 209; Nesselrath 2017, 184.

[47] Wilkinson 1843, 428.

[48] Wilkinson 1843, 429-430.

[49] Westberg 1915, 338-339; Gulbekian 1987, 359-360.

[50] Wilkinson 1843, 428.

[51] Naville 1891, 60.

[52] For a commented translation of all fragments see: Lange-Athinodorou 2019(b).

[53] Naville 1891, 61; BAR IV, 362; Kitchen 1996, 303, §262.

[54] GDG IV, 127-128; Helck 1958, 112-114; Gomaà 1987, 185; Raue 1999, 157, 197, 346 no. 4.

[55] Raue 1999, 14, 35, 88, 94, 95, Abb. 10.

[56] Lange-Athinodorou 2019(b), 576-580.

[57] Lange-Athinodorou, 2019(b), 556-557.

[58] Lange-Athinodorou, 2019(b), 551-552.

[59] Leitz 1994, 134-135, 206-207, 213-215.

[60] Dean et al. 2018.

[61] Naville 1891, 60-61.

[62] Habachi 1957, 119-120.

8. The Festivals of the Feline Goddess: Bubastis from the Saite to the Ptolemaic Period

Following the Libyan kings of the Twenty-second and Twenty-third Dynasties, came the reign of Tefnakht and his son Bokchoris (*Bakenrene*), who formed the short-lived Twenty-fourth Dynasty (727-751 BCE). These rulers were of Libyan origin too, belonging to a dynasty of '*Great Chiefs of the Libu*', yet their rule saw a power shift from Tanis to another city. Their hometown was Sais, at that time the most important metropolis in the Western Delta with a history reaching back to around 5000 BCE, when it was home to a possible outbranch of the Merimde culture.[1] Already attested at the end of the reign of King Shoshenq V, Tefnakht undertook a military-based expansion of his territory, first to control the whole of the Western Delta and then to move on to Memphis. Further moves to the south beyond Herakleopolis were halted however when Tefnakht's forces clashed with a southern power that had developed at the end of the New Kingdom after the gradual retreat of Egypt from Egyptian-dominated territories in Nubia ('*Kush*' in Egyptian written sources).[2]

Over the course of the ninth century BCE, an indigenous ruling dynasty was able to establish themselves in Napata at Gebel Barkal south of the Fourth Cataract, which would eventually subjugate Egypt and form the Twenty-fifth Dynasty. The first known ruler of this new Kushitic dynasty was Alara (780-760 BCE). While his kingdom was still limited to Nubia, his son Kashta (760-747 BCE) however had greater ambitions. A fragment of a stela dedicated by Kashta to the temple of Khnum at Elephantine has him bearing the traditional titles of an Egyptian king, revealing his assertion to be the legitimate ruler of Egypt. Moreover, Kashta made advances as far north as Aswan in Upper Egypt. His military campaign was facilitated by the unstable political conditions caused by the political fragmentation of Egypt in the late Libyan period.[3]

Kashta's successor Piye (747-716 BCE), a son or relative of Kashta, continued the policy of his predecessor. The key sources on his reign are two stelae from the temple of Amun at Gebel Barkal inscribed with detailed accounts of his activities. According to the inscriptions, after expanding his realm far north of Thebes, Piye set out around his twenty-first regnal year to confront an alliance of Libyan rulers from the north, led by Tefnakht.[4] At that time, Tefnakht was laying siege to Herakleopolis near the entrance to the Fayum. Piye successfully defeated Tefnakht's troops at Herakleopolis after sacking Hermopolis, a city in Middle Egypt loyal to Tefnakht. He then captured Memphis, a major stronghold of Tefnakht, and proceeded to Athribis located in the southern part of the Central Delta. When confronted with the power of the Kushites, a group of Libyan rulers from cities in the Delta region – including King Osorkon (IV) who the stela tells us: "*is in Bubastis and the district of rꜣ-nfr*"[5] – submitted to Piye and pledged their allegiance to him.[6]

Osorkon IV is yet not attested at Bubastis. On the other hand, *rꜣ-nfr* ("*The perfect (river) mouth*") is a place name identified with the site of Tell Tebilla close to the ancient estuary of the Mendesian Nile branch in the Northeastern Delta.[7] Thus, the text clearly defines the region ruled by Osorkon IV in the Eastern Delta with Bubastis at its southern end and *rꜣ-nfr* at its northern end.

At any rate, Tefnakht himself remained in Sais but submitted to the Nubian king by letter, only to carry on with his mission once Piye had returned to Nubia, and succeeded in regaining control over the north of Egypt and Memphis. His son Bokchoris, however, had to face Shabaka (716-702 BCE), the brother of Piye, who reunited Egypt under Kushite rule once again and ended the Twenty-fourth Dynasty by allegedly capturing and killing his opponent.[8] The Kushite dynasty, though, saw the first invasion of the Assyrians, who had already been seeking to subdue Egypt for some time, as Egypt had supported small Palestinian city-states fighting against the Assyrians. This invasion marked the beginning of a prolonged and brutal conflict between the Kushites and the Assyrians.[9] King Assarhaddon's first attack in 673 BCE was fought off by King Taharqa (690-664 BCE), the son of Piye, but in a renewed attack in 671 BCE Assarhaddon was able to penetrate the Eastern Delta and proceed south as far as Memphis, forcing the Kushite ruler to retreat. The remaining Libyan-ruled chiefdoms of the Delta submitted to the Assyrians. Assarhaddon regarded them as allies against the Kushites and allowed them to act as governors, with Necho I (671-664 BCE) of Sais playing an important role in particular. Subsequently, however, Taharqa attempted to reconquer Egypt and was initially able to win back Memphis at which time Necho of Sais broke away from the Assyrians. In the winter of 667/66 BCE, however, Assarhaddon's son, Assurbanipal, came to Egypt and deported the disloyal Libyan rulers of the Delta to Nineveh, pushing Taharqa back to the south. Surprisingly, Necho succeeded in absolving himself of the accusations. The Assyrians did not only reinstall him as king of Sais but made Necho's son, Psamtik I (664-610 BCE), the ruler of Athribis, laying the foundation of a Saite royal line.[10]

After Taharqa's death and burial in the royal cemetery at Nuri in his Nubian homeland, the son of Shabaka, Tanutamun (664-656 BCE) ascended to the throne. Following the example of his predecessor Piye, Tanutamun had a stela erected in the temple of Amun at Gebel Barkal. It was inscribed with the account of a dream supposedly had by Tanutamun, in which the appearance of two snakes, representing the two uraei of the Double Crown of Egypt, caused his move to the north.[11] According to the stela, Tanutamun's military campaign ended victoriously with the recapturing of Egyptian cities. The rulers of the Delta once more submitted to Kushitic rule, while the disloyal Necho I was killed in the battle. Tanutamun's success, if it was real at all,[12] did not last long. The return of the Assyrian army under Assurbanipal in 663 BCE forced the Kushite king back to Thebes and after the city was defeated, he retreated back to Nubia. Thus, the country was divided once again: Upper Egypt was de facto ruled by the governor of Thebes, Montemhet, the famous official who had previously served under Taharqa. The other powerful force also residing at Thebes was the so-called 'God's Wife of Amun' (ḥm.t nṯr n jmn), who at that time was Shepenupet II, a sister of Taharqa. This office goes back to the beginning of the Eighteenth Dynasty and was always borne by women of the royal house. It was of greatest importance in the Twenty-fifth and Twenty-sixth Dynasties when the 'God's Wife of Amun' had royal privileges for performing the cult of the god and was granted titles that were otherwise reserved for the royal consorts.[13]

Despite the formal rule of the Assyrians over Egypt, the surviving son of Necho I, Psamtik I, residing at Sais, took on royal titles. Hiring Greek (Carian) mercenaries, he managed to subdue his competitors and reunited the Delta and the Nile Valley as far south as Thebes. In his ninth regnal year, possibly as part of a treaty with Tanutamun, he appointed his daughter Nitokris as 'God's Wife of Amun'. However, as the holder of the office was not supposed to marry and have children, they had to adopt their intended successor formally. Therefore, in order to assume the office legitimately, Nitokris had to be adopted by the current 'God's Wife *of Amun*', i.e., by the aforementioned Shepenupet II. At that time, Shepenupet II had already adopted Taharqa's daughter, her niece Amenirdis II. Thus, it is unclear if Amenirdis II ever assumed the office briefly between Shepenupet II and the appointment of Nitokris or if she was simply put aside after the death of Shepenupet II.[14]

Finally, Psamtik I had secured the rule of the Saite (Twenty-sixth) Dynasty throughout Egypt, which saw the restitution of large-scale building projects in the country. After fortifying the Western Delta against Libyan incursions, Psamtik I undertook military campaigns in the Levant. His successors Necho II (610-595 BCE) and Psamtik II (595-589 BCE) continued these politics, expanding into Syria and Palestine, and leading campaigns into Nubia up to the Third Cataract, all with the effective help of Greek mercenaries.[15] Military conflict with the Babylonian King Nebuchadnezzar arose in the reign of Psamtik II's son, Apries (589-570 BCE), who fought the Babylonians by land and by sea in Palestine and the Phoenician cities on the coast. However, a mutiny in his army following a defeat against the Greek city-state of Kyrene in Western Libya forced Apries into exile to Babylonia. His general, Amasis, assumed kingship, yet later buried Apries in the royal tombs of the Saite Dynasty in the temple of Neith at Sais.

To stabilize his reign, Amasis forged alliances with Kyrene as well as with other Greek city-states, such as Samos and Rhodos. He also granted important trading privileges to the main Greek settlement in Egypt, the city of Naukratis in the Western Delta. This led to the town's development into a major trading centre of the Mediterranean, and would earn Amasis his reputation as '*Philhellenos*'. Later in his reign, Egypt had to face the rising power of the burgeoning Persian empire, which defeated Babylon and the Phoenician and Greek city-states in Asia and the Levant. Soon after Amasis' death and the accession to the throne of his son, Psamtik III (526-525 BCE), the Persian king Cambyses attacked the northeastern border of Egypt at Pelusium, defeating the army of Psamtik III in 525 BCE. Psamtik III retreated to Memphis but could not hold the city.[16] According to Herodotus[17], he was captured and later, after a failed attempt to lead an uprising against the Persians, was forced to commit suicide.

The death of Psamtik III not only marks the end of the Twenty-sixth Dynasty but the end of the Egypt's sovereignty. For more than a century now, from Cambyses (525-522 BCE) to Darius II (424-404 BCE), Egypt was ruled by Persian kings in name (the Twenty-seventh Dynasty) and by their satraps in reality. However, resistance against the detested Persian overlords rose up again in Sais, the old capital in the Nile Delta, led by Amyrtaeus (404-399 BCE), a possible descendant of the vanished Twenty-sixth Dynasty. He retook Egypt, aided by the fact that after the death of Darius II in Persia, there were squabbles over the succession to the throne and a war between Persia and Sparta. At any rate, Amyrtaeus was destined to be the only king of the dynasty he founded (the Twenty-eighth), as other pretenders to the throne emerged during his reign, with Nepherites I (399-380 BCE) of Mendes eventually prevailing, possibly after having Amyrtaeus captured and killed.[18]

Nepherites I is the first in a dynasty of four kings (the Twenty-ninth Dynasty). They ruled from Mendes in the Northeastern Delta which, like Sais, was an important city that had already existed for around four millennia.[19] Hakoris I (393-380 BCE), Nepherites I's son, renewed Egypt's old alliance with the Greek city-states. The goal was to form a coalition against the Persian threat, which was still looming at the time. This move helped Egypt regain its position as a major power in the Mediterranean.[20] Despite their success, the claim of the Mendesian Dynasty, however, did not remain unchallenged. After a short reign of only four months, Hakoris' son Nepherites II (380 BCE), was deposed by Nectanebo I (*Nekhthorheb*, 380-363 BCE) from Sebennytos in the Central Delta, who in turn founded the Thirtieth Dynasty. In 373 BCE, he fought off a Persian attack which had pushed into the Eastern Delta and continued to support Egypt's allied Greek city-states in Asia as well as those of Athens and Sparta. His nephew, Nectanebo II (360-343 BCE), was the last king of this dynasty and the last indigenous pharaoh of Egypt. His widespread building activities in the Delta and throughout Egypt included the temple of Bastet in Bubastis (see below). However, in 343 BCE, the Persian army under Artaxerxes III (343-338 BCE) overran Egypt's fortresses and penetrated into the Eastern Delta.[21]

After Nectanebo II fled to Nubia, Egypt was once again occupied by the Persians. This changed when the Macedonian army led by Alexander III ('*The Great*') arrived in Egypt in 332 BCE following his successful campaigns against Persia in Asia. Alexander was crowned as pharaoh in Memphis and founded the city Alexandria on the Western Delta coast. Egypt had become part of Alexander's empire. Following the partition of Alexander's realm after his death in 332 BCE, his general and half-brother Ptolemaios I (306-283 BCE) was declared satrap of Egypt. Ptolemaios I was later crowned in Egypt and founded the Ptolemaic dynasty which lasted for 300 years until Cleopatra VII (51-30 BCE), his descendent, was defeated by the Roman Emperor Octavian in 30 BCE.[22]

8. 1 The temple of Bastet and its sacred landscape

It is in the time of the first Persian dominion of Egypt in around 450 BCE, when HERODOTUS seems to have visited Bubastis. His written accounts allow us an intriguing glimpse into the appearance of the temple of Bastet and its setting. HERODOTUS draws a lively picture of the temple as the central part of the city. He also writes about two canals surrounding the temple. These canals were clearly renowned features of the sacred dwelling of Bastet and an essential part of the temple's sacred landscape.

While the respective paragraph in Herodotus' work is cited in Chapter 7.2, it is worth repeating here the part that is essential for the following discussion:

> "*This is her temple: Except for the entrance, the rest is an island. The canals, which come from the Nile, are not joining one another, but each one extends to the entrance of the temple; one surrounds one side, the other the other side, and each one is 100 feet wide and shadowed by trees.*"[23]

To fully comprehend HERODOTUS' words, it is important to understand that the numerous waterways in the Nile Delta were the most prominent feature of the natural landscape. As a result, bodies of water that were linked to a temple, in the form of a stream, canal, lake, or pool, typically formed the main element of a sacred deltaic landscape. HERODOTUS wrote that two canals branching off the Pelusiac branch passed close by Bubastis to create the sacred waters of the temple of Bastet.

Texts of Egyptian origin also refer to these canals at Bubastis, calling them '*Henet*'(*ḥn.t*), a designation for various types of natural bodies of water, such as Nile branches, canals and lakes[24] or, more frequently, '*Isheru*' (*jšrw*, see below). An important source is Papyrus Brooklyn 47.218.84, a mythological compendium on the cities of the Delta from the reign of Psamtik I at the beginning of the Twenty-sixth Dynasty. Here we find two references to the canals of the temple of Bastet while the goddess herself is described as being on her staircase or throne podium (*ḥnd(w)*, see Chapter 6.1). The canals appear as part of the description of the location of the statue of the goddess on a podium:

> "*She is on the staircase of (the name): 'Throwing down the enemies'. A falcon tames her, two hippo deities surround her, a Henet-water is all around her, the length of which is ...7 (?) (cubits) (and) <the width> 42 (cubits).*"[25]

A relief of Bastet kneeling on a throne podium, with a falcon embracing her back and the depiction of hippo deities on the side of the podium can be found in the temple of Hathor at Dendera from the Ptolemaic Period, where it is depicted in the third eastern chapel of Osiris. There, she is referred to as "*Bastet, lady of Bubastis, first of the southern Bubastis, the mistress of life, who dwells in Dendera, the lady of joy, who dwells in Bubastis*".[26] Another paragraph describes the triumphal appearance of Bastet as the saviour of the eye of Horus from Seth in her sacred barque during her annual festival:

> "*And they row her in the Oryx antelope on the Isheru at the moment as she saved the Udjat-Eye from him.*"[27]

Intriguingly, this passage illuminates the existence of a local mythos of Bastet in which the goddess apparently had saved the eye of Horus after Seth had knocked it out during the epic battle of the two gods.

A stela from the cemetery of cats, the sacred animals of the goddess, bears a striking depiction of this event (see fig. 46). The image accurately depicts the description found on the papyrus. It shows the statue of the goddess seated in her shrine, on a barque whose stern is shaped like the head of an Oryx-antelope, which is the animal of Seth, representing the enemy she had vanquished. Zig-zag lines under the barque indicate the water of the *Isheru-canal* (see Chapter 8.3).

Another text from the second register on the eastern wall of the Ptolemaic enclosure of the temple of Horus at Edfu refers to the goddess Bastet of Bubastis as:

> "*Bastet, the Great One, lady of Bubastis (...) under (whose temple) the Nile flows*".[28]

It remains unclear how far back the sacred canals at Bubastis date. A relief block from the temple of Min at Koptos depicts Sesostris I in front of the Bastet with the caption "*Bastet, lady of the Isheru*". Yet, contrary to some scholarly beliefs the *Isheru* mentioned on the block are the sacred canals at Bubastis[29], it could easily refer to another temple of Bastet somewhere else. This term was not reserved for the sacred canals at Bubastis but was a general designation for horseshoe-shaped lakes or canals at temples of lioness goddesses who were believed to be of a strong protective yet dangerous character (see Chapter 1).[30] Due to their predatory nature, lionesses were feared as wild and fiery. Yet, as real-world observations of wildlife at watering holes could easily reveal, lion prides would rest there peacefully. Thus, canals or lakes close to temples of lioness goddesses were seen as a means of cooling the goddess's wild nature and therefore the ideal setting for their cult. Furthermore, there are

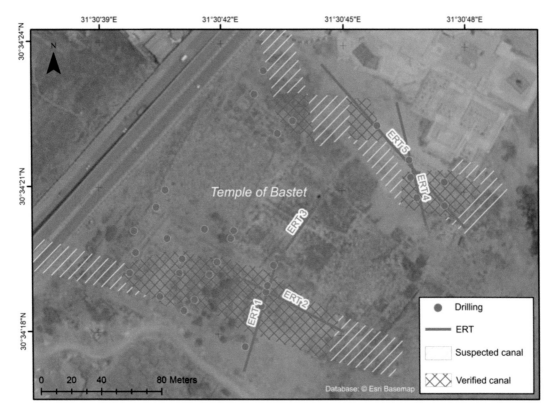

Fig. 44: *Course of the canals around the temple of Bastet, based on core drillings and ERT measurements. (MEISTER et al. 2021, Fig. 7)*

textual sources referring to sacred lakes or canals, i.e., for the temple of Wadjet at Buto, and the temple of Neith at Sais.[31]

An important part of the TELL BASTA PROJECT is the geoarchaeological survey, which has recently enabled us to prove the existence of the sacred *Isheru* of the temple of Bastet and to draw further conclusions regarding their location, shape and course. From 2018 to 2021, the combined geophysical analysis of DCR soundings and ERT measurements conducted by AMR ABD EL-RAOUF and core drillings and sediment analyses led by JULIA MEISTER revealed up to 5 m of thick loamy to clayey deposits that were deposited in a very low-velocity fluvial system, exactly as a lake or canal would appear in the geoarchaeological record.

These fine-grained deposits were detected around 50-60 m to the north and south of the temple where they were distributed in a basin-like shape representing a cross section of two canals, each around 30 m wide, exactly as Herodotus had described them. The integration of 2D ERT depth profiles helped to establish the ancient course of the canals over a length of 150 m. Over this distance, the canals ran parallel to the main east-west axis of the temple.[32]

These canals were the actual *Isheru* of the temple of Bastet, as described in the Egyptian texts and by HERODOTUS. Up to now, it is difficult to decide whether they were a natural feature of the landscape or artificially created. However, relocations of anthropogenic and fluvial sediment observed in the deepest parts of the canals indicate human activities, such as the cleaning out of the canal bed. Such measures were necessary as the low water flow in the canals was not strong enough to disperse fluvial sediments further which would lead to a gradual choking of these waterways. The evidence of human activities to maintain the canal flow matches the testimony of the religious texts, which reveal the important role they played in the cult of Bastet. Therefore, we can conclude that even if the canals were of natural origin, they were certainly seen as the core part of the sacred landscape of Bubastis and labour was invested to preserve their existence for as long as possible.

During the Fourth century BCE, the cult of Bastet was flourishing in the time of King Nectanebo II, who was the last pharaoh of Egypt. This is evident from the great building activities of Nectanebo II at Bubastis. In particular, he renewed the sanctuary of the temple located in the western part of the structure.[33] Even today, many blocks of pink and dark granite and basalt are still visible on the surface, covering an area of around 60 by 60 m to the immediate west of the hypostyle hall.

In 1888, NAVILLE was the first to document some inscriptions in the sanctuary. HABACHI followed in 1939 and 1943-1944, and attempted a reconstruction of the building, suggesting that the sanctuary consisted of several chambers with shrines for Bastet and the connected cults of other deities within them. Like NAVILLE before him, HABACHI observed thousands of fragments of quartzite, many of them carved with reliefs, and argued that they might be all that remained of an entire wall built of quartzite blocks close to the sanctuary's entrance.[34]

In her doctoral thesis, DANIELA ROSENOW investigated the sanctuary building in detail. In spite of the fragmentary state of the structure, she was able to reconstruct its main features: the sanctuary had a façade with a frieze of uraei in high relief and a corridor paved with basalt blocks that surrounded the core building made from pink granite with a ceiling decorated with stars, except for an open court in the centre. Rows of at least three rooms flanked the east and west of the temple's axis. As HABACHI had proposed, these rooms housed naoi for several deities including lioness goddesses closely connected to Bastet, such as Sekhmet, Shesemtet and Wadjit, as well as other divinities of Bubastis, such as Hor-Hekenu, Mihos and Khons-Horus in their role as sons of Bastet. There is also evidence for the existence of a shrine for the sacred barque of Bastet.[35]

A tripartite sanctuary in the western part of the building contained the cult statue of the goddess Bastet in her shrine, fragments of which were found by NAVILLE and are now in London and Cairo. The most recent reconstruction of the shrine by NEAL SPENCER shows that the shrine was fashioned from a single block of pink granite and measured almost 4 m in height. It had a pyramidal roof with a uraei-frieze in front and might have contained an inner shrine made of wood and adorned with glass inlays in which the actual golden cult image of Bastet once stood. The shrine was decorated with reliefs of superior quality, showing for example the kneeling King Nectanebo II offering a figure of Ma'at on the front of the pedestal. The side walls bear dedicatory inscriptions to Bastet as well as several registers containing long rows of deities. Among them are an enthroned lioness goddess, Ma'at, Mut, Apis, the Ogdoad from Hermopolis, Isis, Hathor and prominently Osiris in several forms. The decorative programme thus follows similar patterns found on other naoi of the Thirtieth Dynasty, the most famous example of which comes from Pi-Sopdu (Saft el-Henna), the main cult place of Shesemtet, only a few kilometres east of Bubastis, which also dates to the reign of Nectanebo II.[36]

A fragment of another shrine for Bastet, found reused in Cairo but probably from Bubastis as well and dating to the same period is most interesting as it holds a part of the above-

Fig. 45a: *Relief from the sanctuary of the temple showing the goddess Bastet with the epitheton "Lady of Bubastis, who creates the forms in the 'Field of the-god', privy to the secrets of Atum" on the back side of a frieze of uraei. (TELL BASTA PROJECT 2023)*

discussed (Chapter 7.4) monography dedicated to the seven arrows of Bastet. The preserved text deals with the fourth arrow, connected to the fourth mound of Bubastis:

> *"The fourth mound of Bubastis: '(The One) north of his city' is his name. The god inside him is: 'Horus, who is in his nomes'. The name of the genie of his land is: 'His face is a flame, he who scratches with his claw, the fourth arrow of Bastet".*[37]

8.2 Private statues at the temple of Bastet

During his cleaning work in the area of the temple's sanctuary, HABACHI discovered two private statues. The first was a limestone statue of a standing man, of which only the upper part was preserved. He sports the so-called *Khat*-wig, a kind of a kerchief holding the hair like a bag, and a kilt. Both shoulders are inscribed with cartouches of Psamtik I. An inscription on the belt gives his titles and filiation: *"The acquaintance of the king, his beloved, Horkhui, son of Panrui"*. The inscription on the dorsal pillar of the statue has the so-called 'Saite formula' which connects the statue of the owner with the local deity of the town[38], reading:

> *"The deity of the town of the jrj-p^c.t and h3tj-^{c}, the sealer of the king of Lower Egypt, the sole friend, beloved by his lord, Horkhui, vindicated, [is set behind him]. He is one equipped with a statue, his feet may not be hindered, his heart*

Fig. 45b: *Fragment of the upper part of a naos from the sanctuary of Nectanebo II. (TELL BASTA PROJECT 2022)*

may not be restrained. He may give for him that he strides [...].'[39]

The second statue found by HABACHI at the same locality is a fragment of a dark granite naophor, consisting of the naos containing the figure of the goddess Bastet in the shape of a lioness-headed standing woman in the traditional tight dress. The inscription on the dorsal pillar gives the titles of a high official whose name is lost:

"[...] the jrj-pꜥ.t and ḥꜣtj-ꜥ, the sealer of the king of Lower Egypt, the sole beloved friend, who follows the way of the lord of the Two Lands[40] *[...] of every good thing from you. May the king give slaughter (of offering animals) [...]."*

The inscription around the frames of the naos contains the usual offering formula addressed to Bastet and the deities of Bubastis:

"An offering that the king gives and Bastet, lady of Bubastis that she may give food and provisions and everything what the sky gives, the earth creates, and the inundation brings from its cavern for the Ka of the venerated one with Bastet [...]. An offering that the king gives and the gods of Bubastis that they may give provisions and all that comes forth on the altar at the third time of her offering ritual for the Ka of the venerated one, the jrj-pꜥ.t with the gods [...]."[41]

A number of private statues of the Saite Period from Bubastis are now to be found in several museums. Although their exact find spots are not documented, it seems reasonable to assume that they once stood in the temple of Bastet to partake in the offerings for the goddess, similar to the two aforementioned statues. Of all the statues now housed in collections all over the world[42], one is a naophor in the Brooklyn Museum. This naophor contains interesting inscriptions that provide information on the local cults and mythologies of Bubastis. It is made of highly polished black diorite and shows the headless statue of a kneeling man wearing a pleated kilt and holding a naos on his front. Standing within the naos is the figure of the goddess in a tight dress and with the head of a lioness. The object is inscribed on the frame and sides of the naos and the base of the statue with the above-mentioned '*Saite formula*', as well as the name, title and filiation of the statue's owner.[43] The inscription on the frame of the naos reads:

> "*An offering that the king gives and the gods who are in Bubastis for the sealer of the king of Lower Egypt, the sole friend, the priest of Bastet, Pawerem, made by Peftjauawybastet, possessor of reverence. An offering that the king gives and the gods who are in Bubastis for the sealer of the king of Lower Egypt, the sole friend, the priest of Bastet Pawerem, made by the lady of the house, Tanettawemet, justified.*"

On the left side of the base of the naos:

> "*His brother, his beloved one, priest of Bastet, priest of the mound: 'The One, who produces the flame', priest of Bastet, mistress of the breath of life, priest of Horus of Akhbit in Bubastis, priest of Mut, fourth priest of Horus, Harsiese, born of the lady of the house Tanettawemet.*"

The content of the second inscription shows that both Pawerem and his brother Harsiese held the priesthood of Bastet at Bubastis, which indicates that this office could run in families. Moreover, Harsiese also held the title of '*priest of the mound: The One, who produces the flame*'. This is most interesting because this mound appears in the temple monograph of the seven arrows of Bastet from the time of Osorkon I, inscribed on some blocks found at the presumed location of the so-called '*Temple of Hermes*' (see Chapter 7). As discussed above, each arrow is paired with the name of a mythical mound at Bubastis. '*The One, who produces the flame*' is an epithet of the goddess Bastet herself, and the mound of this name is the seventh, paired with the seventh arrow: '*Red bull, who creates chaos*'.[44]

It is uncertain what the mounds ($j\mathitbf{3}.t$) named in the text actually refer to. For example, topographical inscriptions in the temples of the Graeco-Roman Period list constituents of the religious topography of each nome, amongst them the '*divine mounds*' ($j\mathitbf{3}.t\ n\underline{t}r.t$). It has been suggested that they are a designation of the mythical necropolises of local deities. A connection to the seven mounds of Bubastis named in the temple monographs referring to the arrows of the dangerous goddesses of Bastet, is, however, uncertain.[45]

From the titles of Pawerem's brother Harsiese, we also learn that there was a cult of '*Horus of Akhbit*' at Bubastis. Akhbit ($\mathitbf{3}\underline{h}\ bjt$), which translates as the "*papyrus thicket of the bee*", appears in written sources since the time of the Pyramid Texts (ca. 2350 BCE).

Especially in mythological texts, Akhbit, the later Greek '*Chemmis*', is referred to as papyrus thicket near the Western Delta town of Buto. More precisely, it is the hiding place of the goddess Isis where she raised her infant son Horus. Isis was in hiding to prevent the god Seth, Horus' murderous uncle, from harming him, because Horus was the son of Osiris and the rightful successor to the throne of Egypt.[46] Geoarchaeological investigations over the last few decades have proved that from the Fifth to the Fourth millennium BCE, a large semi-marine lagoon did in fact exist just a few kilometres north of Buto.[47] This environment could be the Akhbit mentioned in early texts. Such a connection between the real palaeo-landscape of Buto and the mythos illuminates how impressive marshlands with forest-like papyrus thickets standing up to five metres high could have undergone a mythological interpretation which endured even after the original lagoon had diminished due to environmental changes.[48] At Bubastis however, the cult of Horus of Akhbit was certainly linked to the local mythos of Bastet as the saviour of Horus' eye from Seth. Moreover, a specific form of Horus, Horus-Hekenu, was worshipped as the son of Bastet in Bubastis, thus showing that Horus in his many manifestations was an essential member of the Bubastite constellation of divinities.

8.3 The festivals of Bastet in the context of a local Bubastite mythology

Herodotus, whose accounts have been most informative on the subject of the appearance of the temple and its canals was obviously also very intrigued by the cult of Bastet and her famous festivals. He gives a detailed description of how people from all over the country gathered for orgiastic feasts, drinking bouts and other debaucheries in honour of the goddess:

> "*When the people come to Bubastis, they do the following – as they journey by river, men and women together, a great number of each in every boat: Some of the women have rattles which they rattle, some men play flutes all the way, while the rest of the women, and the men, sing and clap their hands. Whenever they come near any other town they bring their boat near the bank and they do the following: some of the women do as I have said, while others shout mockery of the women of the town; others dance, and others stand up and lift their garment. This they do at any riverside town. However, when they have reached Bubastis, they make a festival with great sacrifices, and more wine is drunk from the grape wine at this feast than in the whole year. Altogether, men and women (except the children) assemble then to the number of seven hundred thousand, as the local people say.*"[49]

The earliest known attestation of the festival of Bastet is the biographical inscription of the *wab*-priest of Sekhmet at Bubastis, Iun-Ka, discussed in Chapter 6.1. He describes that King Amenhotep III performed offerings during this specific festival. On a stela from Abydos dedicated to Osiris, Ramses IV (1156-1150 BCE) states that he did not hunt lions at the time of the festival of Bastet.[50] Nevertheless, the festival of Bastet might easily be much older and it seems reasonable to assume that they date back to the time of the establishment of the cult of Bastet at Bubastis at least during the Old Kingdom.

As colourful as the above-cited description of Herodotus is, it lacks any information on the meaning and motifs of the festival. Fortunately, other textual sources and imagery provide us with deeper insights into the religious context. Scholars have generally argued that there was a close connection between the high fertility of cats and their peculiar behaviour during mating season. Based on this reasoning, festival participants sought to share in the goddess' fertility and protection, possibly inspired by cats' nurturing behaviour towards their young.

The available sources, however, focus on different themes: music, dance and intoxication as the means of expressing devotion and connecting with the divine sphere. These were considered to be especially pleasing to Egyptian goddesses, principally Hathor, but also Sekhmet, Bastet, Tefnut and Mut, all of whom could appear as lionesses, a guise closely associated with the sun god Ra.[51] As said above, accordingly, their epithets often refer to them as the '*Eye of Ra*' or '*Daughter of Ra*'. The so-called '*Myth of the Sun's Eye*'[52] tells the gripping story of the daughter of Ra, angered by her father, who takes the form of a large wild cat and goes to live far away from him in the deserts of Nubia. The sun god finally sends the god Thoth disguised as a baboon to appease her and escort her back to him. To placate the fiery goddess, the monkey plied her with alcohol and song.

The so-called '*Tell Basta Treasure*' contained luxurious vessels made from silver and gold. As was shown in Chapter 6.4, they were inscribed with toasts to their owners and were certainly used during the festival of Bastet within the courts of her temple and temples of associated goddesses. Scholars have also drawn attention to several vessels found outside of Egypt which may also be connected to the festival at Bubastis: A stone jar inscribed with a toast to the ka of a King Osorkon discovered in a Phoenician period tomb in Spain and a silver bowl of the same date from a cemetery at Agios Georgios at Cyprus, which shows people celebrating in boats with the figure of a sitting cat.[53]

The festival of Bastet at Bubastis, however, was deeply rooted in local mythology and was not just an occasion for drinking to please the goddess. This is evident in the above-mentioned paragraph of Papyrus Brooklyn 47.218, which reads in full:

> "*And they row her in the Oryx antelope on the Isheru at the moment as she saved the Udjat-Eye from him, when Seth created his form at the stealing of the Udjat-Eye in Mehet. He came to Bubastis with the things he had swallowed, (but) Horit saved the Udjat-Eye of her father.*"[54]

The paragraph describes the sacred canals around the temple as the location of the appearance of the triumphant Bastet, here named '*Horit*' because she acts as the daughter of Horus and victress over Seth. Horus and Seth, however, are two gods who were engaged in a mythical violent conflict over the kingship of Egypt. According to the Bubastite myth, after Seth had knocked out one of Horus' eyes (the so-called '*Udjat-Eye*'), Seth carried it to Bubastis where Bastet saved it and healed Horus. Afterwards, Bastet appeared in her barque on the *Isheru*-canals surrounding her temple in a triumphal ride. In the text, her barque is called "*Oryx-antelope*", denoting the antelope form of the stern of the ship, exactly as a depiction on the fragment of a stela from the cemetery of cats at Bubastis illustrates (see Chapter 8.4). This is a perfect reference to the god Seth, whose symbolic animals included the antelopes living in the *Sethic* refuge of the desert. The picture on the stela thus captures the humiliation and subjugation of Seth by Bastet in an intriguing way.

It is obvious that the festival of Bastet at Bubastis was essentially a celebratory repetition of the salvific moment of the goddess' victory over Horus' adversary Seth. The rowing of Bastet in her sacred barque on the canals surrounding her temple by priests and other cult personnel was a transition of the mythos into the real world of the participants. It was certainly the culmination of the rituals and celebrations duly accompanied by her followers in all expressions of joy, including wine, feasts and orgies.

Although celebrated in a local context, the mythos of Bastet represents the most important core aspects of an all-Egyptian salvation story where the goddess stands at the dramatic turning point of a narrative actually aimed at pharaonic legitimation. Several texts from the Ptolemaic temple at Edfu, where the connections between Bastet and the eyes of Horus are clearly expressed, prove that knowledge of Bastet's special role was also known elsewhere in Egypt. For example, the goddess is described as:

> *"The Great One in northern Bubastis, the lady of the two Udjat-Eyes, who illuminates the Two Lands."*[55]

Another inscription from the same temple pays even more specific attention to Bastet as the saviour of the eye of Horus and her triumphant appearance on the sacred canals at Bubastis. Under the heading *"To kill the Oryx antelope"*, a clear reference to Seth, it continues:

> *"The Udjat-Eye is safe, o Mighty One, lady of Bubastis, the thief of the Udjat-Eye does not exist anymore. Your majesty is rowed on the Isheru, while your enemy is under you as a ship."*[56]

8.4 The sacred cats of Bubastis and their cemetery

As mentioned in Chapter 1, the original appearance of Bastet was a lioness-headed female. Her depiction as a cat seems to be an invention of the New Kingdom. The numerous cat statues in bronze, stone and wood found in museums and collections today date mainly from the later First millennium BC. These figurines represent the change in religious concepts over time, whereby the dangerous lioness goddess is joined by her gentler cat version. The latter can still display dangerous and unpredictable traits, but embodies the gentle and caring side of the feline deity, which makes for a more accessible figure to humans.

The sacred cats of Bastet were apparently kept at the temple of the goddess and buried in their own necropolis. On this subject, HERODOTUS writes:

> *"The cats on their decease are taken to the city of Bubastis, where they are embalmed, after which they are buried in certain sacred repositories"*.[57]

In 1889, in the northwestern part of the ancient city, about 200 m northwest of the temple of Bastet, NAVILLE discovered a heavily robbed cat cemetery dating to the Late Period (see fig. 3). Its exact location is difficult to identify. However, a map published by EL-SAWI in 1979 shows an area of around 200 by 150 m west of the Coptic cemetery designated as *"Cemetery of Cats"*, most probably referring to NAVILLE's earlier works. In an area that is now completely overbuilt but still visible on earlier cartographic material,[58] NAVILLE excavated two large pits filled with the remains of the animals, which he described thus:

"The bones are heaped up in large subterraneous pits, the walls and bottoms of which are made of bricks or hardened clay. Near each pit is seen the furnace in which the bodies of the animals were burnt; its red or blackened bricks indicate clearly the action of the fire, which is confirmed by the circumstance that the bones often form a conglomerate with the ashes and charcoal. (...) Here and there among the bones have been thrown bronze cats or statuettes of Nefertum, which are but rarely intact; the feet are generally broken off. Some of the pits were very large; we emptied one containing over 720 cubic feet of bones. This gives an idea of the quantity of cats necessary for filling it."[59]

NAVILLE's observation indicates that the cats' bodies were burnt at some point, yet is unclear if this happened ante-mortem or post-mortem. As examples from other cat cemeteries, such as Saqqara, show, cats were not buried after they had succumbed to old age but were intentionally killed at a young age, mostly by blows to the head or strangling.[60]

Such archaeological discoveries present us with problems. Why was the sacred incorporation of Bastet cruelly killed and then buried in large numbers? How can we reconcile this historical reality with the picture painted by HERODOTUS on the sacredness of animals in Egypt[61] and other textual sources such as the above-mentioned '*Myth of the Sun's Eye*', which describes the temple cats as recipients of fish, poultry, beef and milk, of worship and devoted care? It is obvious that the so-called Egyptian animal cult is a very complex and multi-layered religious phenomenon that we are still far from fully comprehending. According to DIETER KESSLER, who has conducted extensive research on this topic, the killing of many animal species was part of a ritualistic practice aimed at rejuvenating the king and protecting him from danger. According to his hypothesis, the temple animals temporarily took on the role of gods in order to be able to act effectively. In the case of cats, which in pharaonic times were larger, stronger and only semi-domesticated animals compared to today's domestic cats, their physical appearance and dangerous and demonic aspects attributed to them ensured that these animals were regarded as having particularly potent apotropaic and protective powers.[62]

NAVILLE also sent some skeletons to the famous Berlin physician and anthropologist RUDOLF VIRCHOW for taxonomic studies. The latter found that the burnt animals were mostly of the species *Felis maniculata* (African wild cat). Surprisingly however, a considerable number of skulls could be attributed to Ichneumons (*Herpestes ichneumon*), a small, weasel-like predator who belongs to the large family of feline animals (*Feliforma*). Their presence can be explained by the fact that the creator god Atum, who enjoyed an important cult in Bubastis as the consort of Bastet, was believed to appear in the form of an Ichneumon in the same way as Bastet could manifest herself in the form of a cat.[63]

In 1970, EL-SAWI conducted excavations south of the Coptic cemetery and discovered further cat burials. Whether or not this was just an extension of the cat cemetery discovered by NAVILLE or an entirely separate resting place is difficult to determine. There were, however, different characteristics: the animals were interred in cylindrical jars laid out side by side in regular rows, unlike the brick-lined pit burials mentioned by NAVILLE.[64] One could believe that EL-SAWI was excavating a different cemetery entirely, but another possibility is that the discovered burials might simply date to different periods.

Both NAVILLE and EL-SAWI found a number of objects associated with the burials, such as bronze statuettes of cats and of the goddess Bastet, as well as amulets, ushabtis, and

Fig. 46: *Relief of the lower part of a stela from the cemetery of the cats, showing Bastet in her sacred barque with digitally superimposed line-drawing. (LANGE-ATHINODOROU 2021)*

jewellery, none of which are published in detail.[65] EL-SAWI's most interesting discovery is the above-mentioned part of a limestone stela showing a depiction of the statue of Bastet as a seated lioness-headed goddess in her sacred barque on the canals of the temple (see fig. 46).[66] The stela is believed to date to somewhere between the Twenty-second and Twenty-fifth Dynasties and is thus a vivid illustration of the mythos of Bastet as the saviour of the eye of Horus and her triumphant appearance at the *Isheru* of Bubastis as described in Papyrus Brooklyn 47.218 (see Chapter 8.1). A Late Period round-topped stela in the August Kestner Museum Hannover shows what the complete stela must have looked like. The lower register has exactly the same depiction of Bastet in her barque on the Isheru, while the upper register shows a king offering to a lioness goddess Bastet/Tefnut, her companion Shu, and her lion-headed son Mihos.[67]

8.5 A temple city: Bubastis in Ptolemaic and Roman times

While the rebuilding of the sanctuary of the temple in splendid quality and on a grander scale in the Thirtieth Dynasty shows that the cult of Bastet was of great importance then, there are few remains of the subsequent Ptolemaic Period to be found in the temple. However, to conclude from this that the cult had diminished would be wrong. The discovery of a decree of a priestly synod held in the reign of Ptolemaios III Euergetes (246-222 BCE) proves the cult of the feline goddess continued to flourish.

In March 2004, the mission of the University Potsdam discovered a fragment of a bilingual

Fig. 47: *General plan of excavated buildings in Area A. (LANGE-ATHINODOROU 2022, Fig. 2)*

stela of dark granite at the eastern side of the first court, very close to the entrance and in the immediate vicinity of the main axis of the temple. The piece was inscribed with 24 lines of a Demotic and 67 lines of a Greek inscription. The text is a copy of the so-called '*Decree of Canopus*', which is the record of an assembly of priests chiefly celebrating the king's achievements and ordering honours for the king's deceased daughter Arsinoe. The Bubastis stela is the third known copy of this decree. The others were found in 1861 at Tanis and at Kom el-Hisn in 1881. The text from Bubastis adds some new variations to the known text, but its real importance lies in the fact that the text clearly states that the decree is to be erected at the entrances of "*temples of the first, second and third order*", thus proving that at this time, the temple of Bastet was among the most important temples in Egypt.[68]

8.5.1 The Ptolemaic casemate buildings[69]

The temple of Bastet was, however, not an isolated building, but stood in the heart of the city, which must have flourished as well. In order to gain a clearer picture of the spatial and functional connection between city and temple, the TELL BASTA PROJECT initiated an excavation in the immediate environs of the temple in 2008. Apart from some clearance work by HABACHI in 1943 in a small area of 25 by 15 m east of the temple entrance, this area had never been investigated before. HABACHI discovered what he thought were the remains of a Roman temple: a building of fired bricks, a limestone slab pavement and a pedestal of limestone blocks with fragments of a pink granite column.[70]

HABACHI's short-term excavations provided a valuable starting point for our own research in the area. HERODOTUS describes how the temple of Bastet was connected to the city and the '*Temple of Hermes*' to the east via the processional route to the temple and main street of the city, known as the dromos (see Chapter 7.4). This description helped us to identify the area where temple and city once merged. Obviously, the dromos would have crossed in front of the temple entrance (Area A), making it a promising area for the excavations, which lasted until 2017.

In theory, Area A would have been well situated within the yet unidentified enclosure wall and would have included the first pylon. However, the recent geophysical reconstruction of the sacred canals situated only around 10 m from the temple building makes the existence of a massive enclosure wall doubtful. Furthermore, there are no traces of the pylon which was built either of stone or of mudbrick but must have been completely dismantled in antiquity.

We found that the pedestal discovered by HABACHI was aligned to the main axis of the temple of Bastet, indicating the location and main axis of the dromos of the temple (cf. fig. 47). The opening of the area in grid squares V/2-3, W/2-3 and U/2-3 showed the above-mentioned rectangular limestone slabs [101] at 4.57-5.23m/asl in an area of 17.60 x 12.53m. North and south of the pavement lie the remains of buildings (see below), while the pavement extends into the still unexcavated area to the south. A good archaeological comparison for a temple dromos exists at the Graeco-Roman site of Hermopolis Magna, referred to as the '*Dromos of Hermes*' in Greek papyri. As at Bubastis, it is the main street of the city and is likewise made of limestone slabs on a foundation of sand and gypsum.[71] Another limestone-paved dromos can be found to the south of the temple at Soknopaiou Nesos.[72]

The above-mentioned pedestal consists of six rectangular blocks of limestone, sitting on a base of five layers of fired bricks. The column of pink granite, once placed on top of the pedestal, was found in its vicinity. It was probably a so-called '*single column monument*' with a statue of an emperor or a votive on top. Such monuments were a typical element of open courts in Roman cities and temples.[73] Thus, it seems that in Roman times, the limestone slabs of the dromos were reused to pave an open court in front of the temple at Bubastis.

At the southern part of the open court (grids squares U/3–W/3) a vaulted water conduit built of fired bricks covered with white plaster [112] was discovered on 4.93–4.16 m/asl. Detailed investigation showed that at the time of the installation, the limestone slabs were

Fig. 48a-b: *Fragments of limestone reliefs from Area A. (TELL BASTA PROJECT 2013)*

partly cut but patched up later with lime mortar to preserve the appearance of the white pavement. The preserved part of the conduit measures 13.70 by 0.62 m with a depth of 1.10 m. Very intriguing was the discovery of a fragment of a tombstone with a Greek epitaph, saying: "*Lochion (?), free of suffering (?), fare well! (Died) 14 years of age*". It was used to

Fig. 49: *Vessels discovered in house unit 2 in Area A. (Reimann 2022, Fig. 7-8).*

Fig. 50: *Room paved with limestone slabs in house unit 10. (Tell Basta Project 2017)*

Fig. 51a-c: *Head of a statuette of limestone from the construction level in Area A IV, Phase Vc from the Late Period. (TELL BASTA PROJECT 2017)*

cover the top of the conduit. The palaeography of the inscription dates the tombstone to the early First century CE.[74] In order to reconstruct the chronology of the area, it is safe to assume that the tombstone was not new when it was used on the conduit, which was installed after the construction of the paved Roman court. The latter, on the other hand, made use of the original dromos, which dates back at least into the time of Herodotus (around 450 BCE).

No limestone slabs were preserved east of grid square W2 and the stratigraphy of the excavated grid squares in that area (Y/2 and Z/2) was heavily disturbed. Within a layer with mixed pottery dating from Ptolemaic to Late Roman times, we discovered two triad statues of the Ramesside Period, which had been dumped there in late antiquity. A level on 5.99-5.48 m/asl in grid square Y/2 contained a few limestone fragments with reliefs showing royal iconography, an uraeus with original colouring still preserved (see fig. 48a-b). These fragments were obviously once part of temple architecture, but it is impossible to say whether they come from the temple of Bastet or another structure nearby.

An east-west oriented trench (TS1, 8.70 by 3.85 m) in grid squares W/1 and X/1 revealed details about the stratigraphy of the dromos area: the upper levels consisted of several loamy sand layers with a few tumbled mud bricks, indicating that after the removal of the dromos pavement, this place laid open for some time. The associated pottery was a mixed assemblage of Ptolemaic, Roman, and Late Roman dates. Densely packed limestone chips, which were

Fig. 52a-b: *TB 4a Y/4. NS 4: Vase with applied relief decoration of Bes from an occupation level in Area A, Phase VI from the Late Period (TELL BASTA PROJECT 2012)*

used to level the area before rebuilding in Ptolemaic times, followed on level 4.72-4.50 m/ asl. It is from this level that the faience fragments with the cartouche of King Shoshenq Meriamun from the Twenty-second Dynasty were found (see Chapter 7.3). At 4.21 m/asl, two north-south oriented massive mud-brick walls (TS1-M1and TS1-M2) appeared, sitting on an older layer of domestic waste. The pottery of these levels dates mostly to the Late Dynastic Period (Twenty-seventh to Thirtieth Dynasties) with a few sherds from the Third Intermediate Period. At the deepest level at 2.42 m/asl we reached the original building ground as indicated by the appearance of Gezira sand.

To the north and south of the pavement, we discovered the remains of several buildings. These are older than the Roman open court and date into Ptolemaic times. Of the houses to the north of the dromos-axis, two house units (A/III.7, A/III.6, A/III.6a) were excavated. Their ground plan shows a sequence of rectangular, north-south oriented rooms with entrances in the south. Some of the rooms had a preserved pavement of fired bricks with lime mortar. Domestic architecture in Egypt was mostly built of unfired, sun-dried mud bricks. A fired brick and lime mortar pavement could thus point to a function of these structures as rooms for washing and bathing, as these materials were better equipped to deal with the destroying effects of water. The closeness of these rooms to the temple and the existence of a water conduit (albeit the latter apparently being of a younger date) indicates that they were structures for cultic cleansing used by people prior to entering the temple of Bastet. Another interesting fact revealed by our excavation was that the Ptolemaic houses built next to the dromos were in fact encroaching on to this main street, thus blocking the main connection between temple and city. The temple, however, was still flourishing, as the above-discussed Decree of Canopus proves. Therefore, we have to consider that at that time the main entrance to the temple was no longer in the east but somewhere else.

To the south of the dromos, five house units (AIV/ 1-5, 8-10, see fig. 47) were discovered, but given the limits of the excavation area, they could all only be partially exposed. The northernmost houses still stood up to relatively high levels. Their walls were eroded and had collapsed to form massive blocks of bricks obscuring the course of individual walls, making the reconstruction of their ground plan difficult. All buildings had a general north-south axis with a slight deviation to the northwest. In general, they show the same ground plan as the house units to the north. However, AIV/1 is the best-preserved structure of the whole area. It is a typical casemate foundation with its square (14.5 by 14.5 m) floor plan consisting of massive outside walls and small internal compartments filled with rubble. The same type of building exists at many other sites in the Nile Delta such as Tell el-Balamun[75], Tell el-Herr[76], Tell el-Dab'a[77], Naukratis[78] and Buto[79].

Casemate foundations were not restricted to one building type but widely spread. They are found in tower houses, generally fortified buildings and the so-called šnᶜ-wᶜb-buildings (lit.: "*the pure storehouse*") of the temple administration and economy. In addition, palaces and small temples show casemate foundations as well.[80] Given the fact that unit AIV/1 is located close to the temple, it could have been the foundations of a small peripheral temple or barque-station and might have been the origin of fragments of limestone reliefs discovered in the fill of the cellular structures (see fig. 48a-b).

As the pottery shows, the houses in Area A/IV date mainly to the Ptolemaic Period. In fact, room R28 in house unit 2, contained imported vessels of the early Ptolemaic Period (number 417) which may have fallen down from a room on a higher level or from a shelf.[81] The pottery also indicates that the structures further to the south (units 2 and 1) are slightly older and date to the end of the Late Period and the early Ptolemaic Period. The pottery and remains of painted wall plaster and mosaics (see fig. 53) found in the buildings show that these were houses of the elite class of Bubastis at that time.

In sum, Area A in front of the temple of Bastet was occupied for the more than a millennium. The history of this long usage reveals the continuing importance of the temple of Bastet as the centre of the city of Bubastis well into the Ptolemaic Period.

Fig. 53: *Fragment of a mosaic floor from house unit 2 (TELL BASTA PROJECT 2010).*

Phase	Action	Dating	Area
Phase I	Destruction of the dromos	After Fifth century AD	A/I, A/II
Phase II	Water conduit south of open court	Fourth/Fifth century AD	A/I
Phase IIIa	Column monument and paved open court; building of fired bricks with columns of shaped fired bricks and re-use of unit 10	Third to Fourth/Fifth century AD	A/I
Phase IIIb	Building activities: paving of open court re-using stone slabs of dromos (?)	First to Third century AD	A/I
Phase IVa (Level I in TS.2)	House units blocking the dromos	Later Ptolemaic Period (end of Second / beginning of First century BCE)	A/III
Phase IVb (Level II in TS.2)	House units north and south of the dromos; dromos mostly still in function	Ptolemaic Period (Third to Second century BCE)	A/IV
Phase Vc (Level III in TS.2)	Construction level of limestone chips	End of Late Period/Early Ptolemaic Period (Fourth to Third century BCE)	A/IV
Phase VI	Casemate building A/IV.1 (?)	Late Dynastic Period (Fourth century BCE)	A/IV

Phase VII (Level IV in TS.2)	Infill after levelling building directly south of the dromos	Persian Period (Fifth to Fourth century BCE), (probably the time of HERODOTUS' description of the city)	A/IV
Phase VIII (Level V in TS.2)	Building directly south of the dromos	Saite Period (Sixth to Fifth century BCE)	A/IV
Phase IX	Undetermined building activities	Third Intermediate to Saite Period (Twenty-second to Twenty-sixth Dynasties)	A/II

Table 3: *Periods of occupation and usage in Area A.*

Fig. 54: *A Ramesside triad statue, depicting the king between Ptah to his right and Hathor to his left as disovered in grid square Y/2. (TELL BASTA PROJECT 2013)*

Fig. 55a: *Limestone pavement and conduit in Area A, grid square W/2. View to the south. (TELL BASTA PROJECT 2014)*

Fig. 55b: *Preserved part of the conduit in Area A, grid square W/2. View to the east. (TELL BASTA PROJECT 2015)*

Endnotes

[1] Wilson et al. 2014.

[2] Kitchen 1986, 369-377.

[3] Leclant 1963; Kitchen 1986, 151; Naunton 2010, 124-125; Dodson 2012, 146-149.

[4] Kitchen 1986, 151-152, 369-371.

[5] Cairo JE 48862, line 19: Grimal 1981, Pl. VI.

[6] Dodson 2012, 146-148.

[7] Bietak 1975, 143; Coutellier, Stanley 1987, 268-271, Fig. 7; Mumford 2013, 38, 39, Fig. 1.

[8] Kitchen 1986, 153-154, 378-383; Dodson 2012, 153-154.

[9] Onasch 1994.

[10] Kitchen 1986, 161-172, 387-393; Naunton 2010, 126-127; Dodson 2012, 161-168; Karlsson 2022.

[11] Grimal 1981b; Dodson 2012, 169-170.

[12] Jansen-Winkeln 2017(b), 37.

[13] Koch 2012; Dodson 2012, 169-172.

[14] Caminos 1964; Dodson 2012, 170-172, 175-176.

[15] Dodson 2012, 176-177.

[16] Spalinger 1977; Leahy 1988; Dodson 2012, 177-180; Wilson 2016.

[17] Hd. III.15.1: Wilson, 2015, 237-238; Nesselrath, 2017, 213-214.

[18] Wojciechowska 2016, 22-29.

[19] Redford 2010.

[20] Redford 2004; Wojciechowska 2016, 29-38.

[21] Dodson 2012,180; Wojciechowska 2016, 39-72.

[22] Hölbl 2004; Wojciechowska 2016, 83-07.

[23] Hd. II. 138.1-4: Wilson 2015, 208-209; Nesselrath 2017, 184.

[24] Yoyotte, 1962, 88.4; Geßler-Löhr, 1983, 407.1348; Meeks 2006, 100-101.

[25] pBrooklyn 47.218.84; IX.4: Meeks 2006, 20.

[26] Cauville 1997, 201, pl. 97; Leitz 2017, 567, Abb. 10.

[27] pBrooklyn 47.218.84, IX.7-8: Meeks, 2006, 20.

[28] Chassinat 1932, 263.18-264.2; Kurth 2004, 495.

[29] Sauneron 1964, 52.3; Yoyotte 1962, 103-104.

[30] Sauneron, 1964, 50-57; Geßler-Löhr 1983, 47, 401.

[31] Montet 1966; Geßler-Löhr 1983, 233-240, 403-404, 437-438; Wilson 2006, 256-257; Wilson 2019, 5, 17; Leclère 2008, 442-443; Tillier 2010.

[32] Lange-Athinodorou et al. 2019; Meister et al. 2021.

[33] Perdu 2020.

[34] Naville 1891, 56-59; Habachi 1957, 71-92.

[35] Rosenow 2008(a-b).

[36] Spencer 2006.

[37] Rondot 1989, Lange-Athinodorou 2019(b), 555-559.

[38] Jansen-Winkeln 2000(b).

[39] Cairo TN 22/10/48/14: Habachi 1957, 94; Jansen-Winkeln 2014, 59.108.

[40] Vittmann 2012, 286-287.

[41] Cairo JE 88636: Habachi 1957, 95.

[42] Jansen-Winkeln 2014, 59-60, 305, 848-851.

[43] Brooklyn Museum 3736E: O'Rourke 1989; Jansen-Winkeln 2000(b); Jansen-Winkeln 2014, 850-851.

[44] Lange-Athinodorou 2019(b), 557-560.

[45] Waitkus 2010, 152.

[46] Gardiner 1944, 53-58.

[47] Wunderlich 1989, 93-94, 106-110, 127; Wunderlich, Ginau 2014/2015, 494; Ginau et al. 2019.

[48] Lange-Athinodorou 2021.

[49] Hd. II, 60: Wilson 2015, 162; Nesselrath 2015, 144-145.

[50] Cairo JdE 48831: Mariette 1880, Pl. 55; KRI VI, 20-25.

[51] Liliquist 2012, 20-21.

[52] Preserved in a demotic manuscript of the Second century AD: Spiegelberg 1917.

[53] Morenz 2006.

[54] pBrooklyn 47.218.84, IX.7-8: Meeks 2006, 20.

[55] Chassinat 1932, Tab.3d.XXX, 163,10-11.

[56] Chassinat 1932, Tab.2g.IX, 263,10-13.

[57] Hd. II. 67.1: Wilson 2015, 166; Nesselrath 2017, 148.

[58] Lange et al. 2016, 388 Fig. 3.

[59] Naville 1891, 52.

[60] Zivie, Lichtenberg 2005, 117-118.

[61] Hd. II. 65-67: Wilson 2015, 164-170; Nesselrath 2017, 147-148.

[62] Kessler 1989, 150-152; Kessler 1991.

[63] Naville 1891, 52.

[64] El-Sawi 1977, 129.

[65] Naville 1891, 52; El-Sawi 1977, 129.

[66] El-Sawi 1977, 129.

[67] Hannover 1935.200.142: Schorsch 2015, 574-575.

[68] Lange 2005.

[69] For the detailed report see Lange-Athinodorou 2022.

[70] Habachi 1957, 93-94.

[71] Spencer 1989, 34-35, 74-75.

[72] Davoli 2010, 57 Fig. 1, 61 Fig. 4, 63-67; Capasso, Davoli 2012, 83-109; cf. also Rondot 2004, 145, 202; Lehmann 2020, 47, 376.

[73] Jordan-Ruwe 1995, 124-202.

[74] With many thanks to GREGOR STAAB (University of Cologne) for translation and dating.

[75] Spencer 1996, 51-59, Pl. 1, Pl. 6, Pl. 26-32; Spencer 1999, 295.

[76] Marchi 2014.

[77] Lehmann 2019.

[78] Thomas, Villing 2013, 83, 97-99.

[79] Marouard 2015, 106-113.

[80] Traunecker 1987, 147-62; Spencer 1999, 296; Lehmann 2020, 67-70

[81] Reimann 2022.

Abbreviations

BAR: Breasted J. H., *The twentieth to the twenty-sixth dynasties. Ancient records of Egypt: historical documents from the earliest times to the Persian conquest IV*, 1906, Chicago; London; Leipzig: University of Chicago Press; Luzac; Otto Harrassowitz.

GDG: Gauthier, H., *Dictionnaire des noms géographiques contenus dans les textes hiéroglyphiques Tome 1-7.* Le Caire: Société Royale de Géographie d'Égypte 1925-1931.

PM IV: Porter, B., R. L. B. Moss, *Topographical bibliography of ancient Egyptian hieroglyphic texts, reliefs, and paintings IV: Lower and Middle Egypt (Delta and Cairo to Asyût).* Oxford: Clarendon 1934.

RITA II: Kitchen, K. A., *Ramesside inscriptions, translated & annotated: translations, volume II. Ramesses II, royal inscriptions.* Oxford; Cambridge, MA: Blackwell 1996.

RITA VI: Kitchen, K. A., *Ramesside inscriptions, translated & annotated: translations, volume VI. Ramesses IV to XI, & contemporaries.* Malden, MA; Oxford: Wiley-Blackwell 2012.

Urk. I: Sethe, K., *Urkunden des Alten Reichs [I,1-308].* Urkunden des Ägyptischen Altertums I (1-4 [= Band 1]). Leipzig: J. C. Hinrichs 1932-1933.

Urk. IV, 1443: Helck, W.. *Urkunden der 18. Dynastie: biographische Inschriften von Zeitgenossen Thutmosis' III. und Amenophis' II. [IV,1369-1539].* Urkunden des Ägyptischen Altertums IV (18). Berlin: Akademie-Verlag 1956.

Urk. IV, 1840: Helck, W., *Urkunden der 18. Dynastie: Inschriften von Zeitgenossen Amenophis' III. [IV, 1776-1954]*, Berlin: Akademie-Verlag 1958.

Bibliography

Adams, M. J., "An interim report on the Naqada III - First Intermediate Period stratification at Mendes 1999-2005", in: D. Redford (ed.), *Delta reports (research in Lower Egypt), vol. I.* Oxford: Oxbow 2009, 121-206.

Adams, M. J., "The Naqada III-First Intermediate Period stratification", in: D. Redford, S. Redford (eds.), *Excavations at Mendes, 2: The dromos and temple area.* Leiden; Boston: Brill 2020, 48-72.

Adams, M. J., *The Early Dynastic through Old Kingdom stratification at Tell Er-Rub'a, Mendes.* (PhD dissertation: The Pennsylvania State University) 2007.

Alexanian N., W. Bebermeier, D. Blaschta, "Untersuchungen am unteren Aufweg der Knickpyramide in Dahschur", *Mitteilungen des Deutschen Archäologischen Instituts, Abteilung Kairo*, 68, 2012, 1-30.

Alexanian, N., *Die provinziellen Mastabagräber und Friedhöfe im Alten Reich.* (PhD dissertation: Universität Heidelberg) 2016.

Allen, J. P., D. T. Mininberg (eds.) *The Art of Medicine in Ancient Egypt.* New York: The Metropolitan Museum of Art 2005.

Andres, W., J. Wunderlich, "Late Pleistocene and Holocene Evolution of the Eastern Nile Delta and Comparisons with the Western Delta", in: H. Brückner; U. Radtke (ed.), *Von der Nordsee bis zum Indischen Ozean. Ergebnisse der 8. Jahrestagung des Arbeitskreises „Geographie der Meere und Küsten, 13.-15. Juni 1990, Düsseldorf.* Erdkundliches Wissen 105, Stuttgart 1991, 121-130.

Andres, W., J. Wunderlich, "Environmental Conditions for Early Settlement at Minshat Abu Omar, Eastern Nile Delta, Egypt", in: E. C. M. van den Brink (ed.), *The Nile delta in transition; 4th.-3rd. millennium BC*, Tel Aviv 1992, 157-166.

Anthes, R., *Mit Rahineh 1955.* Museum Monographs, Philadelphia: The University Museum, University of Pennsylvania 1959.

Anthes, R., *Die Felseninschriften von Hatnub nach den Aufnahmen Georg Möllers.* Untersuchungen zur Geschichte und Altertumskunde Aegyptens 9 (Nachdr. d. Ausg. Leipzig 1928), Hildesheim: Olms 1964.

Arbouille, D., J. D. Stanley. "Late Quaternary evolution of the Burullus lagoon region, north-central Nile delta, Egypt", *Marine Geology* 99 (1-2), 1991, 45-66.

Arnold, D., "Amenemhat I and the early twelfth dynasty at Thebes", *Metropolitan Museum Journal* 26, 1991, 5-48.

Arnold, D., "Hypostyle halls of the Old and Middle Kingdom?", in: P. Der Manuelian, (ed.), *Studies in honor of William Kelly Simpson 1*. Boston: Dept. of Ancient Egyptian, Nubian and Near Eastern Art, Museum of Fine Arts 1996, 39-54.

Arnold, D., *Lexikon der ägyptischen Baukunst*. Zürich: Artemis & Winkler 1994.

Arnold, D., P. Jánosi, "The move to the north: establishing a new capital", in: A. Oppenheim, D. Arnold, D. Arnold, K. Yamamoto (eds.), *Ancient Egypt transformed: the Middle Kingdom*. New Haven, London: Yale University Press 2015, 54-57.

Ashmawy A. A., "Tell Basta before the Old Kingdom: a newly discovered cemetery from the Early Dynastic settlement", *Egyptian Archaeology* 58, 2021, 18-20.

Ashmawy A. A., "Tell Basta during the Second Intermediate Period", *Ägypten und Levante* 26, 2016, 145-156.

Aston, D. A., *Burial assemblages of dynasty 21 - 25: chronology - typology – developments*. Contributions to the Chronology of the Eastern Mediterranean 21; Österreichische Akademie der Wissenschaften, Denkschriften der Gesamtakademie 54, Wien: Verlag der Österreichischen Akademie der Wissenschaften 2009.

Aston, D. A., M. Bietak. *Tell el-Dab'a VIII: the classification and chronology of Tell el-Yahudiya ware*. Untersuchungen der Zweigstelle Kairo des Österreichischen Archäologischen Institutes 12; Österreichische Akademie der Wissenschaften, Denkschriften der Gesamtakademie 66, Wien: Verlag der Österreichischen Akademie der Wissenschaften 2012.

Auenmüller, J. 2021, "The Ramesside vizier Iuty from Bubastis", *Ägypten und Levante* 31, 2021, 15-43.

Awady, T. el-, *Abusir XVI: Sahure - the pyramid causeway: history and decoration program in the Old Kingdom*. Excavations of the Czech Institute of Egyptology, Prague; Czech Institute of Egyptology, Faculty of Arts: Charles University in Prague 2009.

Bakr, M., "New excavations of Zagazig University", in: Anonymous (ed.), *L'Égyptologie en 1979: axes prioritaires de recherches 1*, Paris: Éditions du Centre national de la Recherche scientifique 1982, 153-167.

Bakr, M. I., "The Old Kingdom at Bubastis: excavations since 1978: Outline", in: A. Nibbi (ed.), *Proceedings of colloquium "The archaeology, geography and history of the Egyptian Delta in pharaonic times": Wadham College, 29-31 August, 1988, Oxford*. Oxford: DE Publications 1989, 29-52.

Bakr, M. I., H. Brandl, F. Kalloniatis (eds.), *Egyptian antiquities: from Kufur Nigm and Bubastis*. Museums in the Nile Delta 1, Berlin: Opaion 2010.

Bakr, M. I., H. Brandl, F. Kalloniatis (eds.), *Egyptian antiquities: from the eastern Nile Delta*. Museums in the Nile Delta 2, Berlin: Opaion 2014.

Bakr, M. I., *Tell Basta I: Tombs and burial customs at Bubastis. The area of the so-called Western Cemetery*. Cairo: E.A.O. Press 1992.

Bakr, M. I.; E. Lange, "Die Nekropolen des Alten Reiches in Bubastis", in: F. Feder, G. Sperveslage, F. Steinborn (eds), *Ägypten begreifen: Erika Endesfelder in memoriam*. London: Golden House, 2017, 31-48.

Bárta, M., "In mud forgotten: Old Kingdom Palaeo ecological evidence from Abusir", *Studia quaternaria* 30.2, 2013, 75-82.

Bárta, M., *Analyzing collapse: the rise and fall of the Old Kingdom*. The AUC History of Ancient Egypt 2, Cairo; New York: American University in Cairo Press 2019.

Barta, W., "Die Sedfestdarstellung Osorkons II. im Tempel von Bubastis", *Studien zur Altägyptischen Kultur* 6, 1978, 25-42.

Baud, M., "The Old Kingdom", in: A. B. Lloyd (ed.), *A companion to ancient Egypt 1*, Chichester; Malden, MA: Wiley-Blackwell 2010, 63-80.

Baud, M., "The relative chronology of Dynasties 6 and 8", in: E. Hornung, R. Krauss, D. A. Warburton (eds.), *Ancient Egyptian Chronology*. Handbook of Oriental Studies, section 1: The Near and

Middle East 83, Leiden; Boston: Brill 2006, 144-158.

Baud, M., V. Dobrev, "De nouvelles annales de l'Ancien Empire égyptien: une "Pierre de Palerme" pour la VIe dynastie", *Bulletin de l'Institut Français d'Archéologie Orientale* 95, 1995, 23-92.

Bell, B., "The dark ages in ancient history, I: the first dark age in Egypt", *American Journal of Archaeology* 75 (1), 1971, 1-26.

Ben-Tor, D., *Scarabs, chronology, and interconnections: Egypt and Palestine in the Second Intermediate Period*. Orbis Biblicus et Orientalis, Series Archaeologica 27, Fribourg: Göttingen: Academic Press; Vandenhoeck & Ruprecht 2007.

Bernhauer, E., *Hathorsäulen und Hathorpfeiler: altägyptische Architekturelemente vom Neuen Reich bis zur Spätzeit*. Philippika 8, Wiesbaden: Harrassowitz 2005.

Bernhauer, E., *Innovationen in der Privatplastik: die 18. Dynastie und ihre Entwicklung*. Philippika 27, Wiesbaden: Harrassowitz 2010.

Bierbrier, M. L., W. R. Dawson, E. P. Uphill, *Who was who in Egyptology*, 3rd revised ed. London: The Egypt Exploration Society 1995.

Bietak, M., "Egypt and the Levant", in: T. Wilkinson (ed.), *The Egyptian world*. London; New York: Routledge 2007, 417-448.

Bietak, M., "Harbours and coastal military bases in Egypt in the second millennium B.C.: Avaris, Peru-nefer, Pi-Ramesse", in: H. Willems, J.-M. Dahms (eds.), *The Nile: natural and cultural landscape in Egypt*. Bielefeld: transcript 2017, 53-70.

Bietak, M., "Houses, palaces and development of social structure in Avaris" in: M. Bietak, E. Czerny, I. Forstner-Müller (eds.), *Cities and urbanism in ancient Egypt: papers from a workshop in November 2006 at the Austrian Academy of Sciences*. Wien: Verlag der Österreichischen Akademie der Wissenschaften 2010, 11-68.

Bietak, M., "Nord und Süd - königlich und profan: Neues zum Palast des Mittleren Reiches von Bubastis", *Mitteilungen des Deutschen Archäologischen Instituts, Abteilung Kairo* 70-71, 2014-2015, 49-57.

Bietak, M., "Der Friedhof in einem Palastgarten aus der Zeit des späten Mittleren Reiches und andere Forschungsergebnisse aus dem östlichen Nildelta (Tell el-Dabʻa 1984-1987)" *Ägypten und Levante* 2, 1991, 47-109.

Bietak, M., "Zum Königreich des ʿḥ-zḥ-Rʿ Neḥesi", *Studien zur Altägyptischen Kultur* 11, 1984, 59-75.

Bietak, M., E. Lange, "Tell Basta: the palace of the Middle Kingdom", *Egyptian Archaeology* 44, 2014, 4-7.

Bietak, M., E. Strouhal, „Die Todesumstände des Pharaos Seqenenreʿ (17. Dynastie)", *Annalen des Naturhistorischen Museums in Wien* 78, 1974, 29-52.

Bietak, M., I. Forstner-Müller, "Der Hyksos-Palast bei Tell el-Dabʻa: zweite und dritte Grabungskampagne (Frühling 2008 und Frühling 2009). Mit einem Beitrag von Frans van Koppen und Karen Radner", *Ägypten und Levante* 19, 2009, 91-119.

Bietak, M., J. Dorner, "Der Tempel und die Siedlung des Mittleren Reiches bei ʻEzbet Ruschdi: Grabungsvorbericht 1996", *Ägypten und Levante* 8, 1998, 9-49.

Bietak, M., J. Dorner, I, Hein, P. Jánosi, "Neue Grabungsergebnisse aus Tell el-Dabʻa und ʻEzbet Helmi im östlichen Nildelta (1989-1991)", *Ägypten und Levante* 4, 1994, 9-80.

Bietak, M., N. Math, V. Müller, "Report on the excavations of a Hyksos palace at Tell el-Dabʻa/Avaris (23rd August - 15th November 2011)", *Ägypten und Levante* 22-23, 2012-2013, 17-53.

Bietak, M., *Tell el-Dabʻa II: der Fundort im Rahmen einer archäologisch-geographischen Untersuchung über das ägyptische Ostdelta*. Mit einem geodätischen Beitrag von Josef Dorner und Heinz König. Untersuchungen der Zweigstelle Kairo des Österreichischen Archäologischen Institutes 1; Österreichische Akademie der Wissenschaften, Denkschriften der Gesamtakademie 4, Wien: Verlag der Österreichischen Akademie der Wissenschaften 1975.

Bietak, M., *Avaris, the capital of the Hyksos: recent excavations at Tell el-Dabʻa*. London: British Museum Press 1996.

Blackman, A. M., *The story of King Kheops and the magicians: transcribed from Papyrus Westcar (Berlin Papyrus 3033). Edited by W. V. Davies*. Reading: J. V. Books 1988.

Borchardt, L., *Das Grabdenkmal des Königs Nefer-ir-ke-Re*. Ausgrabungen der Deutschen Orient-

Gesellschaft in Abusir 1902-1908 5; Wissenschaftliche Veröffentlichungen der Deutschen Orient-Gesellschaft 11, Leipzig: J.C. Hinrichs'sche Buchhandlung 1909.

Broekman, G. P. F., "Falcon-headed coffins and cartonnages", *Journal of Egyptian Archaeology* 95, 2009, 67-81.

Broekman, G. P. F., "The 21st Dynasty: the theocracy of Amun, and the position of Theban priestly families", in: L. Weiss (ed.), *The coffins of the priests of Amun: Egyptian coffins from the 21st dynasty in the collection of the National Museum of Antiquities in Leiden*. Leiden: Sidestone; Rijksmuseum van Oudheden 2018, 13-19.

Broekman, G. P. F., R. J. Demarée, O. E. Kaper, "Summary of the discussion sessions", in: G. P. F. Broekman, R. J. Demarée, O. E. Kaper (eds.), *The Libyan period in Egypt: historical and cultural studies into the 21st-24th Dynasties. Proceedings of a conference at Leiden University, 25-27 October 2007*, Leiden, Leuven: Nederlands Instituut voor het Nabije Oosten, Peeters 2009, 441-447.

Bryan, B. M., "The 18th Dynasty before the Amarna Period (*c.* 1550-1352 BC)", in: I. Shaw (ed.), *The Oxford history of ancient Egypt*. Oxford: Oxford University Press 2000, 218-271.

Budge, E. A. W., *Hieroglyphic texts from Egyptian stelae, &c., in the British Museum, part V*. London: British Museum 1914.

Bunbury, J., "Geomorphological development of the Memphite floodplain over the past 6,000 years", *Studia quaternaria* 30, 2013, 61-67.

Bunbury J., *The Nile and ancient Egypt: changing land- and waterscapes, from the Neolithic to the Roman Era*. Cambridge: Cambridge University Press 2019.

Bussmann, R., *Die Provinztempel Ägyptens von der 0. bis zur 11. Dynastie*. Probleme der Ägyptologie 30, Leiden: Brill 2010.

Butzer, K. W., *Quaternary stratigraphy and climate in the Near East*. Bonner Geographische Abhandlungen 24, Dümmler 1958.

Butzer, K. W., "Some recent geological deposits in the Egyptian Nile valley", *The Geographical Journal* 125.1, 1959(a), 75-79.

Butzer, K. W., "Environment and human ecology", *Geography* 4, 1959(b), 43-87.

Butzer, K. W., "Climatic change in arid regions since the Pliocene", in: L. D. Stamp (ed.), *A History of Land use in arid regions*, UNESCO Arid Zone Research XVII, 1961, 31-56.

Caminos, R.A., "Amenophis III's vizier Amenhotep at Silsilah East", *Journal of Egyptian Archaeology* 73, 1987, 207-210.

Caminos, R.A., "The Nitocris adoption stela", *Journal of Egyptian Archaeology* 50, 1964, 71-101.

Capasso, M., P. Davoli (eds.), *Soknopaiou Nesos Project I (2003-2009)*. Biblioteca degli "Studi di egittologia e di papirologia" 9, Pisa: Fabrizio Serra Editore 2012.

Chassinat, É., *Le temple d'Edfou, tome septième*. Mémoires publiés par les membres de la Mission Archéologique Française au Caire 24. Le Caire: Institut Français d'Archéologie Orientale 1932.

Cauville, S., *Le temple de Dendara 10: les chapelles osiriennes*, 2 vols. Le Caire: Institut Français d'Archéologie Orientale 1997.

Chłodnicki, M. "Tell el-Farkha: the changes in spatial organisation of the settlement - from the Predynastic to the Early Dynastic periods", in: A. Mączyńska (ed.), *The Nile Delta as a centre of cultural interactions between Upper Egypt and the Southern Levant in the 4th millennium BC*, Poznań 2014, 57-72.

Ciałowicz K. M., "New discoveries at Tell el-Farkha and the beginnings of the Egyptian state", *Études et Travaux* 30, 2017, 231-250.

Cílek, V., M. Bárta, L. Lisá, A. Pokorná, L. Juříčková, V. Brůna, A.M. A. Mahmud, A. Bajer, J. Novák, J. Beneš, "Diachronic development of the Lake of Abusir during the third millennium BC, Cairo, Egypt", *Quaternary International* 266, 2012, 14-24.

Cordova, C., *Geoarchaeology: The human-environmental approach*. London; New York: Bloomsbury Publishing 2018.

Coutellier, V., J.-D. Stanley, "Late Quaternary stratigraphy and paleogeography of the eastern Nile Delta, Egypt", *Marine geology* 77.3-4, 1988, 257-275.

Czerny E., *Tell el-Dab'a IX: eine Plansiedlung des frühen Mittleren Reiches*, Untersuchungen der Zweigstelle Kairo des Österreichischen Archäologischen Institutes 15; Österreichische Akademie der Wissenschaften, Denkschriften der Gesamtakademie 16, Wien: Verlag der Österreichischen Akademie der Wissenschaften 1999.

Czerny E., *Tell el-Dab'a XXII: „Der Mund der beiden Wege": die Siedlung und der Tempelbezirk des Mittleren Reiches von Ezbet Ruschdi*, 2 vols. Untersuchungen der Zweigstelle Kairo des Österreichischen Archäologischen Institutes 38; Österreichische Akademie der Wissenschaften, Denkschriften der Gesamtakademie 77, Wien: Verlag der Österreichischen Akademie der Wissenschaften 2015.

Davoli, P., "Archaeological research in Roman Soknopaiou Nesos: results and perspectives", in: K. Lembke, M. Minas-Nerpel, S. Pfeiffer (eds.), *Tradition and transformation: Egypt under Roman rule. Proceedings of the international conference, Hildesheim, Roemer- and Pelizaeus-Museum, 3-6 July 2008*. Leiden; Boston, MA: Brill 2010, 53-77.

Dean, K. R., F. Krauer, L. Walløe, O. C. Lingjærde, B. Bramanti, N. C. Stenseth, B. V. Schmid, "Human ectoparasites and the spread of plague in Europe during the Second Pandemic", *Proceedings of the National Academy of Sciences* 115.6, 2018, 1304-1309.

Dee, M. W., "A radiocarbon-based chronology for the Old Kingdom", in: A. J. Shortland, C. Bronk Ramsey (eds.), *Radiocarbon and the chronologies of ancient Egypt*. Oxford: Oxbow Books 2013, 209-217.

Dee, M. W., "Absolutely dating climatic evidence and the decline of Old Kingdom Egypt", in: F. Höflmayer (ed.), *The late third millennium in the ancient Near East: chronology, C14, and climate change*. Chicago: Oriental Institute of the University of Chicago 2017, 323-332.

Dijk, J. van., "The Amarna Period and the later New Kingdom (*c.* 1352-1069 BC)", in: I. Shaw (ed.), *The Oxford history of ancient Egypt*. Oxford: Oxford University Press 2000, 272-313.

Dodson, A., *Afterglow of empire: Egypt from the fall of the New Kingdom to the Saite renaissance*. Cairo; New York: American University in Cairo Press 2012.

Dodson, A., *The royal tombs of ancient Egypt*. Barnsley: Pen & Sword 2016.

Downes, D., *The excavations at Esna, 1905-1906*. Warminster: Aris and Phillips 1974.

Dreyer, G., *Elephantine VIII: Der Tempel der Satet. Die Funde der Frühzeit und des Alten Reiches*. Archäologische Veröffentlichungen, Deutsches Archäologisches Institut, Abteilung Kairo 39, Mainz: Philipp von Zabern 1986.

Dreyer, G., *Umm el-Qaab I: Das prädynastische Königsgrab U-j und seine frühen Schriftzeugnisse*. Archäologische Veröffentlichungen, Deutsches Archäologisches Institut, Abteilung Kairo 86, Mainz: Philip von Zabern 1998.

Edgar, C. C., "The treasure of Tell Basta", in: E. Grébaut, G. Maspero (eds.), *Le Musée Égyptien: recueil de monuments et de notices sur les fouilles d'Égypte 2*. Le Caire: Institut français d'archéologie orientale 1907, 93-108.

Edwards, I. E. S., *Hieroglyphic texts from Egyptian stelae, etc., part 8*. London: British Museum 1939.

Eigner, D., "A palace of the early 13th Dynasty at Tell el-Dab'a", in: M. Bietak (ed.), *Haus und Palast im Alten Ägypten / House and palace in ancient Egypt*. Wien: Verlag der Österreichischen Akademie der Wissenschaften 1996, 73-80.

Eigner, D., "Tell Ibrahim Awad: divine residence from Dynasty 0 until Dynasty 11", *Ägypten und Levante* 10, 2000, 17-36.

Endesfelder, E., *Beobachtungen zur Entstehung des altägyptischen Staates*. Internet-Beiträge zur Ägyptologie und Sudanarchäologie 14. Berlin; London: Golden House 2011.

Erman, A., H. Grapow (eds.), *Wörterbuch der aegyptischen Sprache im Auftrage der Deutschen Akademien: zweiter Band*. Leipzig: J. C. Hinrichs 1928.

Fakhry, A., "The search for texts in the western desert", in: S. Sauneron (ed.), *Textes et langages de l'Égypte pharaonique: cent cinquante années de recherches 1822 - 1972. Hommage à Jean-François Champollion 2*. Le Caire: Institut français d'archéologie orientale 1973, 207-222.

Fakhry, A., "Wâdi-el-Natrûn", *Annales du Service des Antiquités de l'Égypte* 40, 1940, 837-848.

Faltings, D., "Recent excavations in Tell El-Fara'in Buto: new finds and their chronological implications", in: C. J. Eyre (ed.), *Proceedings of the Seventh International Congress of Egyptologists, Cambridge, 3-9 September 1995*, Leuven: Peeters, 1998, 365-375.

Farid, S., "Preliminary report on the excavations of the Antiquities Department at Tell Basta (Season

1961)", *Annales du Service des Antiquités de l'Égypte* 58, 1964, 85-98.

Feldman, M. H., "Luxurious Forms: Redefining a Mediterranean "International Style" 1400–1200 BCE", *The Art Bulletin* 84.1, 2002, 6-29.

Fischer, H. G., "An Old Kingdom monogram: 𓏏 ". *Zeitschrift für ägyptische Sprache und Altertumskunde* 93, 1966, 56-69.

Fischer, H. G., "Some early monuments from Busiris, in the Egyptian delta", *Metropolitan Museum Journal* 11, 1976, 5-24.

Fischer, H. G., "Tomb Z and its contents", in: R. Anthes (ed.), *Mit Rahineh 1955*. Philadelphia: The University Museum, University of Pennsylvania 1959, 15-20.

Forstner-Müller, I., "Central power and the harbour: some thoughts on the main harbour of Avaris in the Middle Kingdom and Second Intermediate Period", in: A. Tenu, M. Yoyotte (eds.), *Le roi et le fleuve: exemples d'usages pluriels de l'espace*. Paris: Khéops 2021, 109-123.

Forstner-Müller, I., "Ritual activity in a palace of the 15th Dynasty (Hyksos) at Avaris", in: R. Gundlach, K. Spence (eds.), *Palace and temple: architecture - decoration - ritual. 5. Symposium zur ägyptischen Königsideologie / 5th symposium on Egyptian royal ideology. Cambridge, July, 16th-17th, 2007*. Wiesbaden: Harrassowitz 2011, 1-21.

Forstner-Müller, I., N. Moeller (eds.), *The Hyksos ruler Khyan and the early Second Intermediate Period in Egypt: problems and priorities of current research. Proceedings of the workshop of the Austrian Archaeological Institute and the Oriental Institute of the University of Chicago, Vienna, July 4 - 5, 2014*. Ergänzungshefte zu den Jahresheften des Österreichischen Archäologischen Institutes in Wien 17, Wien: Holzhausen 2018.

Forstner-Müller, I., *Tell el-Dabʿa XVI: die Gräber des Areals A/II von Tell el-Dabʿa*. Untersuchungen der Zweigstelle Kairo des Österreichischen Archäologischen Institutes 28; Österreichische Akademie der Wissenschaften, Denkschriften der Gesamtakademie 44. Wien: Verlag der Österreichischen Akademie der Wissenschaften 2008.

Franke, D., "The Middle Kingdom in Egypt", in: J. M. Sasson, J. Baines, G. Beckman, K. S. Rubinson (eds.), *Civilizations of the ancient Near East 2*. New York: Charles Scribner's; Macmillan Library Reference; Simon & Schuster Macmillan 1995, 735-748.

Franke, D., "Zur Chronologie des Mittleren Reiches. Teil II: die sogenannte „Zweite Zwischenzeit" Altägyptens", *Orientalia* 57 (3), 1988, 245-274.

Franzmeier, H., "The landscape(s) of Pi-Ramesse: living and dying in the capital of Ramesside Egypt", in: L. Weiss, N. Staring, H. T. Davies (eds.), *Perspectives on lived religion II: the making of a cultural geography*. Leiden: Sidestone Press 2022, 109-123.

Friedman, R. F., "The Early Dynastic and transitional pottery of Mendes: the 1990 Season", in: E. C. M. van den Brink (ed.), *The Nile Delta in transition: 4th - 3rd millennium BC. Proceedings of the seminar held in Cairo, 21 - 24 October 1990, at the Netherlands Institute of Archaeology and Arabic Studies*. Tel Aviv: E. C. M. van den Brink 1992, 199-205.

Gabolde, M., "Les écritures cryptographique et ptolémaïque: quand un signe peut en cacher un autre", in: L. Bazin Rizzo, A. Gasse, F. Servajean (eds.), *À l'école des scribes: les écritures de l'Égypte ancienne*. Milano: Silvana Editoriale 2016, 87-97.

Gardiner, A. H., "Horus the Beḥdetite", *Journal of Egyptian Archaeology* 30, 1944, 23-60.

Gardiner, A.H., *Late-Egyptian stories*. Bibliotheca Aegyptiaca 1, Bruxelles: Fondation Égyptologique Reine Élisabeth 1932 (Reprint 1981).

Gardiner, Alan H. 1947. *Ancient Egyptian onomastica*, 3 vols. Oxford: Oxford University Press.

Gauthier, H., "Le titre 𓂋𓏏𓎛𓏤 (*imi-ra âkhnouti*) et ses acceptions diverses", *Bulletin de l'Institut Français d'Archéologie Orientale* 15, 1918, 169-206.

Gauthier, H., "Un vice-roi d'Éthiopie enseveli à Bubastis", *Annales du Service des Antiquités de l'Égypte* 28, 1928, 129-137.

Gessler-Löhr, B., *Die heiligen Seen ägyptischer Tempel: ein Beitrag zur Deutung sakraler Baukunst im alten Ägypten*. Hildesheimer Ägyptologische Beiträge 21, Hildesheim: Gerstenberg 1983.

Gestermann L., *Kontinuität und Wandel in Politik und Verwaltung des frühen Mittleren Reiches in Ägypten*. Göttinger Orientforschungen 4, Ägypten, vol. 18, Wiesbaden: Harrassowitz 1987.

Ginau, A., R. Schiestl, J. Wunderlich, "Integrative geoarchaeological research on settlement patterns in the dynamic landscape of the northwestern Nile delta", *Quaternary International* 511, 2019,

51-67.

Goedicke, H., *Königliche Dokumente aus dem Alten Reich*. Ägyptologische Abhandlungen 14, Wiesbaden: Harrassowitz 1967.

Gomaà, F., el-S. Hegazy, "Neue Funde aus dem Nildelta", *Cahiers caribéens d'égyptologie* 9, 95-111, 2006.

Gomaà, F., *Die Besiedlung Ägyptens während des Mittleren Reiches II: Unterägypten und die angrenzenden Gebiete*. Beihefte zum Tübinger Atlas des Vorderen Orients, Reihe B (Geisteswissenschaften) 66 (2), Wiesbaden: Reichert 1987.

Gordon, A., "Who was the southern vizier during the last part of the reign of Amenhotep III?", *Journal of Near Eastern Studies* 48 (1), 1989, 15-23.

Grajetzki, W., "Setting a state anew: the central administration from the end of the Old Kingdom to the end of the Middle Kingdom", in: J. M. Moreno García (ed.), *Ancient Egyptian administration*. Leiden: Brill 2013, 215-258.

Grajetzki, W., *Burial customs in ancient Egypt: life in death for rich and poor*. Duckworth Egyptology, London: Duckworth 2003.

Grajetzki, W., *Court officials of the Egyptian Middle Kingdom*. Duckworth Egyptology. London: Duckworth 2009.

Grajetzki, W., *Die höchsten Beamten der ägyptischen Zentralverwaltung zur Zeit des Mittleren Reiches: Prosopographie, Titel und Titelreihen*. Achet A 2, Berlin: Achet 2000.

Grimal, N.-C., *La stèle triomphale de Pi('ankh)y au Musée du Caire: JE 48862 et 47086-47089*. Mémoires publiés par les membres de l'Institut français d'archéologie orientale 105, Le Caire: Institut français d'Archéologie Orientale 1981(a).

Grimal, N.-C., *Quatre stèles napatéennes au Musée du Caire, JE 48863-48866: textes et indices*. Mémoires publiés par les membres de l'Institut français d'archéologie orientale 106, Le Caire: Institut français d'archéologie orientale 1981(b).

Gulbekian, E., "The Origin and Value of the Stadion Unit used by Eratosthenes in the Third Century B.C.", Archive for History of Exact Science 37/4, 1987, 359-363.

Habachi, L., "The jubilees of Ramesses II and Amenophis III with reference to certain aspects of their celebration", *Zeitschrift für ägyptische Sprache und Altertumskunde* 97, 1971, 64-72.

Habachi, L., "The so-called Hyksos Monuments reconsidered: apropos of the discovery of a dyad of sphinxes", *Studien zur Altägyptischen Kultur* 6, 1978, 79-92.

Habachi, L., P. Ghalioungui, "The "House of Life" of Bubastis", *Chronique d'Égypte* 46 (91), 1971, 59-71.

Habachi, L., *Tell Basta*. Supplément aux Annales du Service des Antiquités de l'Egypte 22, Le Caire: Imprimerie de l'Institut français d'archéologie orientale 1957.

Habachi, L., *The second stela of Kamose and his struggle against the Hyksos ruler and his capital*. Abhandlungen des Deutschen Archäologischen Instituts Kairo, Ägyptologische Reihe 8, Glückstadt: Augustin 1972.

Habachi, L., *Tell el-Dab'a I: Tell el-Dab'a and Qantir. The site and its connection with Avaris and Piramesse*. Edited by E.-M. Engel, P. Jánosi, C Mlinar. Untersuchungen der Zweigstelle Kairo des Österreichischen Archäologischen Institutes 2; Österreichische Akademie der Wissenschaften, Denkschriften der Gesamtakademie 23, Wien: Österreichischen Akademie der Wissenschaften 2001.

Hamdan, M. A., F. A. Hassan, R. J. Flower, E. M. Ebrahim, "Climate and collapse of Egyptian Old Kingdom: a geoarchaeological approach", in: C. Vittozzi, G. and F. Porcelli (eds.), *Archaeology and environment: understanding the past to design the future: a multidisciplinary approach. Proceedings of the international workshop "Italian days in Aswan", 16th-18th November 2013*. Rome: Consiglio Nazionale delle Ricerche, Istituto di Studi sul Mediterraneo Antico 2016, 89-99.

Hartung, U., "Recent investigations of Early Dynastic building structures at Tell el-Fara'in/Buto", in: M. Bietak, S. Prell (eds.), *Ancient Egyptian and ancient Near Eastern palaces, volume I: proceedings of the conference on palaces in ancient Egypt, held in London 12th-14th June 2013, organised by the Austrian Academy of Sciences, the University of Würzburg and the Egypt Exploration Society*. Vienna: Austrian Academy of Sciences 2018, 101-112.

Hassan, F. A., "Droughts, famine and the collapse of the Old Kingdom: re-reading Ipuwer.", in: Z. A.

Hawass, J. E. Richards (eds.), *The archaeology and art of ancient Egypt: essays in honor of David B. O'Connor 1*. Le Caire: Conseil Suprême des Antiquités de l'Egypte 2007, 357-377.

Helck, W., *Zur Verwaltung des Mittleren und Neuen Reichs*. Probleme der Ägyptologie 3, Leiden; Köln: E. J. Brill 1958.

Helck, W., *Die altägyptischen Gaue*. Beihefte zum Tübinger Atlas des Vorderen Orients, Reihe B (Geisteswissenschaften) 5, Wiesbaden: Ludwig Reichert 1974.

Hendrickx, S., „Predynastic - early Dynastic chronology", in: E. Hornung, R. Krauss, D. A. Warburton (eds.), *Ancient Egyptian chronology*. Leiden; Boston: Brill 2006, 55-93.

Hoffmeier, K. J., M. Abd el-Maksoud, "A new military site on 'The Ways of Horus': Tell el-Borg 1999-2001: a preliminary report", *Journal of Egyptian Archaeology* 89, 2003, 169-197.

Hölbl, G., *Geschichte des Ptolemäerreiches: Politik, Ideologie und religiöse Kultur von Alexander dem Großen bis zur römischen Eroberung*. Stuttgart: Theiss 2004.

Hölzl, R., *Ägyptische Opfertafeln und Kultbecken: eine Form- und Funktionsanalyse für das Alte, Mittlere und Neue Reich*. Hildesheimer Ägyptologische Beiträge 45, Hildesheim: Gerstenberg 2002.

Hornung, E., E. Staehelin. *Neue Studien zum Sedfest*. Aegyptiaca Helvetica 20, Basel: Schwabe 2006.

Hornung, E., R. Krauss, D. A. Warburton (eds.), *Ancient Egyptian chronology*. Handbook of Oriental Studies, section 1: The Near and Middle East 83, Leiden; Boston: Brill 2006.

Jacquet-Gordon, H. K., "The inscription on the Philadelphia-Cairo statue of Osorkon II", *Journal of Egyptian Archaeology* 46, 1960, 12-23.

Jánosi, P., *Die Pyramidenanlagen der Königinnen: Untersuchungen zu einem Grabtyp des Alten und Mittleren Reiches*. Österreichische Akademie der Wissenschaften, Denkschriften der Gesamtakademie 13, Untersuchungen der Zweigstelle Kairo des Österreichischen Archäologischen Institutes 13, Wien: Verlag der Österreichischen Akademie der Wissenschaften 1996.

Jansen-Winkeln, K., "Das Ende des Neuen Reiches", *Zeitschrift für ägyptische Sprache und Altertumskunde* 119, 1992, 22-37.

Jansen-Winkeln, K., "Der Beginn der libyschen Herrschaft in Ägypten", *Biblische Notizen* 71, 1994, 78-97.

Jansen-Winkeln, K., "Die Fremdherrschaften in Ägypten im 1. Jahrtausend v. Chr.", *Orientalia* 69 (1), 2000(a), 1-20.

Jansen-Winkeln, K., "Zum Verständnis der 'Saitischen Formel' ", *Studien zur Altägyptischen Kultur* 28, 2000(b), 83-124.

Jansen-Winkeln, K., "Der thebanische 'Gottesstaat' ", *Orientalia* 70 (2), 2001, 153-182.

Jansen-Winkeln, K., *Inschriften der Spätzeit, Teil II: Die 22.-24. Dynastie*. Wiesbaden: Harrassowitz 2007.

Jansen-Winkeln, K., "Der Untergang des Alten Reiches", *Orientalia* 79 (3), 2010, 273-303.

Jansen-Winkeln, K., *Inschriften der Spätzeit, Teil IV: Die 26. Dynastie*, 2 vols. Wiesbaden: Harrassowitz 2014.

Jansen-Winkeln, K.,„„Libyerzeit" oder „postimperiale Periode"? Zur historischen Einordnung der Dritten Zwischenzeit", in: C. Jurman, B. Bader, D. A. Aston (eds.), *A true scribe of Abydos: essays on first millennium Egypt in honour of Anthony Leahy*. Leuven: Peeters 2017(a), 203-238.

Jansen-Winkeln, Karl. Beiträge zur Geschichte der Dritten Zwischenzeit, *Journal of Egyptian History* 10(1), 2017(b), 23-42.

Jéquier, G., *Tombeaux de particuliers contemporains de Pepi II*. Fouilles à Saqqarah, Le Caire: Institut français d'Archéologie Orientale 1929.

Jeuthe, C., "The governor's palaces at Ayn Asil/Balat (Dakhla Oasis/Western Desert)", in: M. Bietak, S. Prell (eds.), *Ancient Egyptian and ancient Near Eastern palaces, volume I: proceedings of the conference on palaces in ancient Egypt, held in London 12th-14th June 2013, organised by the Austrian Academy of Sciences, the University of Würzburg and the Egypt Exploration Society*, 125-140. Vienna: Austrian Academy of Sciences 2018.

Jones, D., *An index of ancient Egyptian titles, epithets and phrases of the Old Kingdom*, 2 vols. BAR International Series 866 (1-2), Oxford: Archaeopress 2000.

Jordan-Ruwe, M., *Das Säulenmonument: Zur Geschichte der erhöhten Aufstellung antiker Porträt-*

statuen. Vol. 19, R. Habelt: Münster 1995.

Jucha, M. A., "The Nile Delta since the end of the Lower Egyptian culture until the beginning of Egyptian state", in: M. A Jucha, J. Dębowska-Ludwin, P. Kołodziejczyk (eds.), *Aegyptus est imago caeli: studies presented to Krzysztof M. Ciałowicz on his 60th birthday.* Kraków: Institute of Archaeology, Jagiellonian University in Kraków; Archaeologica Foundation 2014, 19-35.

Junker, H., *Gîza VI: Bericht über die von der Akademie der Wissenschaften in Wien auf gemeinsame Kosten mit Dr. Wilhelm Pelizaeus unternommen Grabungen auf dem Friedhof des Alten Reichs bei den Pyramiden von Gîza. Die Maṣṭaba des nfr (Nefer), qdfjj (Kedfi), kAhjf (Kahjef) und die westlich anschließenden Grabanlagen.* Österreichische Akademie der Wissenschaften, Denkschriften der Philosophisch-Historischen Klasse 72 (1), Wien; Leipzig: Hölder-Pichler-Tempsky 1943.

Kahl, J., "Inscriptional evidence for the relative chronology of Dyns. 0-2", in: E. Hornung, R. Krauss, D. A. Warburton (eds.), *Ancient Egyptian chronology*, Leiden; Boston: Brill 2006, 94-115.

Kaiser, W., "Stand und Probleme der ägyptischen Vorgeschichtsforschung", *Zeitschrift für ägyptische Sprache und Altertumskunde* 81, 1956, 87-109.

Kaiser, W., "Zur Entstehung des gesamtägyptischen Staates". *Mitteilungen des Deutschen Archäologischen Instituts, Abteilung Kairo* 46, 1990, 287-299.

Kamil, J., *Labib Habachi: the life and legacy of an Egyptologist.* Cairo; New York: American University in Cairo Press 2007.

Kanawati, N., *Conspiracies in the Egyptian palace: Unis to Pepy I.* London, New York: Routledge 2003.

Känel, F. von, *Les prêtres-ouâb de Sekhmet et les conjurateurs de Serket.* Bibliothèque de l'École des hautes études. Sciences religieuses 87, Paris: Presses Universitaires de France 1984.

Kantor, H. J. "Syro-Palestinian Ivories", *Journal of Near Eastern Studies* 15.3, 1956, 153-174.

Kantor, H. J. "Ivory carving in the Mycenaean period", *Archaeology* 13.1, 1960, 14-25.

Karlsson, M., "Taharqa, vanquisher of the Assyrians", *Der Antike Sudan. Mitteilungen der Sudanarchäologischen Gesellschaft zu Berlin* 33, 2022, 87-90.

Kemp, B. J., "The Osiris temple at Abydos", in: *Mitteilungen des Deutschen Archäologischen Instituts, Abteilung Kairo* 23, 1968, 138-155.

Kemp, B. J., *Ancient Egypt: anatomy of a civilization*, 3rd revised and updated ed. London; New York: Routledge 2018.

Kessler, D., *Die heiligen Tiere und der König, Teil I: Beiträge zu Organisation, Kult und Theologie der spätzeitlichen Tierfriedhöfe.* Ägypten und Altes Testament 16, Wiesbaden: Harrassowitz 1989.

Kessler, D., "Herodot II, 65-67 über heilige Tiere in Bubastis", *Studien zur Altägyptischen Kultur* 18, 1991, 265-289.

Khaled, M. I., *Abusir XXVI: The funerary domains in the pyramid complex of Sahura: an aspect of the economy in the late third millennium BCE.* Prague: Charles University, Faculty of Arts 2020.

Kitchen K. A., *The Third Intermediate Period in Egypt (1100-650 B.C.)*, 2nd ed. Warminster 1986.

Koch, C., „Die den Amun mit ihrer Stimme zufriedenstellen": Gottesgemahlinnen und Musikerinnen im thebaischen Amunstaat von der 22. bis zur 26. Dynastie. Studien zu den Ritualszenen altägyptischer Tempel 27, Dettelbach: Röll 2012.

Koch, R., *Die Erzählung des Sinuhe.* Bibliotheca Aegyptiaca 17, Brüssel: Ed. de la Fondation Egyptologique 1990.

Köhler, E. C., "Of culture wars and the clash of civilizations in prehistoric Egypt: an epistemological analysis", *Ägypten und Levante* 30, 2020, 17-58.

Köhler, E. C., "The development of social complexity in early Egypt: a view from the perspective of the settlements and material culture of the Nile Valley", *Ägypten und Levante* 27, 2017, 335-356.

Köhler, E. C., *Tell el-Fara'în-Buto. Band 3: die Keramik von der späten Naqada-Kultur bis zum frühen Alten Reich (Schichten III bis VI).* Archäologische Veröffentlichungen, Deutsches Archäologisches Institut, Abteilung Kairo 94, Mainz: Zabern 1998.

Kopetzky, K., M. Bietak, "A seal impression of the Green Jasper Workshop from Tell el-Dab'a", *Ägypten und Levante* 26, 2016, 357-375.

Kroeper K., D. Wildung, *Minshat Abu Omar. Ein vor- und frühgeschichtlicher Friedhof im Nildelta, I: Gräber 1-114*. Mainz 1994.

Kroeper, K., "The excavations of the Munich East-Delta Expedition in Minshat in Abu Omar", in: E. C. M. van den Brink (ed.), *The archaeology of the Nile Delta, Egypt: problems and priorities. Proceedings of the seminar held in Cairo, 19-22 October 1986, on the occasion of the fifteenth anniversary of the Netherlands Institute of Archaeology and Arabic Studies in Cairo*. Amsterdam: Netherlands Foundation for Archaeological Research in Egypt 1988, 11-46.

Krzyżaniak, L., "New data on the late prehistoric settlement at Minshat Abu Omar, eastern Nile Delta", in: L. Krzyżaniak; M. Kobusiewicz; J. Alexander (eds.), *Environmental change and human culture in the Nile Basin and Northern Africa until the second millennium B.C*, Poznań 1993, 321-325.

Kurth, D., *Edfou VII*. Die Inschriften des Tempels von Edfu: Abteilung I Übersetzungen 2, Wiesbaden: Harrassowitz 2004.

Lacau, P., H. Chevrier, *Une chapelle de Sésostris Ier à Karnak*, 2 vols. Service des Antiquités de l'Égypte, Le Caire: Imprimerie de l'Institut français d'archéologie orientale 1956-1969.

Landgráfová, R., *It is my good name that you should remember: Egyptian biographical texts on Middle Kingdom stelae*. Prague: Faculty of Arts, Charles University in Prague, Czech Institute of Egyptology 2011.

Lange, E., "Ein neuer König Schoschenk in Bubastis", *Göttinger Miszellen* 203, 2004, 65-72.

Lange, E., "Die Ka-Anlage Pepis I. in Bubastis im Kontext königlicher Ka-Anlagen des Alten Reiches", *Zeitschrift für ägyptische Sprache und Altertumskunde* 133, 2006, 121-140.

Lange, E., "Khenemet Nefer Hedjet Weret in the great temple of Tell Basta (Bubastis)", in: S. Grallert, W. Grajetzki (eds.), *Life and afterlife in ancient Egypt during the Middle Kingdom and Second Intermediate Period*. London: Golden House 2007, 91-93.

Lange, E., "Legitimation und Herrschaft in der Libyerzeit: eine neue Inschrift Osorkons I. aus Bubastis (Tell Basta)", *Zeitschrift für ägyptische Sprache und Altertumskunde* 135, 2008, 131-141.

Lange, E., "King Shoshenqs at Bubastis", *Egyptian Archaeology* 37, 2010, 19-20.

Lange, E., "The EES Amelia Edwards Projects Fund: Tell Basta", *Egyptian Archaeology* 39, 2011, 7–9.

Lange, E., "The so-called governors' cemetery at Bubastis and provincial elite tombs in the Nile Delta: state and perspectives of research", in: G. Miniaci, W. Grajetzki (eds.), *The world of Middle Kingdom Egypt (2000-1550 BC): contributions on archaeology, art, religion, and written sources. Volume I*. London: Golden House 2015, 187-203.

Lange, E., "The lioness goddess in the Old Kingdom Nile Delta: a study in local cult topography", in: S. L. Lippert, M. Schentuleit, M. A. Stadler (eds.), *Sapientia Felicitas: Festschrift für Günter Vittmann zum 29. Februar 2016*. Montpellier: Équipe "Égypte Nilotique et Méditerranéenne" 2016, 301-324.

Lange-Athinodorou, E., "Palaces of the ancient mind: the textual record versus archaeological evidence", in: M. Bietak, S. Prell (eds.), *Ancient Egyptian and ancient Near Eastern palaces, volume I: proceedings of the conference on palaces in ancient Egypt, held in London 12th-14th June 2013, organised by the Austrian Academy of Sciences, the University of Würzburg and the Egypt Exploration Society*. Vienna: Austrian Academy of Sciences 2018(a), 39-63.

Lange-Athinodorou, E., "Palace cemeteries of the eastern Delta", in: M. Bietak, S. Prell (eds.), *Ancient Egyptian and ancient Near Eastern palaces, volume I: proceedings of the conference on palaces in ancient Egypt, held in London 12th-14th June 2013, organised by the Austrian Academy of Sciences, the University of Würzburg and the Egypt Exploration Society*. Vienna: Austrian Academy of Sciences 2018(b), 157-168.

Lange-Athinodorou, E., *Sedfestritual und Königtum: die Reliefdekoration am Torbau Osorkons II. im Tempel der Bastet von Bubastis*. Ägyptologische Abhandlungen 75. Wiesbaden: Harrassowitz 2019(a).

Lange-Athinodorou, E., "Der „Tempel des Hermes" und die Pfeile der Bastet: zur Rekonstruktion der Kultlandschaft von Bubastis, in: M. Brose, P. Dils, F. Naether, L. Popko, D. Raue (eds.), *En détail - Philologie und Archäologie im Diskurs: Festschrift für Hans-Werner Fischer-Elfert 1*,. Berlin; Boston: De Gruyter. 2019(b), 549-585.

Lange-Athinodorou, E., "The issue of residence and periphery in the Middle Kingdom: surveying the Delta", in: A. Jiménez-Serrano, A. J. Morales (eds.), *Middle Kingdom palace culture and its echoes in the provinces: regional perspectives and realities*, 256-283. Leiden; Boston: Brill 2021(a).

Lange-Athinodorou, E., "Implications of geoarchaeological investigations for the contextualization of sacred landscapes in the Nile Delta", *E&G Quaternary Science Journal* 70, 2021(b), 73-82.

Lange-Athinodorou, E., "Preliminary report on the excavation in the precinct of the temple of Bastet in Bubastis/Tell Basta (Area A), seasons 2009-2017", in: A. Wahby, P. Wilson (eds.), *The Delta survey workshop: proceedings from conferences held in Alexandria (2017) and Mansoura (2019)*. Oxford: Archaeopress 2022, 115-139.

Lange-Athinodorou, E., "A provincial residence at Bubastis from the 4th and 5th Dynasty and the issue of the administration of the Old Kingdom Nile Delta", Mitteilungen des Deutschen Archäologischen Instituts Kairo 79, 2023.

Lange, E., T. Ullmann, R. Baumhauer. Remote sensing in the Nile Delta: spatio-temporal analysis of Bubastis/Tell Basta, *Ägypten und Levante* 26, 2016, 377-392.

Lange-Athinodorou, E., A. Abd El-Raouf, T. Ullmann, J. Trappe, J. Meister, R. Baumhauer, "The sacred canals of the temple of Bastet at Bubastis (Egypt): new findings from geomorphological investigations and Electrical Resistivity Tomography (ERT)", *Journal of Archaeological Science: Reports* 26 (101910), 2019.

Lange-Athinodorou, E., A. el-Senussi, "A royal *ka*-temple and the rise of Old Kingdom Bubastis", *Egyptian Archaeology* 53, 2018, 20-24.

Lange-Athinodorou, E., A. el-Senussi, "First preliminary report on the excavations in the ka-temple of Pepi I in Tell Basta/Bubastis: the discovery of a residential building of the fourth and fifth dynasties", *Journal of Egyptian Archaeology* 108 (1-2), 2022, 23-43.

Laube, K., "The forgotten excavation at Tell Basta: new information on the Graeco-Egyptian bath and the context of gold and silver objects discovered in 1906", *Journal of Egyptian Archaeology* 109 (1-2), 2023, 77-87.

Leahy, A., "The earliest dated monument of Amasis and the end of the reign of Apries", *Journal of Egyptian Archaeology* 74, 1988, 183-199.

Leclant, J., "Fouilles et travaux en Egypte et au Soudan", *Orientalia* 35 (2), 1966, 127-178.

Leclant, J., "Kashta, pharaon, en Egypte", *Zeitschrift für ägyptische Sprache und Altertumskunde* 90, 1963, 74-81.

Leclère, F., *Les villes de Basse Égypte au Ier millénaire av. J.-C.: analyse archéologique et historique de la topographie urbaine*, 2 vols. Bibliothèque d'étude 144, Le Caire: Institut français d'archéologie orientale 2008.

Lehmann, M., *Tell el-Dab'a XXV: die materielle Kultur der Spät- und Ptolemäerzeit im Delta Ägyptens am Beispiel von Tell el-Dab'a*, 2 vols. Mit einem Beitrag von Günther Karl Kunst. Untersuchungen der Zweigstelle Kairo des Österreichischen Archäologischen Institutes 40, Denkschriften der Gesamtakademie 87, Wien: Verlag der Österreichischen Akademie der Wissenschaften 2020.

Lehner, M., "Lake Khufu: on the waterfront at Giza: modelling water transport infrastructure in Dynasty IV", in: M. Bárta, J. Janák (eds.), *Profane landscapes, sacred spaces: urban development in the Bronze Age southern Levant*. New directions in Anthropological Archaeology. Sheffield; Bristol, CT: Equinox 2020, 191-292.

Lehner, M., "The name and nature of the Heit el-Ghurab Old Kingdom site: worker's town, pyramid town, and the port hypothesis", in: I. Hein, Irmgard, N. Billing, E. Meyer-Dietrich (eds.), *The pyramids: between life and death. Proceedings of the workshop held at Uppsala University, Uppsala, May 31st - June 1st, 2012*. Uppsala: Uppsala Universitet, 2016, 99-160.

Lehner, M., Z. Hawass, *Giza and the pyramids: the definitive history*. London: Thames & Hudson 2017.

Leitz, C., *Die Gaumonographien in Edfu und ihre Papyrusvarianten: ein überregionaler Kanon im spätzeitlichen Ägypten. Soubassementstudien III*, 2 vols. Studien zur spätägyptischen Religion 9, Wiesbaden: Harrassowitz 2014.

Leitz, C., *Die regionale Mythologie Ägyptens nach Ausweis der geographischen Prozessionen in den späten Tempeln: Soubassementstudien IV*, 2 vols. Studien zur spätägyptischen Religion 10, Wiesbaden: Harrassowitz 2017.

Lichtenberg, R., A.-P. Zivie, „The cats and the goddess Bastet", in: S. Ikram (ed.), *Divine creatures: animal mummies in ancient Egypt*. Cairo; New York: American University in Cairo Press 2005, 106-119.

Lilyquist, C., "Treasures from Tell Basta: goddesses, officials, and artists in an international age", *Metropolitan Museum Journal* 47, 2012, 9-72.

Lorand, D., "*Amenemhat-Itj-Taouy*: quelques réflexions sur la compréhension d'un toponyme", in: S. Dhennin, C. Somaglino (eds.), *Décrire, imaginer, construire l'espace: toponymie égyptienne de l'Antiquité au Moyen Âge*. Le Caire: Institut français d'archéologie orientale 2016, 30-48.

Loth, M. "Vorarbeiten zu einem Katalog des Skulpturengartens", in: C. Tietze, *Tell Basta-Vorläufiger Bericht der XIV. Kampagne*. Unpublished excavation report Potsdam: 2003, 134-198.

Lourenço Gonçalves, P. M., *Landscape and environmental changes at Memphis during the dynastic period in Egypt*. (PhD dissertation: University of Cambridge, 2019).

Mączynska, A., "The Lower Egyptian-Naqada transition: a view from Tell el-Farkha", in: R. F. Friedman, P. N. Fiske (eds.), *Egypt at its origins 3: proceedings of the Third International Conference "Origin of the state: predynastic and early dynastic Egypt", London, 27th July - 1st August 2008*. Leuven: Peeters 2011, 879-908.

Mączynska, A., *Lower Egyptian communities and their interactions with Southern Levant in the 4th millennium BC*. Studies in African Archaeology 12, Poznań: Poznan Archaeological Museum 2013.

Mahmoudi, A. el-, A. Gabr, "Geophysical surveys to investigate the relation between the Quaternary Nile channels and the Messinian Nile canyon at East Nile Delta, Egypt", *Arabian Journal of Geosciences* 2(1), 2009, 53-67.

Maksoud, M. Abd el-, D. Valbelle, "Tell Héboua II: rapport préliminaire sur le décor et l'épigraphie des éléments architectoniques découverts au cours des campagnes 2008-2009 dans la zone centrale du *khétem* de Tjarou", *Revue d'égyptologie* 62, 2011, 1-39.

Marchi, S., *L'habitat dans les forteresses de Migdol (Tell el-Herr) durant les Ve et IVe siècles avant J.-C.: étude archéologique*. Mission franco-égyptienne de Tell el-Herr (Nord-Sinaï), Paris: Presses de l'université Paris-Sorbonne 2014.

Mariette, A., *Catalogue général des monuments d'Abydos découverts pendant les fouilles de cette ville*. Paris: Imprimerie Nationale 1880.

Marks, L., F. Welc, B. Woronko, J. Krzymińska, A. Rogóż-Matyszczak, M Szymanek, J Holuša, J. Nitychoruk, Z. Chen, A. Salem, "High-resolution insight into the Holocene environmental history of the Burullus Lagoon in northern Nile delta, Egypt", *Quaternary Research* 107, 2022, 87-103.

Marouard, G., "Maisons-tours et organisation des quartiers domestiques dans les agglomérations du Delta: l'exemple de Bouto de la Basse Époque aux premiers lagides", *NeHeT* 2, 2015, 105-133.

Martinet, É., *L'administration provinciale sous l'Ancien Empire égyptien*, 2 vols. Probleme der Ägyptologie 38 (1-2), Boston: Brill, 2019.

Martin-Pardey, E. *Untersuchungen zur ägyptischen Provinzialverwaltung bis zum Ende des Alten Reiches*. Hildesheimer Ägyptologische Beiträge 1, Hildesheim: Gerstenberg 1976.

Meeks, D., *Mythes et légendes du Delta d'après le papyrus Brooklyn 47.218.84*. Mémoires publiés par les membres de l'Institut français d'archéologie orientale 125, Le Caire: Institut Français d'Archéologie Orientale 2006.

Meister, J., P. Garbe, J. Trappe, T. Ullmann, A. es-Senussi, R. Baumhauer, E. Lange-Athinodorou, A. Abd el-Raouf, "The sacred waterscape of the temple of Bastet at ancient Bubastis, Nile Delta (Egypt)", *Geosciences* 11 (9), 2021.

Moeller, N., "The First Intermediate Period: a time of famine and climate change?", *Ägypten und Levante* 15, 2005, 53-167.

Moeller, N., G. Marouard, "The context of the Khyan sealings from Tell Edfu and further implications for the Second Intermediate Period in Upper Egypt" in: I. Forstner-Müller, N. Moeller (eds.), *The Hyksos ruler Khyan and the early Second Intermediate Period in Egypt: problems and priorities of current research. Proceedings of the workshop of the Austrian Archaeological*

Institute and the Oriental Institute of the University of Chicago, Vienna, July 4 – 5, 2014. Wien: Holzhausen 2018, 173-197.

Moeller, N., *The archaeology of urbanism in ancient Egypt: from the Predynastic period to the end of the Middle Kingdom.* New York: Cambridge University Press 2016.

Montet, P., *Les énigmes de Tanis.* Bibliothèque historique, Paris: Payot, 1952.

Montet, P., *Le lac sacré de Tanis.* Mémoires de l'Académie des inscriptions et belles-lettres 44, Paris: Imprimerie Nationale, C. Klincksieck 1966.

Moreno García, J. C., "The territorial administration of the kingdom in the 3rd millennium", in: J. C.

Moreno García (ed.), *Ancient Egyptian administration.* Leiden: Brill 2013, 85-151.

Morenz, L. D., ",… wobei mehr Wein getrunken wird als im ganzen Jahre": altägyptische Weingefäße im Licht Herodots kontextualisiert", *Chronique d'Égypte* 81 (161-162), 2006, 45-61.

Morenz, L., *Die Zeit der Regionen im Spiegel der Gebelein-Region: kulturgeschichtliche Re-Konstruktionen.* Probleme der Ägyptologie 27, 2010.

Morris, E., *Ancient Egyptian imperialism.* Hoboken, NJ; Chichester: Wiley Blackwell, 2018.

Morris, E., *Famine and feast in ancient Egypt.* Cambridge Elements: Elements in Ancient Egypt in Context, Cambridge: Cambridge University Press 2023.

Müller-Wollermann, R., *Krisenfaktoren im ägyptischen Staat des ausgehenden Alten Reichs.* (PhD dissertation: Eberhard-Karl-Universität Tübingen, 1986).

Mumford, G., "A Late Period riverine and maritime port town and cult center at Tell Tebilla (Ronefer)", *Journal of Ancient Egyptian Interconnections* 5 (1), 2013, 38-67.

Naunton, C., "Libyans and Nubians", in: A. B. Lloyd (ed.), *A companion to ancient Egypt 1*, 120-139. Chichester; Malden, MA: Wiley-Blackwell.

Naunton, C., *Searching for the lost tombs of Egypt.* London; New York: Thames & Hudson; W. W. Norton 2018.

Naville, E., *Bubastis (1887-1889).* Memoir of the Egypt Exploration Fund 8, London: Kegan Paul, Trench, Trübner & Co 1891.

Nesselrath, H.-G., *Herodot: Historien.* Alfred Kröner Verlag: Stuttgart 2017.

Nuzzolo, M., *The Fifth Dynasty sun temples: kingship, architecture and religion in third millennium BC Egypt.* Prague: Charles University, Faculty of Arts 2018.

O'Connor, D., "The status of early Egyptian temples: an alternative theory", in: R. Friedman, B. Adams (eds.), *The followers of Horus: studies dedicated to Michael Allen Hoffman.* Oxford: Oxbow Books 1992, 83-98.

Onasch, H.-U., *Die assyrischen Eroberungen Ägyptens. Teil 1: Kommentare und Anmerkungen. Teil 2: Texte in Umschrift.* Ägypten und Altes Testament 27, Wiesbaden: Harrassowitz 1994.

Pantalacci, L., "Local contacts: traces of desert culture(s) in Egyptian contexts of the Dakhla oasis (late 3rd millennium BCE)", in: R. Bußmann, I. Hafemann, R. Schiestl, D. A. Werning (eds.), *Spuren der altägyptischen Gesellschaft: Festschrift für Stephan J. Seidlmayer.* Berlin; Boston: De Gruyter 2022, 23-32.

Papazian, H., "The central administration of the resources in the Old Kingdom: departments, treasuries, granaries and work centers", in: J. C. Moreno García (ed.), *Ancient Egyptian administration*, Leiden: Brill 2013, 41-83.

Papazian, H., "The state of Egypt in the Eighth Dynasty", in: P. Der Manuelian, T. Schneider (eds.), *Towards a new history for the Egyptian Old Kingdom: perspectives on the pyramid age.* Leiden; Boston: Brill 2015, 393-428.

Papazian, H., *Domain of pharaoh: the structure and components of the economy of Old Kingdom Egypt.* Hildesheimer Ägyptologische Beiträge 52, Hildesheim: Gerstenberg 2012.

Parkinson R.B., *The Tale of Sinuhe and Other Ancient Egyptian Poems 1940-1640 BC.* Oxford World's Classics, Oxford 1997.

Parkinson, R. B., *Poetry and culture in Middle Kingdom Egypt: a dark side to perfection.* Athlone Publications in Egyptology and Ancient Near Eastern Studies, London; New York: Continuum 2002.

Pennington, B. T., F. Sturt, P. Wilson, J. Rowland, A. G. Brown, "The fluvial evolution of the Holocene Nile Delta", *Quaternary Science Reviews* 170, 2017, 212-231.

169

Petrie, W. M. F., *Abydos II*. Memoir of the Egypt Exploration Fund 24, London: Egypt Exploration Fund, Kegan Paul, Trench, Trübner & Co 1903.

Petrie, W. M. F., J. E. Quibell, *Naqada and Ballas: 1895*. British School of Archaeology in Egypt and Egyptian Research Account [1] (1st year), London: Bernard Quaritch 1896.

Petrie, W. M. F., *The making of Egypt*. British School of Archaeology in Egypt and Egyptian Research Account [61], London: Sheldon Press 1939.

Petrie, W. M. F., *The royal tombs of the First Dynasty*, 3 vols. Memoir of the Egypt Exploration Fund 18; 21; [21] special extra publication, London: Egypt Exploration Fund; Kegan Paul, Trench, Trübner & Co 1900-1901.

Phillips, D. W., "Cosmetic spoons in the form of swimming girls", *Bulletin of the Metropolitan Museum of Art* 36 (8), 1941, 173-175.

Poiron, P., "Being the son of a Goddess: the claim for legitimacy of the Bubastite kings", in: M. Peterková Hlouchová, D. Bělohoubková, J. Honzl, V. Nováková (eds.), *Current research in Egyptology 2018: proceedings of the Nineteenth Annual Symposium, Czech Institute of Egyptology, Faculty of Arts, Charles University, Prague, 25-28 June 2018*. Oxford: Archaeopress 2019, 130-140.

Polz, D., "The territorial claim and the political role of the Theban state at the end of the Second Intermediate Period: a case study", in: I. Forstner-Müller, N. Moeller (eds.), *The Hyksos ruler Khyan and the early Second Intermediate Period in Egypt: problems and priorities of current research. Proceedings of the workshop of the Austrian Archaeological Institute and the Oriental Institute of the University of Chicago, Vienna, July 4 – 5, 2014*. Wien: Holzhausen 2018, 217-233.

Polz, D., "Upper Egypt before the New Kingdom", in: K. Radner, N. Moeller, D. T. Potts (eds.), *The Oxford history of the ancient Near East, volume III: from the Hyksos to the late second millennium BC*, New York: Oxford University Press 2022, 48-100.

Poole, F., "Tanis (San el-Haggar)", in: K. A. Bard, S. B. Shubert (eds.), *Encyclopedia of the archaeology of ancient Egypt*. London; New York: Routledge 1999, 755-757.

Posener-Kriéger, P., *Les archives du temple funéraire de Néferirkarê-Kakaï (Les papyrus d'Abousir): traduction et commentaire*, 2 vols. Bibliothèque d'étude 65, Le Caire: Institut français d'Archéologie orientale 1976.

Priglinger, E., *The enigma of the Hyksos, volume V: Zwischen den Zeiten. Überlegungen zum Ende der drei Reiche im alten Ägypten*. Contributions to the Archaeology of Egypt, Nubia and the Levant 13, Wiesbaden: Harrassowitz 2021.

Pusch E., A. Herold, "Quantir/Pi-Ramesse", in: K. A. Bard, S. B. Shubert (eds.), *Encyclopedia of the archaeology of ancient Egypt*. London; New York: Routledge 1999, 647-649.

Quack, J. F., *Studien zur Lehre für Merikare*. Göttinger Orientforschungen, 4, Reihe: Ägypten 23, Wiesbaden: Harrassowitz 1992.

Quack, J. F., "Irrungen, Wirrungen? Forscherische Ansätze zur Datierung der älteren ägyptischen Literatur", in: G. Moers, Gerald, K. Widmaier, A. Giewekemeyer, A. Lümers, R. Ernst (eds.), *Dating Egyptian literary texts*. Hamburg: Widmaier 2013, 405-469.

Quibell, J. E., F. W. Green. *Hierakonpolis*, 2 vols. British School of Archaeology in Egypt and Egyptian Research Account [4-5], London: Bernard Quaritch 1900-1902.

Quirke, S., *The administration of Egypt in the Late Middle Kingdom: the hieratic documents*. New Malden: SIA 1990.

Ranke, H., *Die ägyptischen Personennamen. Band I: Verzeichnis der Namen*. Glückstadt: J. J. Augustin 1935.

Raue, D., *Heliopolis und das Haus des Re: eine Prosopographie und ein Toponym im Neuen Reich*. Abhandlungen des Deutschen Archäologischen Instituts Kairo, Ägyptologische Reihe 16, Berlin: Achet 1999.

Redford, D. B. (ed.), *Excavations at Mendes, 1: The royal necropolis*. Culture and History of the Ancient Near East 20, Leiden: Brill 2004.

Redford, D. B., *City of the ram-man: the story of ancient Mendes*. Princeton; Oxford: Princeton University Press 2010.

Reimann, R., "Preliminary report on the pottery from Area A in Tell Basta", in: A. Wahby, P. Wilson (eds.), *The Delta survey workshop: proceedings from conferences held in Alexandria (2017) and Mansoura (2019)*. Oxford: Archaeopress 2022, 141-163.

Revel, M., E. Ducassou, C. Skonieczny, C. Colin, L. Bastian, D. Bosch, S. Migeon, J. Mascle, "20,000 years of Nile River dynamics and environmental changes in the Nile catchment area as inferred from Nile upper continental slope sediments", *Quaternary Science Reviews* 130 (2015), 200-221.

Richards, J., "Text and context in late Old Kingdom Egypt: the archaeology and historiography of Weni the Elder", *Journal of the American Research Center in Egypt* 39, 2002, 75-102.

Ricke, H., "Zur ägyptischen Baukunst des Alten Reiches 2", in: H. Ricke (ed.), *Beiträge zur ägyptischen Bauforschung und Altertumskunde* 5, Kairo: Schweizerisches Institut für ägyptische Bauforschung und Altertumskunde in Kairo 1950, 1-128.

Römer, M., *Gottes- und Priesterherrschaft in Ägypten am Ende des Neuen Reiches: ein religionsgeschichtliches Phänomen und seine Grundlagen.* Ägypten und Altes Testament 21, Wiesbaden: Harrassowitz 1994.

Rondot, V., "Une monographie bubastite", *Bulletin de l'Institut Français d'Archéologie Orientale* 89, 1989, 249-270.

Rondot, V., *Tebtynis II: Le temple de Soknebtynis et son dromos.* Fouilles de l'Institut Français d'Archéologie Orientale 50, Le Caire: Institut français d'archéologie orientale 2004.

Rosenow, D., Das Tempelhaus des Großen Bastet-Tempels in Bubastis (Doctoral dissertation: Humboldt-University Berlin 2008(a)).

Rosenow, D., "The naos of 'Bastet, lady of the shrine' from Bubastis", *Journal of Egyptian Archaeology* 94, 2008(b), 247-266.

O'Rourke, P. F., "A Late Period naophoros from Bubastis", *Bulletin of the Egyptological Seminar* 10, 1989-1990, 109-128.

Ryholt, K. S. B. *The political situation in Egypt during the Second Intermediate Period* c. *1800-1550 BC.* CNI Publications 20, Copenhagen: The Carsten Niebuhr Institute of Near Eastern Studies, University of Copenhagen; Museum Tusculanum Press 1997.

Ryholt, K., "The Late Old Kingdom in the Turin King-list and the identity of Nitocris", *Zeitschrift für ägyptische Sprache und Altertumskunde* 127.1, 2000, 87-119.

Sabbahy, L. K., *Kingship, power, and legitimacy in ancient Egypt: from the Old Kingdom to the Middle Kingdom.* Cambridge: Cambridge University Press 2021.

Sagrillo, T. L., "The geographic origins of the 'Bubastite' dynasty and possible locations for the royal residence and burial place of Shoshenq I.", in: G. P. F. Broekman, R. J. Demarée, O. E. Kaper (eds.), *The Libyan period in Egypt: historical and cultural studies into the 21st-24th Dynasties. Proceedings of a conference at Leiden University, 25-27 October 2007.* Leiden; Leuven: Nederlands Instituut voor het Nabije Oosten, Peeters 2009, 341-359.

Sauneron, S., "Villes et légendes d'Égypte", *Bulletin de l'Institut Français d'Archéologie Orientale* 62, 1964, 33-57.

Sawi, A. el-, "Preliminary report on Tell Basta excavations: seasons 1969, 1970, 1971", *Zeitschrift für ägyptische Sprache und Altertumskunde* 104, 1977, 127-131.

Sawi, A. el-, *Excavations at Tell Basta: report of seasons 1967 - 1971 and catalogue of finds.* Prague: Charles University 1979.

Scharff, A., "Ein Rechnungsbuch des königlichen Hofes aus der 13. Dynastie (Pap. Boulaq Nr. 18)", *Zeitschrift für ägyptische Sprache und Altertumskunde* 57, 1922, 51-68.

Schenkel, W., *Memphis, Herakleopolis, Theben: die epigraphischen Zeugnisse der 7.-11. Dynastie Ägyptens.* Ägyptologische Abhandlungen 12, Wiesbaden: Otto Harrassowitz 1965.

Schiestl, R., *Tell el-Dab'a XVIII: Die Palastnekropole von Tell el-Dab'a. Die Gräber des Areals F/I der Straten d/2 und d/1.* Untersuchungen der Zweigstelle Kairo des Österreichischen Archäologischen Institutes 30, Österreichische Akademie der Wissenschaften, Denkschriften der Gesamtakademie 47, Wien: Verlag der Österreichischen Akademie der Wissenschaften 2009.

Schipper, B. U., *Die Erzählung des Wenamun: ein Literaturwerk im Spannungsfeld von Politik, Geschichte und Religion.* Orbis Biblicus et Orientalis 209, Fribourg; Göttingen: Academic Press; Vandenhoeck & Ruprecht 2005.

Schneider, T., "The Old Kingdom abroad: an epistemological perspective: with remarks on the biography of Iny and the Kingdom of Dugurasu", in: P. Der Manuelian, T. Schneider (eds.), *Towards a new history for the Egyptian Old Kingdom: perspectives on the pyramid age*, 429-455. Leiden, Boston: Brill 2015.

Schneider, T., *Lexikon der Pharaonen*, revised ed. München: Deutscher Taschenbuch Verlag 1996.

Schneider, T., "Überlegungen zur Chronologie der thebanischen Könige in der Zweiten Zwischenzeit", in: E. Czerny, I. Hein, H. Hunger, D. Melman, A. Schwab (eds.), *Timelines: studies in honour of Manfred Bietak 1*. Leuven: Peeters, Departement Oosterse Studies 2006, 299-305.

Schorsch, D., "Bastet goes boating", *Bulletin of the Egyptological Seminar* 19, 2015, 571-584.

Schulman, A. R., "The battle scenes of the Middle Kingdom", *Journal of the Society for the Study of Egyptian Antiquities* 12 (4), 1982, 165-183.

Schulz, R., *Die Entwicklung und Bedeutung des kuboiden Statuentypus: eine Untersuchung zu den sogenannten „Würfelhockern"*. Hildesheimer Ägyptologische Beiträge 33-34, Hildesheim: Gerstenberg 1992.

Seidlmayer, S. J., "Die staatliche Anlage der 3. Dyn. in der Nordweststadt von Elephantine: archäologische und historische Probleme", in: M. Bietak (ed.), *Haus und Palast im Alten Ägypten / House and palace in ancient Egypt*. Wien: Verlag der Österreichischen Akademie der Wissenschaften 1996, 195-214.

Seidlmayer, S. J., "The First Intermediate Period (*c.* 2160-2055 BC)", in: I. Shaw (ed.), *The Oxford history of ancient Egypt*. Oxford: Oxford University Press 2000, 118-147.

Selve, V., "Les fonctions religieuses des nomarques au Moyen Empire", *Cahiers de Recherches de l'Institut de Papyrologie et d'Égyptologie de Lille* 15, 1993, 73-81.

Sheisha, H., D. Kaniewski, N. Marriner, M. Djamali, G. Younes, Z. Chen, G. El-Qady, A. Saleem, A. Véron, C. Morhange, "Nile waterscapes facilitated the construction of the Giza pyramids during the 3rd millennium BCE", *Proceedings of the National Academy of Sciences*, 119 (37) e2202530119.

Siddall M., E. J. Rohling, A. Almogi-Labin, C. Hemleben, D. Meischner, I. Schmelzer, D. A. Smeed, "Sea-level fluctuations during the last glacial cycle", *Nature* 423.6942, 2003, 853-858.

Silverman, D. P., W. K. Simpson, J. Wegner (eds.), *Archaism and innovation: studies in the culture of Middle Kingdom Egypt*. New Haven, CT, Philadelpia, PA: Department of Near Eastern languages and civilizations, Yale University, University of Pennsylvana Museum of Archaeology and Anthropology 2009.

Simpson, W. K., "The vessels with engraved designs and the repoussé bowl from the Tell Basta treasure", *American Journal of Archaeology* 63 (1), 1959, 29-45.

Snape, S. 2019, "Memorial monuments at Abydos and the 'Terrace of the Great God'", in: I. Regulski (ed.), *Abydos: the sacred land at the western horizon*, Leuven: Peeters 2019, 255-272.

Soukiassian, G., "Balat, un palais des gouverneurs de l'oasis de Dakhla (VIe dynastie - Première Période intermédiaire): travaux de l'IFAO", *Bulletin de la Société Française d›Égyptologie* 206, 2022, 43-65.

Sourouzian, H., "Standing royal colossi of the Middle Kingdom reused by Ramesses II", *Mitteilungen des Deutschen Archäologischen Instituts, Abteilung Kairo* 44, 1988, 229-254.

Spalinger, A., 1977. "The concept of kingship in Dynasty XXVI", *Newsletter of the American Research Center in Egypt* 1977, 99-100.

Spence, K., "Architecture", in: T. Wilkinson (ed.), *The Egyptian world*. London, New York: Routledge 2007, 366-387.

Spencer, A. J., *The temple area. Excavations at el-Ashmunein 2*. London: The Trustees of the British Museum, British Museum Expedition to Middle Egypt 1989.

Spencer, A. J., *Early Egypt: the rise of civilisation in the Nile Valley*. London: British Museum Press 1993.

Spencer, A. J., *Excavations at Tell el-Balamun 1991-1994*. London: British Museum Press 1996.

Spencer, A. J., "Casemate foundations once again", in: A. Leahy, J. Tait (eds.), *Studies on ancient Egypt in honour of H. S. Smith*. London: Egypt Exploration Society 1999, 295-300.

Spencer, A. J., "An elite cemetery at Tell el-Balamun", *Egyptian Archaeology* 18, 2001, 18-20.

Spencer, A. J., *Excavations at Tell el-Balamun, 1999-2001*. London: British Museum 2003.

Spencer, N., *A naos of Nekhthorheb from Bubastis: religious iconography and temple building in the 30th Dynasty. With a contribution by Daniela Rosenow*. British Museum Research Publication 156, London: The Trustees of the British Museum 2006.

Spencer, N., *Kom Firin II: The urban fabric and landscape*, London: The British Museum Press 2014.

Spiegelberg, W., 1917, *Der ägyptische Mythus vom Sonnenauge (der Papyrus der Tierfabeln - „Kufi"): nach dem Leidener demotischen Papyrus I 384*. Strassburg: Schultz 1917.

Stadelmann, R., "Das Grab im Tempelhof: der Typus des Königsgrabes in der Spätzeit", *Mitteilungen des Deutschen Archäologischen Instituts, Abteilung Kairo* 27, 1971, 111-123.

Stadelmann, R., "The development of the pyramid temple in the Fourth Dynasty", in: S. Quirke (ed.), *The temple in ancient Egypt: new discoveries and recent research*, 1-16. London: British Museum Press 1997.

Stanley, D. J., "Egypt's Nile Delta in late 4000 years BP: Altered flood levels and sedimentation, with archaeological implications", *Journal of Coastal Research* 35(5), 2019, 1036-1050.

Stanley, D. J., J. E. McRea, J. C. Waldron, *Nile Delta drill core and sample database for 1985-1994: Mediterranean Basin (MEDIBA) Program*. Smithsonian Contributions to the Marine Sciences 37, 1996.

Stanley, D. J., A. G. Warne, "Nile Delta in its destruction phase", *Journal of Coastal Research* 14 (3), 1998, 795-825.

Stanley, D. J., T. F. Jorstad, "Short contribution: Buried Canopic channel identified near Egypt's Nile delta coast with radar (SRTM) imagery", *Geoarchaeology* 21(5), 2006, 503-514.

Stanley, D. J., S. E. Wedl, "Significant depositional changes offshore the Nile Delta in late third millennium BCE: relevance for Egyptology", *E&G Quaternary Science Journal* 70(1), 2021, 83-92.

Stierlin, H., C. Ziegler, *Tanis: Vergessene Schätze der Pharaonen. Translated by Dietrich Wildung*. München: Hirmer 1987.

Strudwick, N., "The Old Kingdom and First Intermediate Period" in: I. Shaw, E. Bloxam (eds.), *The Oxford handbook of Egyptology*. Oxford: Oxford University Press 2020, 619-637.

Szafrański, Z. E., "Two new royal inscriptions from Tell el-Dab'a", in: E. Czerny, I. Hein, H. Hunger, D. Melman, A. Schwab (eds.), *Timelines: studies in honour of Manfred Bietak 1*. Leuven: Peeters, Departement Oosterse Studies 2006, 377-380.

Tallet, P., *Les papyrus de la mer Rouge I: Le « journal de Merer » (Papyrus Jarf A et B)*. Mémoires publiés par les membres de l'Institut français d'archéologie orientale 136, Le Caire: Institut français d'Archéologie Orientale 2017.

Tavares, A., "Village, town and barracks: a fourth dynasty settlement at Heit el-Ghurab, Giza", in N. Strudwick, H. Strudwick (eds.), *Old Kingdom, new perspectives: Egyptian art and archaeology 2750-2150 BC*. Oxford: Oxbow Books 2011, 270-277.

Thomas, R. I., A. Villing, "Naukratis revisited 2012: integrating new fieldwork and old research", *British Museum Studies in Ancient Egypt and Sudan* 20, 2013, 81-125.

Tietze, C., "Tell Basta: die Stadt der Katzengöttin; Grabungen im östlichen Nildelta legen die Kult- und Palastbauten einer Hauptstadt Ägyptens frei", *Antike Welt* 35(5), 2004, 45-52.

Tietze C., L. Martin, *Tell Basta-Report of the third season, part B*. Unpublished excavation report Potsdam: 1993, 64-92.

Tietze, C., E. Lange, K. Hallof, "Ein neues Exemplar des Kanopus-Dekrets aus Bubastis", *Archiv für Papyrusforschung und verwandte Gebiete* 51(1), 2005, 1-29.

Tillier, A., "Notes sur l'*icherou*", *Égypte Nilotique et Méditerranéenne* 3, 2010, 167-176.

Traunecker, C., "Les « temples hauts » de Basse Époque: un aspect du fonctionnement économique des temples", *Revue d'égyptologie* 38, 1987, 147-162.

Tristant Y., B. Midant-Reynes, "The Predynastic Cultures of the Nile Delta", in: E. Teeter, (ed.), *Before the pyramids: the origins of Egyptian civilization*. Oriental Institute Museum Publications 33, Chicago: The Oriental Institute of the University of Chicago, 2011, 45-54.

Tristant Y., *L'occupation humaine dans le delta du Nil aux Ve et IVe millénaires: approche géoarchéologique à partir de la région de Samara (delta oriental)*. Bibliothèque d'Étude 174, Le Caire: Institut français d'Archéologie orientale; Académie royale des sciences d'outre-mer / Koninklijke Academie voor Ovezeese Wetenschappen 2020.

Ullmann, M., *Die Häuser der Millionen von Jahren: eine Untersuchung zu Königskult und Tempeltypologie in Ägypten*. Ägypten und Altes Testament 51, Wiesbaden: Harrassowitz 2002.

Ullmann, T., E. Lange-Athinodorou, A. Göbel, C. Büdel, R. Baumhauer, "Preliminary results on the paleo-landscape of Tell Basta/Bubastis (eastern Nile delta): an integrated approach combining GIS-based spatial analysis, geophysical and archaeological investigations", *Quaternary International* 511, 2019, 185-199.

Van Siclen C. C., "The shadow of the door and the Jubilee Reliefs of Osorkon II from Tell Basta", *Varia Aegyptiaca* 7 (1), 1991(a), 81-87.

Van Siclen III, C. C., "The mayors of Basta in the Middle Kingdom", in: S. Schoske (ed.), *Akten des vierten Internationalen Ägyptologen Kongresses München 1985. Band 4: Geschichte, Verwaltungs- und Wirtschaftsgeschichte, Rechtsgeschichte, Nachbarkulturen*. Hamburg: Buske 1991(b), 187-194.

Vandier, J., *Mo'alla: la tombe d'Ankhtifi et la tombe de Sébekhotep*. Bibliothèque d'étude 18, Le Caire: Institut français d'archéologie orientale 1950.

Verbovsek, A., *Die sogenannten Hyksosmonumente: eine archäologische Standortbestimmung*. Göttinger Orientforschungen, 4, Reihe: Ägypten 46, Wiesbaden: Harrassowitz 2006.

Verner, M., *The pyramids: the archaeology and history of Egypt's iconic monuments*, new and updated ed. Cairo; New York: American University in Cairo Press 2020.

Vicente, C., "Eine löwenköpfige Bronzestatuette des Gottes Nefertem aus dem Ägyptischen Museum und Papyrussammlung in Berlin (ÄM 8988)", *Égypte Nilotique et Méditerranéenne* 9, 2016, 141-153.

Vittmann, G., "Nachlese zur ägyptischen Wegmetaphorik", in: J. Hallof (ed.), *Auf den Spuren des Sobek: Festschrift für Horst Beinlich zum 28. Dezember 2012*. Dettelbach: Röll 2012, 275-294.

Vogel, C., *Ägyptische Festungen und Garnisonen bis zum Ende des Mittleren Reiches*. Hildesheimer Ägyptologische Beiträge 46, Hildesheim: Gerstenberg 2004.

Waddell, W. G., *Manetho*. Cambridge, Massachusetts: Harvard University Press, London: William Heinemann Ltd 1964.

Waitkus, W., "Die Beziehung der Heiligen Schlangen zur Urgötternekropole (*jȝt ntrjt*) und zu den verstorbenen Urgöttern", in D. Kurth, W. Waitkus (eds.), *Edfu: Materialien und Studien*. Gladbeck: PeWe-Verlag 2010, 131-162.

Walker, M. J. C., M. Berkelhammer, S. Björck, L. C. Cwynar, D. A. Fisher, A. J. Long, J. J. Lowe, R. M. Newnham, S. O. Rasmussen, H. Weiss, "Formal subdivision of the Holocene Series/Epoch: a Discussion Paper by a Working Group of INTIMATE (Integration of ice-core, marine and terrestrial records) and the Subcommission on Quaternary Stratigraphy (International Commission on Stratigraphy)", *Journal of Quaternary Science* 27(7), 2012, 649-659.

Ward, W. A., "Egypt and the East Mediterranean in the early second millennium B.C.", *Orientalia* 30(1-2), 1961, 22-45, 129-155.

Ward, W. A., *Index of Egyptian administrative and religious titles of the Middle Kingdom: with a glossary of words and phrases used*. Beirut: American University of Beirut 1982.

Ward, W. A., *Essays on feminine titles of the Middle Kingdom and related subjects*. Beirut: American University of Beirut 1986.

Wegner, J., K. Cahail, *King Seneb-Kay's tomb and the necropolis of a lost dynasty at Abydos. With contributions by Jane Hill, Maria Rosado, and Molly Gleeson*. University Museum monograph 155, Philadelphia, PA: University of Pennsylvania Museum of Archaeology and Anthropology 2021.

Welc, F., L. Marks, "Climate change at the end of the Old Kingdom in Egypt around 4200 BP: New geoarchaeological evidence", *Quaternary International* 324, 2014, 124-133.

Welc, F., M. Zaremba, J. Trzciński, "Holocene lake sediments as a source of building material in ancient Egypt; archeometric evidence from Wadi Tumilat (Nile Delta)", *Studia Quaternaria* 34, 2017, 109-118.

Wenke, R. J., R. W. Redding, A. J. Cagle (eds.), *Kom el-Hisn (ca. 2500-1900 BC): an ancient settlement in the Nile Delta of Egypt*. Atlanta, GA: Lockwood Press 2016.

Westberg, F., "Zur Topographie des Herodot", *Klio-Beiträge zur Alten Geschichte* 14.14, 1915, 338-

174

344.

Wiese, A., *Antikenmuseum Basel und Sammlung Ludwig: die Ägyptische Abteilung. Unter Mitarbeit von Silvia Winterhalter und Andreas Brodbeck*. Zaberns Bildbände zur Archäologie, Sonderbände der Antiken Welt, Mainz: Zabern 2001.

Wilkinson, G., *Modern Egypt and Thebes: being a description of Egypt, including the information required for travellers in that country*, 2 vols. London: John Murray 1843.

Wilkinson, T. A. H., *Early dynastic Egypt*. London; New York: Routledge 1999.

Wilkinson, T. A. H., *Royal annals of ancient Egypt: the Palermo Stone and its associated fragments*. Studies in Egyptology, London, New York: Kegan Paul International 2000.

Willems, H., "The First Intermediate Period and the Middle Kingdom", in: A. B. Lloyd (ed.), *A companion to ancient Egypt 1*. Chichester, Malden, MA: Wiley-Blackwell 2010, 81-100.

Wilson, N. G., *Herodoti Historiae*, Oxford: Oxford University Press, 2015.

Wilson, P., *The survey of Saïs (Sa el-Hagar) 1997-2002*. Egypt Exploration Society, Excavation Memoir 77, London: Egypt Exploration Society 2006.

Wilson, P., *Sais I: The Ramesside-Third Intermediate Period at Kom Rebwa*. Egypt Exploration Society, Excavation Memoir 98, London: Egypt Exploration Society 2011.

Wilson, P., G. Gilbert, G. Tassie, *Sais II: the prehistoric period*. Egypt Exploration Society, Excavation Memoir 107, London: Egypt Exploration Society 2014.

Wilson, P., "A Psamtek ushabti and a granite block from Sais (Sa el-Hagar)", in: C. Price, R. Forshaw, A. Chamberlain, P. T. Nicholson (eds.), *Mummies, magic and medicine in ancient Egypt: multidisciplinary essays for Rosalie David*. Manchester: Manchester University 2016, 75-92.

Wilson, P., "Gateway to the underworld: the cult areas at Sais", *British Museum Studies in Ancient Egypt and Sudan* 24, 2019, 341-364.

Wit, H. E. de, 'The evolution of the eastern Nile Delta as a factor in the development of human culture', in: L. Krzyżaniak; M. Kobusiewicz; J. Alexander (eds.), *Environmental change and human culture in the Nile Basin and Northern Africa until the second millennium B.C*, Poznań 1993, 305-320.

Wojciechowska, A., *From Amyrtaeus to Ptolemy: Egypt in the fourth century B.C.* Philippika 97, Wiesbaden: Harrassowitz 2016.

Wunderlich, J., *Untersuchungen zur Entwicklung des westlichen Nildeltas im Holozän*. Marburger Geographische Schriften 114, Marburg 1989.

Wunderlich, J., A. Ginau, "Paläoumweltwandel im Raum Tell el Fara'in/Buto: Ergebnisse und Perspektiven geoarchäologischer Forschung", *Mitteilungen des Deutschen Archäologischen Instituts, Abteilung Kairo* 70-71, 2014-2015, 485-497.

Yoyotte, J., "Études géographiques, II: les localités méridionales de la région memphite et le « Pehou d'Héracléopolis »", *Revue d'égyptologie* 14, 1962, 75-111.